Anti-Slavery in America

Radcliffe College Monographs

No. 11

Anti-Slavery in America

FROM THE

Introduction of African Slaves to the
Prohibition of the Slave Trade

(1619–1808)

BY

MARY STOUGHTON LOCKE, A.M.

GLOUCESTER, MASS.

PETER SMITH

1965

PREFACE

THE investigation which has resulted in the present monograph was undertaken in connection with the Seminary
in American History at the " Harvard Annex " (now Radcliffe
College) in 1891–1893, under the direction of Professor Albert
Bushnell Hart. Most of the material was accumulated at that
time, and the main outlines were drawn in reports to the Seminary toward the close of the second year. The investigation
of various details and the writing and revision of the monograph have been accomplished at long intervals, as opportunity
occurred. It is hoped, however, that the defects resulting from
this intermittent and fragmentary work have been remedied by
careful revision.

The aims of this investigation have been to trace the early
development of anti-slavery sentiment under the influence of
religious and ethical principles and of political theories; to indicate its practical outcome in the Revolutionary period and
the years immediately following; to discover the relation of
early anti-slavery to that which culminated in universal emancipation, and to determine whether the anti-slavery movement
may be regarded as a continuous growth. In dealing with
certain aspects of the subject, it has been necessary to touch
upon the events of the subsequent period, from 1808 to 1830.
That important period, however, needs a separate treatment,
and it is hoped that a monograph on the subject, which is
now in process of preparation by another former student of
Radcliffe College, may soon be published.   93406P

For the study of early anti-slavery the most important sources are the direct expressions of sentiment by anti-slavery writers. Material of this nature has been found unexpectedly abundant. The *Germantown Friends' Protest* issued in 1688, Sewall's *Selling of Joseph*, in 1701, and the utterances of James Otis, Benjamin Franklin, George Washington, Thomas Jefferson, and other founders of the Republic are well known; the writings of Ralph Sandiford, Benjamin Lay, Anthony Benezet, and John Woolman are familiar, at least in name; and the *Dialogue concerning Slavery* by Dr. Samuel Hopkins is eminent among the early efforts for emancipation.

Other writers of the period preceding the Revolution who deserve special notice are George Keith, who protested against slavery in 1693; John Hepburn, whose *American Defence of the Christian Golden Rule* was published in 1714; William Burling (1718), and Elihu Coleman (1729). In the Revolutionary period were important pamphlets by Nathaniel Appleton, Dr. Benjamin Rush, and James Swan; an interesting *Forensic Dispute at Harvard* in 1773, and a remarkably vigorous *Address to the Rulers of America*, supposed to have been written by John Dickinson. After the close of the Revolution, in connection with movements for emancipation in the States, there were anti-slavery orations by Dr. George Buchanan and William Pinkney in Maryland; Theodore Dwight, Jonathan Edwards, and Zephaniah Swift, in Connecticut; and David Rice, in Kentucky; while Noah Webster, of Connecticut, contributed an important essay on the *Effects of Slavery on Morals and Industry*, and Judge Tucker, of Virginia, prepared an elaborate *Dissertation on Slavery* with a plan for its gradual abolition in the State. To the cause of national emancipation the Quaker philanthropist, Warner Mifflin, contributed by his words as well as his work; and Thomas Branagan, the " Penitential Tyrant," and John Parrish, the forerunner of Joshua R. Giddings, uttered significant prophecies and proposed definite remedies.

Other important sources of information are the books of travel and the magazine and newspaper articles which appeared during the latter part of the period. Of the latter the disunionist letters of "Pelham" and "Gustavus" in *The Connecticut Courant* (1796–1797) are among the most significant.

Among the most important aids in the accumulation of material have been the Collections of the State Historical Societies. Compilations of State and colonial laws, supplemented by colonial records and judicial reports, have also been of service. For the history of the early abolition societies the *Historical Memoir of the Pennsylvania Society*, by Edward Needles, has been very helpful. Of the less important societies it has been impossible to find satisfactory accounts; but important sources of information are the *Minutes of the Proceedings of the American Convention of Delegates from the Abolition Societies*, which were published annually from 1794 to 1806, with the exception of the years 1799 and 1802. Copies of these Minutes, though very rare, are all in existence; so that it has been possible, by consulting various libraries, to obtain a complete record of the work of the Convention during this period.

Most of my material has been found in the Harvard College and Boston Public Libraries. The Massachusetts State Library and the Boston Athenæum contain some important books and pamphlets not found elsewhere; and the collections of the Massachusetts, New York, and Pennsylvania Historical Societies, of the Philadelphia Library Company, and of Yale University have also been useful. The librarians of all these institutions have been most kind and helpful, and I am glad to have an opportunity to express my thanks. I am especially indebted to the authorities of the Harvard College Library, who have given me the utmost freedom of access to their very valuable special collections.

The debts which I owe to those who have already investigated portions of this subject are more difficult to acknowledge, on account of their great number. Recent monographs which have been found particularly useful are those of Professor W. E. B. DuBois, in the Harvard Historical Series; of Mrs. Marion Gleason McDougall, in the series of Radcliffe College monographs; and of Dr. Jeffrey R. Brackett and Dr. Stephen B. Weeks, in the publications of Johns Hopkins University. The works of Mr. Charles Deane, of the Hon. Emory Washburn, of Mr. George H. Moore, and of Judge William Birney have also furnished many facts and helpful references.

For the accomplishment of this work, thanks are due chiefly to Professor Hart, without whose encouragement and assistance it would never have been undertaken or completed; Professor Hart has read both manuscript and proofs, and has made many important criticisms and suggestions. Professor Edward Channing has very kindly read the proof-sheets of the first three chapters; and the proofs of the remaining chapters have been read by Miss Alice D. Adams, who is making a special study of the period from 1808 to 1830. Miss Mary H. Rollins, of the Boston Public Library, has helped me to make the Index. Thanks are due also to other friends who have given their assistance or criticism.

To Radcliffe College, which, through the instructors in that department, inspired me with an interest in historical work and disclosed to me its possibilities, my debt is inestimable. I shall be glad if this monograph proves sufficiently useful to other students to serve in some degree as an adequate expression of my gratitude.

BOSTON, April, 1901.

CONTENTS

INTRODUCTION

CHAPTER I

THE RELIGIOUS AND MORAL MOVEMENT, 1637–1808

CHAPTER II

THE PHILOSOPHICAL MOVEMENT OF THE REVOLUTIONARY PERIOD,
1761-1783

CHAPTER III

THE POLITICAL MOVEMENT IN THE REVOLUTIONARY PERIOD, 1761–1783

[1] For Hopkins's *Dialogue on Slavery*, see §§ 62 . . . 72.

CHAPTER IV

ABOLITIONISTS AND ABOLITION SOCIETIES, 1783–1808

CHAPTER V

GRADUAL EMANCIPATION IN THE STATES, 1783–1808

CHAPTER VI

The Victory over the Slave-Trade, 1783–1808

CHAPTER VII

Check to Anti-Slavery on the Territorial Question, 1783–1808

CHAPTER VIII

Anti–Slavery Literature after the Revolution, 1783–1808

ANTI-SLAVERY IN AMERICA

INTRODUCTION

THE American Revolution is said to have begun with "the first plantation of the country."[1] Anti-slavery agitation in America began almost as early, and its history was equally continuous. The two movements, one tending toward the independence of the white race, and the other toward the freedom of the black, were in fact intimately connected throughout the colonial period. Both had their sources in the principles for which many of the colonists left their European homes.[2] Both were nourished by the economic conditions of a new world in which land was abundant and opportunity comparatively equal. Theological doctrines and philosophical theories contributed to both alike, and it was in the period of the American Revolution that the slender streams of anti-slavery sentiment, which had been flowing in separate channels for nearly a century, united and gathered force for efficient action.

Connection with the American Revolution.

The political theories which had been developing for the three preceding centuries found their most perfect expression in the American Declaration of Independence. This document was, nevertheless, to a great extent only an expression of political theories; and it was, moreover, incomplete in its application. The members of the Second Continental Congress were not thinking in 1776 of the inalien-

Incompleteness of Revolutionary sentiment.

---

[1] John Adams, Letter to Jefferson, in Adams, *Works* (1856), X, 313.

[2] The Mennonites of Germantown, Pennsylvania, fugitives from religious persecution in the Old World, write in 1688: "Here is liberty of conscience, wch is right and reasonable; here ought to be likewise liberty of ye body, except of evil-doers, wch is an other case. . . . In Europe there are many oppressed for conscience sake; and here there are those oppressed wh are of a black colour." *Germantown Friends' Protest against Slavery*, i.

able rights of the negro, and slavery was tolerated in every one of the inchoate States. When the Virginia Bill of Rights was under discussion in the Revolutionary Convention of that State, a few days before the adoption of the Declaration of Independence by Congress, objections were made to the clause, "All men are by nature equally free and independent," as being "the fore-runner of civil convulsion." The clause was defended on the ground that as slaves were not constituent members of our society, they "could never pretend to any benefit from such a maxim," and with that interpretation it was allowed to stand.[1] Almost a century must elapse before the principles of the Revolution could be carried to their logical conclusion, and the liberty of the African was granted only after a war infinitely more terrible and destructive than that which gave independence to the English colonists.

The growth of the moral sentiment which found expression in the Thirteenth Amendment was, however, no less continuous and no less important in the early history of the nation than it had been in the history of the colonies.

National development of anti-slavery sentiment.

The principles of the Declaration of Independence were sometimes shuffled out of sight, but they were never really forgotten. Under their influence the States on which slavery had the weakest hold gradually admitted the rights of " blacke mankind " as well as white, and the steps once taken could never be retraced. After the Revolution there were always individuals to preach the equal rights of all men to " life, liberty, and the pursuit of happiness," and organizations to work for them. The spirit of universal liberty which flooded the country in 1776 was sometimes in later years confined to narrow channels, its course was sometimes uncertain, and its volume comparatively small. But the flow never ceased, and in time the narrowness of the channel served to give greater force to the current.

The history of the opposition to slavery in America may be conveniently divided into three periods. The first, ending with the prohibition of the African slave-trade by Congress in 1807, was that in which emancipation took place among the Society of Friends, and in which the efforts for emancipation by State legislatures or constitu-

Character of the period, 1619-1808.

---

[1] Rowland, *Life of George Mason*, I, 240.

tions culminated and spent their strength, though they did not entirely cease. It was perhaps an era of sentiment rather than of vigorous purpose, and was marked by less bitterness of feeling, especially sectional feeling, than the later period. It may be regarded as the " era of gradual abolition." [1] Reliance was placed chiefly on appeals to the reason and the conscience of the slave-holder, on quiet perseverance, and the " mild spirit of Christianity." [2] Claims of property were regarded to a considerable extent, and the favorite policy was that of gradual emancipation, which was adopted in most of the Northern States. Yet even in this period there were earnest advocates of immediate abolition, uncompromising spirits who believed that what is morally wrong can never be politically right, who held that there is no question as to which is the lesser evil when one of the evils is a moral one, and that no considerations of property or political expediency or self-interest in any form are of consequence in comparison with humanity and justice.[3]

This period includes several movements, originally independent, but gradually interwoven and united or carried along parallel lines. At first the work was confined to individuals or small local groups. Combined action was found only among the Quakers, and they alone achieved important results. By and by, as the spirit of universal liberty became more pervasive, the groups were extended and multiplied. Combinations appeared in other religious denominations, especially among the Methodists and Baptists. Political leaders joined hands with theologians and humanitarians, and the doctrinarianism of the Revolution found a practical outcome in the State prohibitions of the slave-trade, in the abolition of slavery by the Northern States, and then in the national prohibition of the slave-trade in 1807.

With the year 1808 came a pause in the development of the anti-slavery movement. The prohibition of the slave-trade satisfied men's consciences for a time, and it was supposed that

---

[1] Lalor, *Cyclopædia of Political Science*, I, 3.

[2] The American Convention of Delegates from the Abolition Societies, *Minutes of Proceedings*, 1794–1806, Addresses of the Convention to the Societies; *Ibid.*, 1805, p. 18, Report of the Delaware Society.

[3] *E.g.*, among the Quakers, Ralph Sandiford and Benjamin Lay; among the orators before the Abolition Societies, Jonathan Edwards and Theodore Dwight; also Samuel Hopkins and John Parrish.

as slavery was already disappearing it might now die a natural death throughout the land. At about the same time the in-

Anti-slavery after 1808. Interval of comparative inaction, 1808-1815.

creasing unpopularity of anti-slavery sentiment at the South seriously discouraged the organized efforts in that part of the country.[1] The New England States no longer had a slavery question, and the work of the Abolition Societies which had been formed during the period of State emancipation was confined to the Middle Atlantic States, where there was but little to be done. The troubled years of the Embargo policy and afterwards the War of 1812 turned men's thoughts in other directions, just at the time when the cotton-gin was quietly making slavery too profitable to be easily disposed of. During the Revolutionary War there was a similar decline of anti-slavery literature, a similar decadence of organized effort through an Abolition Society.

As the events which followed the Revolutionary War showed that the opposition to slavery had been quietly gathering force,

Revival of activity after 1815.

even during that absorbing contest, so, after the Treaty of Ghent, in 1815, there was a gradual revival of activity which proved the continued efficiency of anti-slavery sentiment. The numerous travellers whose works appeared in this period were wont to notice the antipathy to slavery which they found as far south as Virginia, and occasionally even farther;[2] to urge immigrants to avoid the States where slavery existed;[3] or, if the authors were Northern men

---

[1] American Convention, *Minutes of Proceedings*, 1805, pp. 14, 21-22; 1806, p. 12.

[2] Birkbeck, *Notes on a Journey in America*, 12, 16-18; Ibid., *Letters from Illinois*, 72; Blane, *Excursions through the United States*, 208-217; Bristed, *The Resources of the United States of America*, 149-150; Cooper, *Notions of the Americans*, II, 347-367; J. Flint, *Letters from America*, 167, 309; B. Hall, *Travels in North America*, III, 231-246; F. Hall, *Travels in Canada and the United States*, Appendix I, pp. 322-323; Hodgson, *Letters from North America*, I, 23-27, 112, 186-208; Holmes, *Account of the United States*, 325; Singleton, *Letters from the South and West*, 80; Welby, *A Visit to North America*, 81-82.

[3] Birkbeck, *Notes on a Journey in America*, 3-7; Fearon, *Narrative of a Journey through the Eastern and Western States of America*, 57-61, 98, 168, 227, 248-268, 353, 425-426; Flower, *Letters from Lexington and the Illinois*, 12-15; Harris, *Remarks on a Tour through the United States*, 77 *et passim;* Holditch, *The Emigrants' Guide to the United States of America*, 55, 81, 105-106; Holmes, *Account of the United States*, 329-334; Howitt, *Selections from Letters written during a Tour through the United States*,

travelling in the South, to express their own objections to the institution.[1] Anti-slavery pamphlets became abundant, and newspapers and periodicals took up the work more extensively than ever before.[2] The old Abolition Societies renewed their zeal, and many new ones were formed in the Southern and Border States.[3] Although the Colonization Society, which was formed in 1816, diverted the energies or lulled the consciences of many individuals, the American Convention of Abolition Societies at once perceived the impracticability and mischie-

75-79, 212. The effects of slavery on immigration are noted by Ogden in *Letters from the West*, 80.

[1] Some of the strongest expressions of anti-slavery sentiment are from English emigrants, notably John Bristed, at the time of writing a lawyer in New York, afterwards well known as an Episcopal clergyman (Appleton's *Encyclopedia*), and Morris Birkbeck and Richard Flower, who were afterwards among the leaders in the struggle to preserve the constitution of Illinois against the attacks of the pro-slavery party in 1823-1824 (Washburne, *Sketch of Edward Coles*, 145-189). Bristed, *The Resources of the United States of America*, 149-155, 388-392; Birkbeck, *Letters from Illinois*, 71; Flower, *Letters from Kentucky and Illinois*, 12-28. Other instances are Evans, *A Pedestrious Tour of Four Thousand Miles*, 213-217, including a plan for emancipation with compensation to slave-owners; Ogden, *Letters from the West*, 14-16, 79-80, 101-125; Darby, *A Geographical Description of Louisiana*, 266-268; Royall, *Sketches of History, Life, and Manners in the United States*, 101, 119; Singleton, *Letters from the South and West*, 74-113; Thomas, *Travels through the West*, 80-81. On the other hand, the inefficiency of anti-slavery sentiment is reflected in Cooper, *Notions of the Americans*, II, 340-367; T. Flint, *Recollections of the Last Ten Years*, 70, 341-348; Paulding, *Letters from the South*, I, 119-120; II, 6, 125-130. It is also commented on in Candler, *A Summary View of America*, chapter xix; Duncan, *Travels*, II, 251-257, 332-334; Faux, *Memorable Days in America*, 102-103; Fearon, *Narrative of a Journey*, references as above; B. Hall, *Travels in North America*, III, chapters vii-ix; Hodgson, *Letters from North America*, I, 23; Holmes, *Account of the United States*, 329-330.

[2] A Bibliography of the period before 1830 may be found in Birney, *James G. Birney and his Times*, Appendix A. Appendix B contains a list of anti-slavery newspapers and periodicals and of papers in which anti-slavery articles were published. A catalogue of anti slavery publications in America (1750-1863) has been prepared by Samuel May, Jr., but is incomplete for the early period. A few titles are given in Poole, *Anti-Slavery Opinions in America before 1800*. In an appendix to this monograph will be found an extended list of materials used by the author.

[3] In 1828 one hundred and forty societies are reported, a large proportion of them due to the efforts of Benjamin Lundy. American Convention, *Minutes of Proceedings*, 1828, p. 46, and Reports of Societies, *passim; Ibid.*, 1823, pp. 16-19. It was this activity that led the South to claim that the emancipation movement was set back by Garrison.

vousness of the scheme,[1] and continued its efforts for the emancipation of the enslaved blacks and the education of the free, until the more famous societies of "Anti-Slavery Days" took up the work and carried it to completion.[2]

In some respects the second period of anti-slavery, embracing the years from 1808 to 1830, partook of the character of the previous period, though it may be more properly regarded as a prelude to the great movement inaugurated by Garrison, which characterized the third and final period. It was in fact a time of transition between the earlier and the later movements, for the leading idea was still that of gradual emancipation. The Abolition Societies were still holding Conventions of Delegates; the acts for the emancipation of slaves by State legislatures were not completed till 1817; and between 1817 and 1830 efforts for gradual emancipation were made in Delaware, Maryland, Tennessee, and Kentucky.[3] In this period, however, the sectional issue became more apparent. The Missouri contest and the struggles over the State constitutions of Illinois and Indiana aroused individuals, societies, and legislatures to the importance of the territorial question.[4] The policy of petition-

Transitional character of the period, 1808–1830.

[1] American Convention, *Minutes of Proceedings*, 1818, pp. 38, 48–49, 60–68.

[2] *Ibid.*, 1823 and 1828.

[3] *Ibid.*, 1823, pp. 15, 18; Brackett, *The Negro in Maryland*, 55, 56; Birney, *James G. Birney and his Times*, 76, 97–99.

[4] American Convention, *Minutes of Proceedings*, 1818, pp. 42–43; *Memorial to the Senate and House of Representatives of the United States, prepared in pursuance of a vote of the inhabitants of Boston and its vicinity*, Dec. 15, 1819; Resolutions of a similar nature by citizens of New York, Nov. 16, 1819, quoted in Holmes, *Account of the United States*, 325; Memorials from Newport, Hartford, and other towns, *Annals of Congress*, 16 Cong., 1 sess., 69, 75, 82, 157, 333; *Ibid.*, Appendix, 2452–2463; Resolutions of the Legislatures of Pennsylvania, New Jersey, Delaware, New York, Ohio, and Vermont, *Ibid.*, 70–72, 234–235, 276, 311–312, 361; 16 Cong., 2 sess., 78–80. These are all connected with the Missouri question.

For interest in the Illinois contest, see Washburne, *Sketch of Edward Coles*, 149–164; Needles, *Hist. Mem. Pa. Soc.*, 79; Birney, *James G. Birney and his Times*, 409–411. The agitation over the territorial question led the Legislatures of Ohio (January, 1824), New Jersey (January, 1825), and Pennsylvania (January, 1826) to adopt resolutions in favor of gradual abolition by act of Congress, on the principle "that the evil of slavery is a national one, and that the People and States of this Union ought mutually to participate in the duties and burdens of removing it." *Reports of the American*

ing Congress to abolish slavery in the District of Columbia and to exclude it from all territorial governments and all new States was seriously undertaken between 1818 and 1829,[1] and the slavery question was rapidly becoming a political issue. The connection with the later movements may also be traced in the history of the Abolition Societies. A few of these continued to exist even after the formation of the later Anti-Slavery Societies,[2] and some of their members were prominent in the new organizations.[3] The later societies, though more numerous and more effective than the earlier ones, carried on their work along similar lines and by somewhat similar methods. Moreover, the call for Emancipation total, universal, and immediate, which appeared occasionally in the previous period and which especially characterized the Garrisonian era, was not entirely lacking during these years of transition.[4] Though the burning zeal of Gar-

---

Colonization Society, VIII, 40–41; *Genius of Universal Emancipation*, V, 165, 179; *Annals of Congress*, 18 Cong., 1 sess., 1428. See also Memorial of North Carolina Manumission Society, in *Genius of Universal Emancipation*, IV, 78–79.

[1] References as above for petitions in regard to the Western Territories. See also Needles, *Hist. Mem. Pa. Soc.*, 72; American Convention, *Minutes of Proceedings* (Report from the Manumission Society of Tennessee), 18.

For action in regard to the District of Columbia, see Tremain, *Slavery in the District of Columbia*, 58–67; American Convention, *Minutes of Proceedings*, 1818, pp. 58–59, 1823, pp. 32, 36, 1828, pp. 15, 17–20, 33–35; Needles, *Hist. Mem. Pa. Soc.*, 80, and *Annals of Congress*, 18 Cong., 1 sess., 1756; Memorial from citizens of Baltimore, *Annals of Congress*, 19 Cong., 2 sess., 1099–1101 (Feb. 12, 1827). Resolutions passed by the Legislatures of Pennsylvania and New York, 1828 and 1829, *Niles's Register*, XXXV, 363, 433–434. Address of the Society for the Abolition of Slavery in the District of Columbia to their fellow-citizens, in B. Hall, *Travels in North America*, III, 42–47; *Memorial of Inhabitants of the District of Columbia*, with 1060 signatures, March 24, 1828, 23 Cong., 2 sess., *H. Doc., No.* 140.

[2] The last meeting of the American Convention of Delegates of the Abolition Societies was held in Philadelphia in 1838. The societies represented were those of New York, Pennsylvania, and Delaware. Needles, *Historical Memoir of the Pennsylvania Society*, 96–97.

[3] Pennsylvania Anti-Slavery Convention, *Proceedings*, 1837, pp. 35, 59, 90; Birney's *Birney*, 414.

[4] Interesting accounts of immediate abolitionists for this period (1808–1830) are to be found in Birney, 74–76, and Appendices, *passim*. "Intemperate and inflammatory productions" are deprecated by Timothy Flint, *Recollections of the Last Ten Years*, 341–344, and J. F. Cooper, *Notions of the Americans*, II, 366.

rison and Phillips kindled men's souls as never before, evidences that the way was prepared for them are found at every point. The history of anti-slavery sentiment has no gaps. The anti-slavery conscience was never really lulled to sleep by self-interest. It had a thousand eyes, and while some slept, others were watchful. It had a thousand tongues, and while some were paralyzed by selfishness and fear, others were ready to warn the nation of its sin and to prophesy an avenging doom.

CHAPTER I

THE RELIGIOUS AND MORAL MOVEMENT, 1637–1808

THE institution of slavery was connected with a great variety of the interests, prejudices, and principles of mankind, and the objections to it were accordingly based on a great variety of grounds. It might be regarded as a relation inconsistent with moral laws and religious precepts; it might be criticised as a violation of the abstract rights of mankind, an irregularity and anomaly in a philosophical theory of the universe; it might be looked upon as a political weakness and danger, and therefore opposed on the ground of expediency; or it might be regarded as an economic system of at least doubtful value. Of these four lines of attack, the religious, philosophical, political, and economic, the last undoubtedly had influence in determining or intensifying the sentiment with regard to slavery; but there was no organized movement of importance distinctly based on economic considerations. Some of the chief instances of strong individual opposition on that ground are connected with the plans for founding some of the colonies.

1. Grounds of objection to slavery.

There appears to have been no protest against the introduction of slavery into Virginia in 1619. But in 1624, according to the plan proposed by William Usselinx for the Swedish Trading Company, slaves were not to be introduced into the Swedish colonies because their labor would be less profitable than that of Europeans.[1] Usselinx also questions whether slavery may not be considered contrary to love for one's neighbor, though he refrains

2. Objections to the introduction of slavery. Usselinx.

[1] Slaves, he says, "cost much, work reluctantly, require nothing from mechanics, as they go almost without clothes, and through ill-treatment soon die; whereas the people from different parts of Europe, being free, intelligent, and industrious, having wives and children, require all kinds of merchandise and mechanics, which would increase commerce." Mickley, *Some Account of William Usselinx*, in *Del. Hist. Soc. Papers*, III, 10–11.

from discussing that point.[1] The plan of Usselinx was not carried out at that time, and the colony established in 1638 is not directly connected with it. Slavery, though probably prohibited in the original Swedish settlements, was undoubtedly soon introduced.[2]

The Free Society of Traders in Pennsylvania, who were to hold their first general court in London in May, 1682, in accordance with the plan of William Penn, attempted to provide against perpetual servitude by declaring in their articles that " if the *Society* should receive *Blacks* for *servants*, they shall make them *free* at *fourteen years* end, upon Consideration that they shall give into the *Society's Ware-house two thirds* of what they are Capable of producing on such a *parcel* of *Land* as shall be allotted them by the *Society*." [3] Slaves, however, were soon introduced from the West Indies, and are said to have been tolerated because of the scarcity of laborers.[4] In West Jersey, in the Concessions of the Proprietors, in 1676, it was agreed " that all and every Person and Persons Inhabiting the said Province, shall, as far as in us lies, be free from Oppression and Slavery." [5] This clause, however, can hardly be assumed to apply to the negro without definite provision to that effect.

3. Provisions against perpetual servitude in Pennsylvania.

In Georgia the exclusion of slavery was more seriously attempted. The position of the colony on the Spanish frontier and the difficulties which South Carolina had already experienced led to the feeling that it was a political necessity to have at this point a people vigorous for attack and strong in their own defence. South Carolina was already conscious of the weakness engendered by a large slave

4. Exclusion of slavery from Georgia.

[1] Jameson, *William Usselinx*, in *Am. Hist. Soc. Papers*, 1887–1888, II, 109.

[2] DuBois, *The Suppression of the African Slave-Trade*, 24; Hazard, *Register of Pennsylvania*, IV, 21; *The Danish Laws; or, The Code of Christian the Fifth*, Book II, chapter xiv, on feudal bondsmen. Sale forbidden in § 9. See also Armstrong, *Record of Upland Court*, 27, 29–30; Hazard, *Annals of Pennsylvania*, 372.

[3] *Articles of the Free Society of Traders*, in *Pa. Mag. Hist. and Biog.*, V, 41–50, art. xviii. Dixon, *Life of Penn*, 301; Watson, *Annals of Philadelphia*, 480.

[4] Bettle, *Notices of Negro Slavery in Pennsylvania*, in *Pa. Hist. Soc. Mem.*, I, 380–381.

[5] DuBois, *Suppression of the Slave-Trade*, 24; Leaming and Spicer, *Grants, Concessions*, etc., 398.

population,[1] and it was believed that only a people who had to work for their own support could possess a vigorous and war-like spirit like that of "the old Romans."[2] In this asylum for the distressed the economic objections to slavery also occupied an important place. It was said that "slaves starve the poor laborer."[3] There was a feeling that the labor of slaves was really less profitable than that of whites, and that the whites would be unwilling to work in a country where slave labor existed.[4] It was found also that rice and the other produc-tions of the country could be raised without negroes,[5] and the importation of white servants from Germany for a term of years was considered preferable.[6] These were purely selfish considerations, but there are occasional gleams of moral sen-timent. Thus in a pamphlet published in 1734, the author pleases himself with the idea that no settlement was ever before established on so humane a plan. "Slavery, the mis-fortune, if not the dishonour of other plantations," he says, "is absolutely proscribed. Let avarice defend it as it will, there is an honest reluctance in humanity against buying and selling, and regarding those of our own species as our wealth and possessions."[7]

General Oglethorpe himself seems to have had no scruples about returning fugitives from South Carolina at the time of a negro revolt in that colony in 1739.[8] Yet his inter-est in a learned young African who had been kid-napped by a hostile tribe and sold into slavery in

5. Attitude of General Oglethorpe.

---

[1] This consciousness is expressed in several of the acts of the South Carolina Legislature, *e. g.*, those of Oct. 8, 1698, Dec. 18, 1714, and Dec. 11, 1717. DuBois, *Suppression of the Slave-Trade*, 9–11 and Appendix A ; Cooper, *Statutes at Large of South Carolina*, II, 153, VII, 367, 370.

[2] *Ga. Hist. Soc. Coll.*, I, 226.

[3] *Ibid.*, I, 96.

[4] *Ibid.*, I, 168–169, 172. A summary of the objections to slavery is given in Jones, *History of Georgia*, I, 110–112.

[5] Emigrants from Salzburg write to General Oglethorpe, in 1739 : " We were told by several People, after our Arrival, that it proves quite impossible and dangerous for White People to plant and manufacture any Rice, being a Work only for Negroes, not for European People ; but having Experience of the contrary we laugh at such a Talking." In Jones, *History of Georgia*, I, 306.

[6] *Ga. Hist. Soc. Coll.*, I, 169.

[7] In Bruce, *Life of Oglethorpe*, 99.

[8] Wright, *Memoir of Oglethorpe*, 220–221.

Maryland[1] shows that his humanitarianism was not confined to members of his own race; and it is supposed that his interest in this individual case may have directed his attention more particularly to the subject of slavery and intensified the objections to it which he already felt. At any rate, he refused in 1738 to alter the laws excluding slavery, declaring that he would have nothing to do with the colony if slavery were introduced; and he afterwards speaks of the prohibition of slavery in the colony as having rested on distinctly moral grounds. "Slavery," he says, "is against the gospel, as well as fundamental law of England. We refused, as trustees, to make a law permitting such a horrid crime."[2]

The example of the neighboring colony soon proved more effective than that of "the old Romans;" and the apparent economic advantages speedily outweighed the political, moral, and economic objections of the founders of the colony. The sentiment of the colonists was, however, by no means unanimous; a petition for slave labor, from one hundred and twenty-one of the magistrates and free-holders of Savannah, December 9, 1738, was partially offset by protests from the Salzburgers of Ebenezer and the Scottish Highlanders of New Inverness (Darien). These protests were made chiefly on economic grounds, but the political, philosophical, and moral arguments all appear. "It is shocking to human Nature," write the Scotch of New Inverness to General Oglethorpe (January 3, 1739), "that any Race of Mankind, and their Posterity should be sentenced to perpetual Slavery; nor in Justice can we think otherwise than that they are thrown amongst us to be our Scourge one Day or other for our Sins; and as Freedom to them must be as dear as to us, what a Scene of Horror must it bring about!"[3] The Trustees of the colony emphatically refused (June 20, 1739) to admit the "baneful

6. Introduction of slavery into Georgia.

---

[1] General Oglethorpe discovered this incident through a letter in Arabic, written by the young man to his father, which came into his hands as deputy-governor of the Royal African Company. He had the letter translated at Oxford, and on learning the contents undertook the ransom of Job, who was then brought to England and finally returned to his home under British escort. Bruce, *Life of Oglethorpe*, 132–138.

[2] *Ibid.*, 206, 99.

[3] Jones, *History of Georgia*, I, 302–307, 421–422. Protest from New Inverness, 304–305.

Commodity" which had already brought their "Neighbour Colonies to the Brink of Ruin."¹ They again refused in 1748, suggesting that it would be of service to the colony for those who persist in declaring that they cannot succeed without negroes to retire to some other province.² The prohibition, however, was evaded by hiring negroes from South Carolina for a term of years, sometimes for a hundred years or for life. Then the magistrates and courts connived at open purchase, and finally slavery, with some restrictions, was allowed (1749).³

In early colonial history the most important anti-slavery movements are those of the Puritans and Quakers. Both were founded upon religious principles. "New England," says Mr. George H. Moore, "had to outgrow the theology of the Elizabethan Calvinists before it could understand that the Father of Heaven respected neither person nor color."⁴ Still, the New England Puritans were at least as far advanced in this respect as their neighbors; and the anti-slavery sentiment that does appear among them is the direct outcome of Calvinistic theology. To lay the foundations of democracy was not at all what John Calvin had intended; but he builded better than he knew, for the doctrine of election did away with distinctions of rank and power and no less with distinctions of color. The Puritan, to be sure, was not inclined to yield social equality to his black brethren; but equality before God he was among the first to admit, and in a theocracy this was not far distant from equality before the law.

7. Puritan anti-slavery sentiment.

The first protest against slavery that appears in the colonies is uttered by Roger Williams. His plea for the captive Pequots in 1637, though limited in its application, shows a sense of the injustice of "perpetuall slaverie" which might easily be extended to the case of the African.⁵ It is not surprising, therefore, to find in the colony of Roger Williams the first positive legislation against negro slavery. By a statute enacted in 1652, negroes were to be held

8. Roger Williams and the Providence Plantation.

---

¹ Jones, *History of Georgia*, I, 311.

² *Ibid.*, I, 419, note.

³ *Ibid.*, I, 420–425; McCall, *History of Georgia*, I, 206–209. *Cf.* Du-Bois, *Suppression of the Slave-Trade*, 7–8.

⁴ Moore, *Notes on Slavery in Massachusetts*, 71.

⁵ Roger Williams, *Letter to John Winthrop*, in 4 *Mass. Hist. Soc. Coll.*, VI, 214.

in service only for a limited number of years, and then to be set free in the same manner as English servants.[1] This law, however, is said to have been in operation only in Providence and Warwick.[2] Slavery was soon found to be more profitable in Rhode Island than in other parts of New England, and " the Narragansett planters " developed an industrial system which may fairly be compared with that of the Southern colonies.[3]

The Massachusetts " Body of Liberties " (1641) is regarded by Mr. Moore as " the first statute establishing slavery in

9. Early sentiment in Massachusetts.

America." [4] The Hon. Emory Washburn, on the other hand, points to it with pride as indicating a very early hostility to slavery.[5] The act is perhaps the first that recognizes slavery, but its evident intention was to limit that which already existed, not to create or establish the institution; and it may be noticed that no person could legally be born a slave in Massachusetts. The law provides that "there shall never be any bond slaverie, villinage or Captivitie amongst us unles it be lawfull Captives taken in just warres, and such strangers as willingly selle themselves or are sold to us. . . . This exempts none from servitude who shall be Judged thereto by Authoritie." [6] The repugnance to enslavement by means which were considered unjust appears a few years later when "the Gennerall Courte, conceaving themselves bound by the first optunity to beare witnes agnt ye hainous & crying sinn of man stealing," and to make such redress as to deter all others from such vile and odious courses, send back to Guinea all those unlawfully taken, at the charge of the country, together with a letter expressing the indignation of the Court.[7]

---

1 *Rhode Island Colonial Records*, I, 243.

2 Hurd, *Law of Freedom and Bondage*, I, 275, note.

3 Channing, *The Narragansett Planters*, 5–23.

4 Moore, *Notes on Slavery in Massachusetts*, 11.

5 Washburn, *The Extinction of Slavery in Massachusetts*, in 4 *Mass. Hist. Soc. Coll.*, IV, 334–335; Ibid., *Slavery as it once prevailed in Massachusetts*, 9–15.

6 *Massachusetts Colonial Laws*, 53, 125.   The legal bearing of this statute may be seen in the plea and decision of *James* vs. *Lechmere*, in 1769. Washburn, *Extinction of Slavery in Massachusetts*, in 4 *Mass. Hist. Soc. Coll.*, IV, 335.

7 *Mass. Col. Rec.*, II, 67, 136, 168, 176; III, 46, 49, 58, 84.   Quotation, III, 84.   See also Winthrop, *History of New England*, II, 244–245, 379–380.

The early objections to slavery itself were directed against its common abuses, — harsh treatment of the negro and the neglect of his spiritual welfare. John Eliot, in 1675, memorialized the legislature of the Massachusetts Bay Colony with regard to the sale of Indians into slavery in the West Indies, but his main anxiety was lest they should be deprived of the benefits of the Gospel: "to sell soules for mony," he said, "seemeth to me a dangerous merchandize . . . to sell y^m away frō all meanes of grace, w^n Christ hath pvided meanes of grace for y^m, is the way for us to be active in the destroying their soules, when we are highly obliged to seeke theire convsion, & salvation."[1] Both John Eliot and Cotton Mather were much concerned that the negroes were treated as domestic animals and "that so little care was taken of their precious and immortal Souls," which were left "to a destroying ignorance, meerly for fear of thereby losing the benefit of their Vassalage."[2] Eliot devoted considerable attention to the instruction of the slaves, and Mather published some *Rules for the Society of Negroes*, apparently urging kind treatment and religious instruction:[3] but neither Mather nor Eliot made any public effort in favor of emancipation.

10. John Eliot and Cotton Mather.

More to the point are the directions to slave-owners in the colonies, given by Richard Baxter, the eminent English Nonconformist, who was a contemporary of Mather and Eliot. These directions, which are published in the *Christian Directory*, must have been often in the hands of his fellow Puritans in America and have had some influence. The address certainly embodies the ideas which the Puritans of his age were making their own and converting into living forces. "Remember," he says, in speaking of negroes and other slaves, "that they are of as good a kind as you; that is, They are reasonable Creatures as well as you, and born to as much natural liberty. If their sin have enslaved them to you, yet Nature made them your equals." Slavery he considers justified in the case of crime, and to a certain degree in case of the "necessitated consent" of the innocent or in case

11. Baxter's Directions to Masters In foraign Plantations.

---

[1] *Petition of John Eliot*, in *Plymouth Col. Rec.*, X, 451–453. Quotation from p. 452.
[2] Cotton Mather, *Life of John Eliot*, 151.
[3] *Ibid.*, 163–164; *Pa. Mag. Hist. and Biog.*, XIII, 265.

of captivity in lawful war, thus occupying a similar position to that of the Massachusetts law-makers of 1641. On the subject of man-stealing, his language is considerably stronger than that of the General Court.   "To go as Pirates," he says, " and catch up poor *Negro's* or People of another Land, that never forfeited Life or Liberty, and to make them slaves, and sell them, is one of the worst kinds of Thievery in the World . . . and they that buy them and use them as Beasts, for their meer commodity, and betray, or destroy, or neglect their Souls, are fitter to be called incarnate Devils than Christians, tho they be no Christians whom they so abuse."   Baxter enforces his point by a series of questions and answers in the form of a catechism:

" Quest. *But what if men buy Negro's or other slaves of such as we have just cause to believe did steal them by Piracy, or buy them of those that have no power to sell them, and not hire or buy them by their own consent, or by the consent of those that had power to sell them, nor take them Captives in a lawful War, what must they do with them afterward?*

" Answ. 1. It is their heinous sin to buy them, unless it be in charity to deliver them.   2. Having done it, undoubtedly they are presently bound to deliver them : Because by right the man is his own, and therefore no man else can have just title to him.

" Quest. *But may I not sell him again and make my Money of him, seeing I leave him but as I found him ?*

" Answ. No, because when you have taken possession of him and a pretended propriety, then the injury that is done him is by you ; which before was only by another.

" Quest. *But may I not return him to him that I bought him of ?*

" Answ. No : for that is but injuring him by delivering him to another to continue the injury . . . Gods Law bindeth you to Love, and work of Love, and therefore you should do your best to free him." [1]

Baxter, like Eliot and Mather, is more concerned for the moral and material welfare of the individual than for the abolition of the institution, but it is a long step in advance when natural liberty and equality are allowed to black as well as white, even in theory, and when so decided a stand is taken against vested rights of property in men.

In American literature the high-water mark of early Puritan sentiment is reached by Chief-Justice Sewall. Perhaps for this

[1] Baxter, *Christian Directory*, Part II, ch. xiv. In *Practical Works* I, 438–440.

reason *The Selling of Joseph* has achieved greater fame than it would otherwise have done.   Sewall's tract seems bare and cold in comparison with the contemporary Quaker 12. Sewall's literature.   It breathes of the Old Testament rather *Selling of* than the New, of righteousness and justice rather *Joseph,* *1701.* than love for one's neighbor, and the conclusion is decidedly lame.   Moreover, it is concerned with the slave-trade rather than with slavery, though the arguments applied to the one may generally be applied to the other also.   But Sewall's " Antipathy against Slavery," which lasted to the end of his days,[1] is evidently beyond that of Cotton Mather or John Eliot.

Sewall's argument is based on the proposition that " Liberty *is in real value next unto Life,*" and therefore " *None ought to part with it themselves, or deprive others of it, but upon most mature Consideration.*" [2]   This can hardly be considered extreme after Locke's chapters on natural liberty and the right of resistance to encroachments upon it; but Sewall makes one step forward in regarding liberty for its own sake, while Locke is thinking of it as a means to self-preservation.   Sewall's position is also in some respects more advanced than Baxter's: the English Puritan countenanced slavery arising from voluntary sale or from captivity in just war; Sewall would permit slavery only as a punishment for crime.   The Israelites, he says, were forbidden to enslave one another, and " Christians should carry it to all the World as the *Israelites* were to carry it one towards another." [3]   As for sale, " there is no proportion between Twenty Pieces of Silver, and *LIBERTY*." [4]

Sewall's ideas of liberty and equality rest on a philosophical rather than a practical basis.   " Originally and Naturally," he says, " there is no such thing as Slavery," because " all Men, as they are the sons of *Adam*, are Coheirs; and have equal Right unto Liberty, and all other outward Comforts of Life." [5] But it is not social or even political equality among these children of a common father that Sewall is contending for.

---

[1] Sewall, *Letter-Book,* in 6 *Mass. Hist. Soc. Coll.,* II, 182.   Feb. 25, 172⅘.

[2] Ibid., *The Selling of Joseph,* in 5 *Mass. Hist. Soc. Coll.,* VI, 16.   A significant extract in Hart, *American History told by Contemporaries,* II, § 103, pp. 293–297.

[3] Sewall, *The Selling of Joseph,* in 5 *Mass. Hist. Soc. Coll.,* VI, 19.

[4] *Ibid.,* 17.   [5] *Ibid.*

Indeed, he has a decided antipathy to his black brethren as a part of the "Body Politick."[1]   He simply asserts that "these *Ethiopians*, as black as they are; seeing they are the Sons and Daughters of the First *Adam*, the Brethren and Sisters of the Last ADAM, and the Offspring of GOD; They ought to be treated with a Respect agreeable."[2]

Sewall's tract was the result partly of his religious convictions and partly of the conditions of the time.   The immediate occasion was a combination of circumstances which indicate that people's minds were already somewhat exercised on the subject.   There was pending "a Motion by a Boston comittee" for a law to discourage the importation of negroes.[3]   The plan, perhaps partly under the influence of Sewall's pamphlet, took the form in 1701 of instructions to the Representatives of Boston, "To promote the Encourrageing the bringing of white serv^ts and to put a Period to negros being Slaves."[4]   No practical results are recorded; and in 1703 an act was passed to restrict manumission, not so much from any objection to manumission in itself as from the reluctance to maintain the aged and infirm at the public cost, a form of thrift which prevailed in the early New England towns.[5]

13. Attempt at legislation.

The Selling of Joseph brought some "Frowns and hard Words" upon its author,[6] and even met with a direct reply.[7]

14. Later attitude of Sewall.

In 1705, under the stimulus of this opposition and of a bill before the General Court which he regarded as oppressive to the negroes, Sewall republished an English tract called *The Athenian Oracle* which he had happened to see in a book-seller's shop, and in which the arguments with regard to slavery and the slave-trade are similar to his own,

---

[1] Sewall, *The Selling of Joseph*, in 5 *Mass. Hist. Soc. Coll.*, VI, 18.

[2] *Ibid.*, 20.

[3] *Ibid.*, 16.

[4] *Boston Town Records*, May 26, 1701.   In *A Report of the Record Commissioners, containing the Records of the Boston Selectmen*, 1701 to 1715, p. 5.

[5] *Acts and Resolves of the Province of the Massachusetts Bay*, I, 519. Passed July 28, 1703.

[6] Sewall, Letters to Nathaniel Byfield and Rev. John Higginson, in *Letter-Book*, 6 *Mass. Hist. Soc. Coll.*, I, 322, 326.

[7] Saffin, *A Brief and Candid Answer to a late Printed Sheet entitled The Selling of Joseph*.   In Moore, *Notes on Slavery in Massachusetts*, 88, note, 251–256.

but somewhat warmer in coloring.[1] In 1716 he made an
attempt "to prevent Indians and Negroes being Rated with
Horses and Hogs."[2] His negro servant, Scipio, seems to
have received wages, and was at one time the possessor of at
least £20, which he gave to his master to keep for him, receiv-
ing interest at five per cent.[3] But though Sewall's antipathy
to slavery affected his personal affairs, he made no direct effort
to destroy the institution. He shrank from the logical outcome of his principles and was content with compromises; he
would have been glad to see slavery abolished, but he had not
the burning zeal which fires men to action.

It is not until a generation or two later that a Puritan anti-
slavery writer takes an absolutely uncompromising attitude.
Nathaniel Appleton, son of the pastor of the First
Church in Cambridge,[4] believed not merely that the
Ethiopian should "be treated with a Respect agreeable," but that slavery should be abandoned at any cost. The
West Indies at that time were a most important source of
income to the trading colonies of New England, but if they
cannot be cultivated without slave labor, Appleton says, "let
them sink then." Though fortunes might be ruined by a
change in the industrial system, "'tis more honourable to seek
a support by begging than by theft."[5] As for the purchase of
negroes, he thinks, the excuse that they are already enslaved is
of no value whatever. He does not, like Baxter, discriminate
as to the original cause of enslavement; and the purchaser, he
says, is guilty of a baseness and meanness unredeemed by even
that brute virtue of courage which was possessed by the man-
stealer in Guinea.[6] Though this tract, written several years
before its publication in 1767, deals mainly with scriptural
arguments, the influence of John Locke is to be discerned
here as well as in the literature of the Revolutionary period;
and the political, economic, and moral arguments are of a
more advanced character than those of Chief-Justice Sewall.

15. Nathan-
iel Appleton,
1767.

[1] Sewall, *Letter-Book*, in 6 *Mass. Hist. Soc. Coll.*, I, 322, 326; *The
Athenian Oracle.*

[2] Sewall, *Diary*, in 5 *Mass. Hist. Soc. Coll.*, VII, 87.

[3] *Ibid.*, 296.

[4] Deane, *Letters and Documents relating to Slavery in Massachusetts*,
in 5 *Mass. Hist. Soc. Coll.*, III, 389, note.

[5] Appleton, *Considerations on Slavery*, 8.   [6] *Ibid.*, 11.

The earlier writers had already considered the unprofitableness of slave-labor on account of the comparative cost of importation, the untrustworthy character of the slaves, and the fact that " their continual aspiring after their forbidden Liberty, renders them Unwilling Servants."[1] Mingled with these arguments is the objection to the African race as an element in the population.   The negroes, says Sewall, cannot "be used in the train-bands" or "serve as husbands for our daughters;" while white servants, after their term has expired, can settle on the frontier and serve as a defence to the province.[2] The slave-trade, argues Appleton, not only takes riches from the province "(if rum may be called so)," but the slaves, as the experience of New York and other colonies has recently proved, "instead of being a defence and support of the common wealth, are often its terror and sometimes its destruction."[3]   The fact that slavery was discouraging to white labor was noticed in the time of Sewall,[4] but the case is more strongly stated by Appleton.   The poor whites, he says, "would gladly serve us for a support, but then they must be upon a level with negro slaves; they being born free, can't think of such a disgrace as they esteem it," and pauperism and vagabondage, idleness and vice are the natural consequences, the slave-holders on their part also degenerating in character and becoming imperious and cruel.[5]

16. Political, economic, and moral arguments.

Puritan anti-slavery sentiment, however, was based mainly on concern for the " precious and immortal soul " of the slave, on the sentiment of justice, and on regard for all God's creatures.[6] It expended itself in mitigating the evils of slavery by just and kind treatment of the slave and by care for his religious and moral welfare.   But economic considerations in New England were not such as to lead men far into temptation, and though the slave-trade

17. General character of Puritan anti-slavery sentiment.

---

[1] Sewall, *The Selling of Joseph*, in 5 *Mass. Hist. Soc. Coll.*, VI, 17; *Computation that the Importation of Negroes is not so profitable as that of White Servants*, reprinted from *The Boston News-Letter*, No. 112, June 10, 1706, in Moore, *Notes on Slavery in Massachusetts*, 106–108.

[2] Sewall, *The Selling of Joseph*, in 5 *Mass. Hist. Soc. Coll.*, VI, 17, 18.

[3] Appleton, *Considerations on Slavery*, 13.

[4] *Computation*, etc., Moore, 106–108.   Cf. *Acts and Resolves of the Province of the Massachusetts Bay*, I, 634, 698 (Feb. 26, 170$\frac{8}{9}$, and Aug. 23, 1712).

[5] Appleton, *Considerations on Slavery*, 14–15.   [6] *Ibid.*, 15.

was actively carried on for the benefit or the injury of other colonies, slavery itself had so weak a hold upon New England that when a new impulse was given by the sentiment of the Revolution it could easily be uprooted.

The religious principles of the Quakers carried them far beyond the Puritans, and their history shows what might have been accomplished through religious organizations if other denominations had been as uniformly sincere and unworldly and single-minded as the Society of Friends. The personal influence of George Fox was employed against slavery as early as 1671, and his authority is frequently quoted by anti-slavery writers; but he sanctioned a limited term of servitude, only advising emancipation after that service. The real value of his work is in organizing a Society upon principles which, if sincerely and consistently held, must result in opposition to slavery.[1] Not that the Quakers had new or peculiar ideas; they simply emphasized a principle as old as Christianity, the principle of human brotherhood, and made the Golden Rule a standing rule to live by. Their opposition to slavery was based mainly on the Scriptures, and many of their arguments are similar to those of the Puritans. Still, there are several differences in the theological attitudes of the two sects, which affected their views with regard to slavery. The Puritans thought more of the Old Testament; the religion of the Quakers is filled with the spirit of the New. The Puritans believed that every event is foreordained, including the action of the human will; the Quakers made the freedom of the human will one of their leading arguments against slavery.[2] The Puritans believed in the equality of human souls, but man, as touching nature, was but a worm of this earth; the Quakers believed in the dignity of man and in a human brotherhood which included social equality as well as equality before God and the law: they were in fact as well as in name a Society of Friends.

18. Anti-slavery sentiment in the Society of Friends.

[1] Janney, *History of the Religious Society of Friends*, II, 249–250, 365. Among Fox's bequests are mentioned, " 1 negro man, 1 warming pan, 1 old looking-glass, and 1 gun." *Ibid.*

[2] Hepburn, *American Defence of the Christian Golden Rule*, 1–3; Coleman, *Testimony against that Anti-Christian Practice of Making Slaves of Men*, 14.

Both Quaker and Puritan had a firm belief in the special interpositions of Providence, but the Quakers much earlier than the Puritans came to feel that slavery was the particular offence that called down the avenging wrath.

19. Moral arguments.

They felt more strongly the inconsistency of slavery with the principles of Christianity, regarding it as so perilous to salvation that "for all the Riches and Honours of this world" they would not be guilty of it.[1] They felt more strongly also the evil effects of slavery in promoting pride, idleness, and vanity. Thus John Hepburn, a native of Great Britain residing in New Jersey, and one of the earliest apostles of the anti-slavery cause, writes, in 1714, of the slave-masters: they "can afford to keep themselves with white hands, except at some Times they chance to be besparkled with the Blood of those poor Slaves, when they fall to beating them with their *twisted Hides and Horse-whips,* . . . to go with *fine powdered Perriwigs,* and great bunched [?] *Coats ;* and likewise keep their Wives idle (*Jezebel-like*) to paint *their Faces,* and *Puff,* and *powder their Hair,* and to bring up their Sons and Daughters in *Idleness* and *Wantonness,* and in all manner of *Pride* and *Prodigality,* in *decking* and *adorning* their Carkasses . . . All, and much more, the miserable Effects produced by the Slavery of the Negroes."[2] These effects were perhaps not particularly conspicuous in the regions where even the Chief-Justice has shared the labor of the hay-field, but not even a Puritan could have been so disturbed by the vanities of life as was John Hepburn.

The duty of kindness to all God's creatures, which was a feature of Puritan sentiment, was equally felt by the Quakers. Antipathy to cock-fighting and bear-baiting and the disapproval of slavery are closely allied. In their writings attention is frequently called to the cruel treatment of slaves, to the barbarous punishments, to the severe precautionary measures prompted by the fear of insurrection, and to the vices which resulted from the miserable condition of the slave and the arbitrary power of the master. The demoralization resulting from

[1] Hepburn, *American Defence*, 3; Coleman, *Testimony*, 22.   Coleman's *Testimony* is evidently given under the influence of Hepburn's *Defence*.

[2] Hepburn, *American Defence*, 3.   *Cf.* Coleman, *Testimony*, 16; Lay, *All Slave-Keepers Apostates*, 28.

the lack of employment among the poor whites is also noticed.[1]

Economic arguments, although they received considerable attention among the Quakers, were only supplementary. They were used for the sake of convincing others, not because they had any influence upon the mind of the writer; and emancipation was accomplished in 20. Economic arguments. spite of economic considerations, not because of them.[2] The chief arguments were that slavery " promotes Idleness in the Rich " and " hinders the Poor from Bread; "[3] that it prevents the immigration of industrious laboring people, " the chief Strength and Support of a Community," and interferes with the prosperity of those who have already come into the country.[4] To the argument that slave-labor is necessary, it was replied that " Poverty does not make Robbery lawful; " that if a man can work he can earn a living as well as the negro, and if he cannot, his neighbors should help him.[5] " Man is born to labour," says one, " and Experience abundantly sheweth, that it is for our Good."[6] " Seed sown with the Tears of a confined oppressed People," says the same writer, " Harvest cut down by an overborne discontented Reaper, makes Bread less sweet to the Taste of an honest Man, than that which is the Produce, or just Reward of such voluntary Action, which is one proper Part of the Business of human Creatures."[7]

Among the Quaker anti-slavery writers there were no such scholars as Cotton Mather and John Eliot, Chief-Justice Sewall and Nathaniel Appleton. Their language is often ungrammatical, and their epithets are occasionally 21. Minor arguments. coarse. A few of them indulge in wandering and irrelevant

[1] Benezet, *A Short Account of that Part of Africa Inhabited by Negroes* 79–80; Hepburn, *Defence*, 4–7; A Native of America, in Hepburn, *Defence* Appendix, 35; Woolman, *Some Considerations on the Keeping of Negroes* 15; Ibid., *Considerations*, Part II, 22–24; *Works*, 26, 57–64.

[2] *Ibid.,* 157.

[3] Sandiford, *A Brief Examination of the Practice of the Times*, § xix p. 68.

[4] Benezet, *A Short Account of that Part of Africa Inhabited by Ne groes*, 79.

[5] A Native of America, in Hepburn, *Defence*, Appendix, 29.

[6] Woolman, *Some Considerations on the Keeping of Negroes*, 15.

[7] Ibid., *Considerations*, Part II, 27.

remarks which give evidence of untrained, if not ill-balanced minds; but their arguments, though homely, are usually cogent, and show keenness of humor and practical good sense. "If these Negroes are Slaves of Slaves," says Ralph Sandiford, in 1729, replying to the well-worn argument of the curse of Canaan, "whose Slaves must their Masters be?"[1] Elihu Coleman, of Nantucket, the same year, meets the argument that the negroes must be slaves because they are ignorant and wicked, by saying, "If that plea would do, I do believe they need not go so far for slaves as now they do."[2]

The first distinctly anti-slavery document in America was the protest of the Mennonite exiles who settled in Germantown, Pennsylvania. This protest is typical of the attitude of the Society of Friends of which the Mennonites became members. "Now, tho they are black," wrote these simple-hearted protestants, in 1688, "we can not conceive there is more liberty to have them slaves, as it is to have other white ones. There is a saying, that we shall doe to all men like as we will be done ourselves; making no difference of what generation, descent or colour they are. . . . Here is liberty of conscience wch is right and reasonable. Here ought also to be liberty of ye body."[3]

22. Early anti-slavery literature among the Quakers.

This protest was soon followed by George Keith's *Exhortation and Caution to Friends* (1693), in which the author, just a century before the enactment of the first Fugitive Slave Law, summarily disposes of the question of fugitives. Keith is the first to make use of the passage from the Scriptures which was afterwards so effectively quoted by Wendell Phillips: "Thou shalt not deliver unto his Master the Servant that is escaped from his Master unto thee." "By which it appeareth," explains Keith, "that those which are at Liberty and freed from their Bondage, should not by us be delivered into Bondage again, neither by us should they be oppressed, but being escaped from his Master, should have the Liberty to dwell amongst us, where it liketh him best."[4]

---

[1] Sandiford, *Brief Examination*, § iv, p. 5.

[2] Coleman, *Testimony*, 17.

[3] *Germantown Friends' Protest against Slavery*, 1; reprinted in Hart, *American History told by Contemporaries*, II, § 102, pp. 291–293.

[4] Keith, *An Exhortation and Caution to Friends*, in *Pa. Mag. Hist. and Biog.*, XIII, 268.

Not long afterwards John Hepburn published his *American Defence of the Christian Golden Rule* (1714). An appendix to this tract by "A Native of America" contains the first elaborate proposals for emancipation.[1] Hepburn was followed almost immediately by William Burling, of Long Island (1718); then came the tract of Elihu Coleman (1729) and, from the press of Benjamin Franklin, the more famous productions of Ralph Sandiford (1729) and Benjamin Lay (1737).

The two last-named authors probably had more influence on anti-slavery sentiment than any others of so early a date. Neither was a native of America, but both had developed an antipathy to slavery before their settlement in Philadelphia, and their opposition to it became the leading interest in their lives. Both were eccentric in their habits and manners and curiously wild and incoherent in their writings; but they enjoyed the friendship of Benjamin Franklin and other eminent men.[2] Their simple sincerity and moral earnestness lent a weight to their words which could not have been given by logic of arrangement or elegance of diction; and their writings are marked by a love for mankind and by a simple though homely truthfulness that must have appealed to many of their readers. Their very eccentricities and extravagances served their cause by attracting attention and awakening discussion. Even the violent opposition aroused by Lay is said to have given stimulus to the movement, and he had the satisfaction, before the close of his days, of knowing that the cause he had so much at heart was really advancing.[3]

23. Ralph Sandiford and Benjamin Lay.

Both Sandiford and Lay wrote mainly from religious motives. Their works are full of quotations from both the Old Testament and the New, and the thought and language throughout is that of men whose education has been chiefly through the study of the Bible. ". . . shall we go to Africa for Bread," says Sandiford, "and lay the Burden which appertains to our Bodily Support on their Shoulders? Is this Washing one another's Feet, or living by the Gospel, or Maintaining Liberty and Property?"[4] And again, "How then have they forfeited their Country and

---

[1] See below, § 29.
[2] Vaux, *Memoirs of Lay and Sandiford*, 37.
[3] *Ibid.*, 50–52.
[4] Sandiford, *Brief Examination*, Dedication.

Liberty, to entitle me to them? And if so, must the Children's Teeth also be set on Edge? Is this *just* or equal? And to live on another's Labour by Force and Oppression, is this *Loving Mercy?* And to keep them Slaves to us and our Posterity to all Eternity, is this *Walking Humbly, with thy God?*"[1]

The early Quaker literature teems with sarcasm directed chiefly against the professors of Christianity. John Hepburn

24. Attacks on Christian sects. devotes several pages of his pamphlet to an imaginary conversation between a Christian Negro-Master and a Turk, in which the Turk of course has much the better of the argument, and to an ironical pro-slavery argument based on the practice of the various Christian sects.[2] The Quakers themselves were not exempt from this form of attack, and Benjamin Lay was particularly severe upon his own sect. "*All Slave-Keepers . . . Apostates*" is the motto of his book, and the Friends, as the most inconsistent and hypocritical of all, he regards as worse even than the slave-traders. ". . . do not we kill," he says, "when we receive the Plunder, and send the Villains for more . . . we appear very Religious and Demure, Preaching against Iniquity and Vice; they appear to be what they are . . . how does our Demure Slave-Keepers *remember them that are in Bonds as bound with 'em*, except as Slaves are bound to them, so they to the Devil, and stronger, for as Death loosens one, it fastens the other in eternal Torments if not repented and forsaken."[3]

Even more violent are Lay's attacks upon the preachers, who are represented as "a sort of Devils, that Preach more to Hell than they do to Heaven, and so they will do forever, as long as they are suffered to reign in the worst, and Mother of all Sins, Slave-Keeping."[4] He describes the Minister's starting off "to preach the Gospel of glad Tydings to all Men and Liberty to the Captives" and giving directions to his slaves before he goes.[5] "What do you think of these Things, you brave Gospel Ministers?" he says, "that keep poor Slaves to Work for you to maintain you and yours in Pride, Pride and much Idleness or Laziness, and Fulness of Bread, the Sins of *Sodom:* How

---

[1] Sandiford, *Brief Examination*, § xv, pp. 38–39.

[2] Hepburn, *American Defence*, 9–19.

[3] Lay, *All Slave-Keepers Apostates*, 114, 119.

[4] *Ibid.*, 106.   [5] *Ibid.*, 31.

do these Things become your plain Dress, Demure Appearance, feigned Humility, all but Hypocrisy, which according to Truth's Testimony, must have the hottest place in Hell; to keep those miserable Creatures at hard Labour continually . . . so that Dogs and Cats are much better taken care for, and yet some have had the Confidence or rather Impudence, to say their Slaves or Negroes live as well as themselves. I could almost wish such hardened, unthinking, Sinful devilish Lyars were put into their Places, at least for a time." [1]

In the early Quaker literature the ideas of natural liberty and equality are not conspicuous. The basis of argument is always distinctly religious rather than political or social. Sandiford, like Sewall, argues in behalf of original rights unforfeited by consent or captivity in war; but his mind, like Sewall's, is fixed on the Old Testament, rather than on man in a state of nature.[2] With the approach of the American Revolution, the doctrine of natural rights appears among the Quakers as well as elsewhere. Anthony Benezet, for instance, writes in 1762, "Upon the whole . . . it must appear to every honest unprejudiced Reader, that the Negroes are equally intituled to the common Priviledges of Mankind with the Whites, that they have the same rational Powers; the same natural Affections, and are as susceptible of Pain and Grief as they, that therefore the bringing and keeping them in Bondage is an Instance of Oppression and Injustice of most grievous Nature, such as is scarcely to be parallelled by any Example in the present or former Ages." [3] John Woolman also "believed that liberty was the natural right of all men equally," [4] and that "the Colour of a Man avails nothing, in Matters of Right and Equity." [5]

25. Later literature. Beginnings of political philosophy.

In this later period, Benezet and Woolman stand foremost, outranking predecessors and contemporaries as representatives of the ideals of their sect. Benezet was a French Huguenot whose parents, soon after his birth, in 1713, had fled to Holland, and thence had gone to England,

26. Anthony Benezet and John Woolman.

---

[1] Lay, *All-Slave-Keepers Apostates*, 92–93.
[2] Sandiford, *Brief Examination*, §§ vi, xv, pp. 6–8, 35–40.
[3] Benezet, *Short Account*, 78.
[4] Woolman, *Works*, 57, 221; *Considerations*, Part II, 47–50.
[5] *Ibid.*, 30.

where they adopted the religious opinions of the Quakers. After coming to America Benezet became an instructor in the Friends' English School in Philadelphia; later, becoming interested in the negroes, he started an evening school for their instruction. He published several works against slavery and the slave-trade, the most famous of which, *A Short Account of that Part of Africa Inhabited by Negroes* (1762), directed Thomas Clarkson's attention to the subject and led him to write his famous prize essay, *Anne liceat invitos in servitutem dare* (1786).[1] There is probably no other man in the period of gradual abolition who did so much for the anti-slavery movement in America as Anthony Benezet.

John Woolman's influence was less widely felt. Though he travelled in England as well as in America, his labours were confined to his own sect, and his written works were less widely circulated than those of his contemporary. The gentle charity with which Benezet met " even the unreasonableness of mankind" was equally characteristic of Woolman; and like Benezet he felt the generous enthusiasm for a good cause, the unfaltering devotion to what he believed to be. right, and the refusal to compromise with sin, though making every allowance for the sinner. In the anti-slavery cause they were equally zealous, equally fearless and devoted, and at the same time reasonable and tolerant. With a charity which admitted the possibility of sentiments of justice and humanity even in the slave-holder, they took into account the difficulties of emancipation. They combined extreme conscientiousness and courage with friendliness and tact, and their personal influence must have accomplished at least as much as their published works.

Benezet, regarding the abolition of the slave-trade as the first necessity, made that the chief object of his attention; but 27. **The work of Benezet.** he begs those who hold slaves to consider whether the distinction between slavery and the slave-trade is not " a Plea founded more in Words than supported by Truth." [2] Realizing the unfitness of the slaves for sudden and total emancipation, he yet did more than any one else toward undermining the favorite arguments against it. His

---

[1] Vaux, *Memoirs of Benezet ;* Appleton, *Encyclopedia.*
[2] Benezet, *Short Account,* 64.

free evening-school for negroes convinced him that the African race had not only a right to freedom but a capacity for mental and moral improvement which would make it possible for them to become useful citizens.[1]   His experience and the educational work to which he devoted life and property[2] went far toward disposing of the argument from the essential inferiority of the African race.

John Woolman is one of the most interesting and lovable characters in the history of the anti-slavery movement.   His scruples were first aroused on occasion of the con- **28. The work** veyancing of a negro woman sold by his employer, **of Woolman.** and his modest but firm demeanor and gentle persuasiveness proved very effective in the case of individuals with whom he came in contact in connection with legal business.[3]   He soon found a wider field in systematic work in the anti-slavery cause. His journeys as a "public Friend," or travelling preacher, extended from Rhode Island to North Carolina, and wherever he went he used his influence in behalf of emancipation.   His sympathetic heart beat for both slave and slave-holder.   He travelled sometimes on foot, that he might " have a more lively feeling of the condition. of the oppressed slaves."[4]   His description of the aged slaves is very characteristic: " when they feel pains, and stiffness in their joints and limbs, weakness of appetite, and that a little labour is wearisome, and still behold themselves in the neglected uncomfortable condition of a slave . . . For men to be thus treated from one generation to another, who, besides their own distresses, think of the slavery entailed on their posterity, and are grieved, what disagreeable thoughts must they have of the professed followers of Jesus! and how must their groans ascend to that almighty Being, who ' will be a refuge for the oppressed'! "[5]

In the Southern colonies, especially among those people who "lived in ease on the hard labour of their slaves," he "felt uneasy," and his gentle admonitions and suggestions to the slave-holders were often kindly received and seriously considered.[6]   Like Sandiford and Lay, he would not use the

---

[1] Vaux, *Memoirs of Benezet*, 27–30.
[2] Bettle, *Notices of Negro Slavery*, in *Pa. Hist. Soc. Mem.*, I, 399–404.
[3] Woolman, *Works*, 17–18, 37, 43–45.   Extracts in Hart, *Contemporaries*, II, § 106, pp. 302–308.
[4] Woolman, *Works*, 161.   [5] *Ibid.*, 221.   [6] *Ibid.*, 25, 56–73, 109–114.

products of slave-labor.[1] The discontent of the slaves and the idleness and vices which accompanied the system of slavery seemed to him "as a gloom over the land."[2] "Luxury and Oppression," he says, "have the seeds of War and Desolation in them," and the shadow of coming events was often heavy on his soul.[3] Through his personal appeals to the reason and conscience of individuals, his addresses at Friends' meetings and his activity in connection with the organized efforts of the Society, he did more than any other, except perhaps Benezet, to free his own sect from the burden of responsibility, and the success of the emancipation movement among the Quakers is very largely due to his influence.[4]

The Quakers as a rule made no proposals for emancipation by law. Probably their objections to magistracy prevented their making any extensive use of this resource. Nevertheless, they continually urged manumission by individual owners, and even so early as 1713 there was a definite scheme for freeing the negroes and returning them to Africa.

29. Schemes for emancipation. Proposals for returning negroes to Africa.

It was proposed : —

" 1. That *Subscriptions* be taken of all Masters that will set their Negros free, and of the Number of Negros so to be set free, that they may be sent to their own Country.

" 2. That Subscriptions be taken, what each Man (Negro Master, or others) will give to defray the Charge of sending the Negros home.

" 3. That such Negros as had rather serve their Masters, then [than] go home, may be kept still (it being their Free Act, and it not being safe to have them free in this Country)."

The negroes were also to be instructed in religion, that they might act as missionaries on their return to Africa.[5]

---

1 Testimony of Monthly Meeting of Friends in Burlington, 8 mo. 1st day, 1774, in Woolman, *Works*, xii; Brissot de Warville, *New Travels in the United States*, I, 225.

2 Woolman, *Works*, 26.

3 Ibid., *Considerations on Keeping Negroes*, Part II, 32–34, 50; *Works*, 26, 58–59, 85.

4 *Ibid.*, 65–67, 83–86, 89–92, 102, 126, 157; *A Brief Statement of the Testimony of Friends*, 22; Janney, *History of the Society of Friends*, III, 318.

5 Hepburn, *American Defence*, Appendix, 33–34.

To the Quakers is therefore due the earliest formulation of a definite remedy for the evils of slavery. Nowhere is the duty of emancipation more clearly pointed out than by Benjamin Lay. His plan is entirely typical of the Quaker attitude. Friends, he says, should "bring up their Negroes to some Learning, Reading and Writing, and endeavour to the utmost of their power in the sweet Love of Truth to instruct and teach 'em the principles of truth and righteousness, and learn them some Honest Trade or Imployment, and then set them free; and all the time Friends are teaching of them let them know that they intend to let them go free in a very reasonable time: and that our Religious Principle will not allow of such Severity, as to keep them in everlasting Bondage and Slavery."[1]

> 30. Benjamin Lay's plan.

John Woolman, like most of the Quakers, had no elaborate scheme of emancipation; yet, though appreciating the difficulties, he believed that they offered no excuse, and that whatever inconveniences might ensue were to be charged upon those who were responsible for the situation and should be borne by them.[2] He argued that the negroes, even if set free, were "still liable to the Penalties of our Laws, and as likely to have Punishment for their Crimes as other People," and that "to retain them in perpetual Servitude, without just Cause for it, will produce Effects, in the Event, more grievous than setting them free would do, when a real Love to Truth and Equity was the Motive to it."[3]

> 31. Ideas of John Woolman.

The general features of Quaker schemes for emancipation were the prevention of the increase of slavery; the manumission of slaves already purchased, after a reasonable term of service; and their moral and religious instruction in the mean time.[4] Anthony Benezet's proposals (1762) are more elaborate, and are exceptional in having recourse to law. These proposals were: first, to put an end to the importation of slaves; second, to declare free by law those already purchased, after a certain period of service. If a slave during

> 32. Proposals of Anthony Benezet.

---

[1] Lay, *All Slave-Keepers Apostates*, 54.

[2] Woolman, *Some Considerations on the Keeping of Negroes*, 11–12.

[3] Ibid., *Considerations on Keeping Negroes*, Part II, 50.

[4] Keith, *Exhortation and Caution to Friends*, in *Pa. Mag. Hist. and Biog.*, XIII, 267. Similar ideas are expressed by Elihu Coleman, John Hepburn, and Benjamin Lay.

his term of service had wilfully neglected his duty, he might, through an appeal to a court of justice, be held for a longer term. Benezet did not approve of returning the negroes to Africa. According to his plan the freedmen were to reside for a certain time in the country in which they were freed, subject to the inspection of the overseers of the poor; the children were to receive instruction; and, where the nature of the country would permit, a small tract of land was to be given to each family, and the members, unless they obtained employment in other ways, were to be required to work on it. The region west of the Alleghanies might, he thought, under some conditions be suitable for colonization.[1]

In the practical work of emancipation, even more than in the expression of sentiment, the Society of Friends is far in ad-

33. Practical work of the Society of Friends. vance of other religious denominations. Organized efforts against slavery began very early. The Germantown Protest of 1688 was carried from Monthly to Quarterly Meeting and from Quarterly to Yearly Meeting, and though the latter declined "to give a Positive Judgment in the Case, It having so general a Relation to many other Parts,"[2] the question was not allowed to rest. George Keith entered his protest at a Monthly Meeting held in Philadelphia in 1693.[3] In 1696 occurs the first decided action of the Yearly Meeting, in the form of advice against encouraging the importation of negroes and against neglecting their moral and spiritual welfare.[4] Some efforts in the latter direction were made by William Penn.[5]

The early efforts of the Quakers were directed chiefly against the importation and purchase of slaves, and these were so

34. Efforts against importation and purchase of slaves. effective that by 1715 the market for slaves in Philadelphia was seriously impaired.[6] The Legislature of Pennsylvania is the first to show the influence of anti-slavery sentiment by the imposition of a duty upon slaves which was practically prohibitory.[7] Nor was the

---

[1] Benezet, *Short Account*, 69–72; Vaux, *Memoirs of Benezet*, 39–40.

[2] *Germantown Friends' Protest*, note.

[3] Keith, *Exhortation and Caution to Friends*, in *Pa. Mag. Hist. and Biog.*, XIII, 265–270.

[4] *Brief Statement of the Testimony of Friends*, 8.

[5] *Ibid.*, 9; Dixon, *Life of Penn*, 301–302.

[6] Watson, *Annals of Philadelphia*, 482.

[7] See below, § 76.

movement confined to Pennsylvania. The Monthly Meeting of Dartmouth, Massachusetts, in 1716 sent to the Rhode Island Quarterly Meeting, of which it was a branch, the query " whether it be agreeable to Truth, for Friends to purchase slaves, and keep them term of life? " This query was referred to the various Monthly Meetings for decision. Some gave partial or evasive answers, but the Nantucket Meeting decided absolutely in the negative.[1] In 1729 we find the Pennsylvania Friends and those of New England acting together. The Chester Quarterly Meeting for the fourth time, now reinforced by the Nantucket Meeting, addressed the Yearly Meeting at Philadelphia on the subject of purchasing slaves already imported; and the latter, after some hesitation, advised against the purchase, and suggested that offenders be admonished under the discipline of the Monthly Meetings. This advice was repeated in 1735, and nearly every year from that time till 1743. Reports from the subordinate meetings described the measures taken against the purchase and sale of slaves, and these reports showed that the number of slave-holders was decreasing. In 1743 the Yearly Meeting issued a query with regard to importation, which was to be regularly answered.[2]

So far little had been done toward emancipation; but already there was considerable agitation on the subject. The Germantown Friends (1688) and George Keith (1693), as already noticed, were followed by John Hepburn (1714) and William Burling (1718). Elihu Coleman, of Nantucket, writing in 1729, says, " There are many sober men that have spoke against this practice, both by writing and in their public assemblies."[3] In the same year appeared Ralph Sandiford's *Brief Examination of the Practice of the Times*, followed in 1730 by a second edition, *The Mystery of Iniquity*, and in 1737 appeared Benjamin Lay's *All Slave-Keepers Apostates*. The anti-slavery sentiment of the Puritans, too, although much less conspicuous than that of the Quakers, was felt as far south as Philadelphia. Cotton Mather is quoted by John Hepburn, who also devotes an

35. Influence of anti-slavery literature.

---

[1] *Brief Statement of Testimony*, 43; Macy, *History of Nantucket*, 281.
[2] *Brief Statement of Testimony*, 14-15.
[3] Coleman, *Testimony against that Anti-Christian Practice of Making Slaves of Men*, vii.

appendix to Sewall's reprint of *The Athenian Oracle*. Lay incorporates in his book Sewall's tract on *The Selling of Joseph*. Thus by the middle of the eighteenth century a considerable body of literature had accumulated, and must have had an influence upon the community. Then came the writings of Woolman and Benezet which marked the period of actual emancipation and contributed incalculably towards it.

In the Yearly Meeting, however, no important question could be decided until nearly all were of one mind. The practice of 36. Process of emancipation. individuals was, therefore, far in advance of that of the whole Society, and some of the subordinate meetings were more zealous than the general body.[1] The efforts of Woolman and Benezet were now supplemented by circumstances. The French and Indian War, occurring at a time when the public mind was already agitated on the subject of slavery, led to a general feeling that the event was a dispensation of the Almighty sent to warn people of their sins.[2] Under this stimulus the Friends' Meetings from Rhode Island to Virginia began to take effective action against slave-holding as well as against the importation and purchase of slaves;[3] and the additional impulse given by the Revolutionary War was sufficient to complete the process of emancipation.

The organization and methods of the Society of Friends were well adapted to effective work. The system of queries addressed by the Yearly Meeting to its subordinates was directed toward the discipline of members by the subordinate meetings,[4] which reported to the general body on their success.[5] Committees were appointed to visit Friends who kept slaves and persuade them to abandon the practice. The discipline

---

[1] The Yearly Meeting at Philadelphia, in 1715, issued advice not only against the importation and ill-treatment of slaves, but also against "judging or reflecting on one another, either in public or private, concerning the detaining or keeping them servants." *Brief Statement of Testimony*, 12. Robert Zane, of Gloucester County, New Jersey, was disowned by the Society for the zeal with which he denounced slave-keeping. T. Matlack, *The Abolition of Slavery in Pennsylvania*, in 2 *Mass. Hist. Soc. Coll.*, VIII, 186.

[2] *Brief Statement of Testimony*, 21–22; Parrish, *Remarks on the Slavery of the Black People*, 1.

[3] *Brief Statement of Testimony*, 23–35, 43–55.

[4] *Ibid.*, 21, 47, 53.

[5] *Ibid.*, 23, 47–50; Janney, *History of the Society of Friends*, III, 428.

was at first in the nature of friendly exhortations; in case of persistence in error, members were testified against in open meeting, then partially excluded from the Society, and finally disowned.[1] Cases of contumacy were sometimes carried from Monthly to Quarterly and from Quarterly to Yearly Meeting;[2] but this process seems to have been seldom necessary and few members were actually disowned.[3] Communication between the meetings in different parts of the country was kept up by addresses from one Yearly Meeting to another, as well as from the Yearly Meeting to its subordinates.[4] Travelling elders or "public Friends" also went about from one colony to another.[5] The Quakers of the other colonies were considerably influenced by those of Pennsylvania and usually followed in their wake.

The New England Quakers, however, succeeded in shaking off the incubus of slavery somewhat earlier than those in localities where the conditions were less favorable. The system of committees adopted by the Philadelphia Meeting in 1758 was adopted in New England in 1769, in New York in 1771, and in Virginia in 1780.[6] In New England the work of emancipation was rapidly accomplished. In 1770 the work of committees was followed up by an inquiry of the Yearly Meeting as to whether all negroes of suitable age and condition had been set free.[7] For not freeing their slaves, some Friends were disowned as early as 1772,[8] four years before the adoption of that measure by the Philadelphia Meeting.[9] In 1773 the Society passed a resolution that even the aged and impotent should be set free, " that we do no more claim property in the human race, as we do in the brutes that

37. Emancipation in New England.

---

[1] Woolman, *Works*, I, 86–90, 102, 126; *Brief Statement of Testimony*, 22–26, 29–35, 46–50, 55; Janney, *History of the Society of Friends*, III, 432–433.

[2] *Brief Statement of Testimony*, 30, 48–49, 26.

[3] Some statistics are given in *Brief Statement of Testimony*, 31–35, 47, 50; Weeks, *Southern Quakers and Slavery*, 213.

[4] Woolman, *Works*, 65, 92.

[5] This was the mission on which John Woolman was engaged. Others who had an influence in the same direction were Benjamin Ferris, William Reckitt, John Griffith, Warner Mifflin, and Sarah Harrison. Weeks, *Southern Quakers and Slavery*, 202, 213.

[6] *Brief Statement of Testimony*, 44–45, 48–49, 54–55.

[7] *Ibid.*, 45–46.   [8] *Ibid.*, 46.   [9] *Ibid.*, 29–31.

perish." [1] Most of the slaves of New England Quakers had been manumitted by 1778; by 1782 all were supposed to have been freed; and the following year arrangements were made for compensating them for past services, and for looking after the moral and religious training of free blacks.[2]

A similar policy was pursued in other colonies. In 1776 the Philadelphia Yearly Meeting resolved to disown slave-holders,[3] and the New York Yearly Meeting the same year partially disowned them.[4] The work of committees was continued, and the reports show few cases of slave-holding after this time.[5] Thus, before the close of the Revolutionary War, slavery had been practically abandoned by the Quakers of the Northern and Middle States. Arrangements were generally or at least frequently made for compensation for past services, and for the assistance and religious instruction of the free blacks and the education of the children.[6]

38. Emancipation in the Middle States.

Where slavery was more firmly established, the process was naturally less rapid. A query with regard to the importation and the ill usage of slaves was issued by the Virginia Yearly Meeting as early as 1722, and directions against either importing or holding slaves appear in 1758. During the next ten years Friends became nearly free from the importation and purchase of slaves. The latter practice, as well as the former, was now held to be a breach of discipline, and a few years later (1770, 1772) the offender was disowned.[7] By this time the influence of the impending Revolution was beginning to make itself felt. The times seemed to demand that people should free their hands from every species of

39. Emancipation in Virginia.

---

[1] *Brief Statement of Testimony*, 46.

[2] *Ibid.*, 46–47. The idea that compensation was due not to the master for the loss of the labor, but to the slave for his years of unrequited toil and for the wrong done to himself and his ancestors, appears very early among the Quakers. William Burling, in *An Address to the Elders of the Church*, in 1718, makes this the main point of his argument. For the necessity of restitution, see also Hepburn, *American Defence*, 19–21; A Native of America, in Hepburn, *American Defence*, 34; Benezet, *Short Account*, 64–65.

[3] *Brief Statement of Testimony*, 30.

[4] *Ibid.*, 50.

[5] *Ibid.*, 31, 50.

[6] *Ibid.*, 31–32, 35–41, 47, 50–51.

[7] Weeks, *Southern Quakers and Slavery*, 201–205.

oppression lest the vengeance of the Almighty should be visited upon the land. Those who continued "to withhold from any their just right to freedom" were therefore exhorted to execute manumissions for adults and minors, the latter to take effect at majority.[1] Those continuing to hold slaves were to be admonished. In 1781 they were to be partially disowned, and in 1784 wholly disowned.[2] Quaker emancipation in Maryland and Virginia seems to have been practically completed by 1788.[3] One Monthly Meeting disowned thirteen persons for slave-holding, and some who had sold their slaves were required to redeem them and give them their liberty.[4]

Among those who contributed to this movement by their work as well as their words were Robert Pleasants and Warner Mifflin. The father of the former attempted to free his slaves by will in 1771, but the legal restrictions in Virginia prevented the execution of the will until 1800, when several hundred slaves were set at liberty with their children. Robert Pleasants emancipated eighty slaves of his own, placing them on his lands and supporting them for a year, while allowing them the full benefit of their labor. He probably also established a school for the children and gave land and money for its endowment.[5]

40. Manumissions. Robert Pleasants and Warner Mifflin.

Warner Mifflin was the object of an enthusiastic eulogy by Brissot[6] and of the bitter resentment of slave-holding Congressmen in the early days of the Republic.[7] He was born on the eastern shore of Virginia, in a region where Quakers were few and slave-holders many. He himself, in a *Defence* published in 1796, tells the story of his early conversion to antislavery principles through a suggestion from one of his father's slaves. His resolution never to own a slave was for a time overcome by the pressure of circumstances, and he tells with modest frankness of his triumph over the desire for wealth and position, over the plausible excuses which soothed the consciences of his neighbors, and even over the fear that his family

---

[1] *Brief Statement of Testimony*, 53–54.

[2] *Ibid.*, 54, 55.

[3] *Ibid.*, 56; Janney, *History of the Society of Friends*, III, 432–435.

[4] Weeks, *Southern Quakers and Slavery*, 213.

[5] *Ibid.*, 213–215.

[6] Brissot De Warville, *New Travels in the United States*, I, 156–159.

[7] *Annals of Congress*, 2 Cong., 1 sess., 730–731.

might come to actual want. The manumission was finally completed about 1775, and included the slaves of his wife, who gave him her sympathy and encouragement. Some slaves who had belonged to his father and had come to him of their own accord were also emancipated. Mifflin made restitution to his former slaves and purchased the release of some who had been sold.[1]

During the Revolutionary War Mifflin became very unpopular on account of his peace policy and particularly because of his refusal to use " bills of credit " (the continental currency) on the ground that they were " Engines of War." It was said that he had freed his slaves in order that they might go over to the enemy, or because they were worthless and he was unwilling to support them. In order to disprove the latter statement he arranged with his freedmen to give each a piece of ground and an outfit, in return for which they should give him a share of the produce. It was then said that Mifflin made more money off his negroes than he did when they were slaves, and he determined to give up the attempt to justify himself. Like many others he felt the hand of God in the Revolution and believed that the Almighty was on the side of the oppressed. But he had no special scheme for emancipation and believed that it must be a gradual process, — not because immediate emancipation would wrong the slave-holder, but because the slave would need some preparation for freedom.[2]

In Virginia the process of emancipation, long retarded by adverse legislation, was at last greatly facilitated by an act in 1782 removing restrictions from voluntary manumission. In North Carolina the Friends experienced still greater difficulties. The Yearly Meeting was considerably influenced by that of Virginia and followed in its footsteps. In 1758 it issued an inquiry about the treatment of slaves; ten years later it advised against the buying and selling of negroes and issued queries or recommendations of gradually increasing vigor from year to year;[3] in 1772 it addressed the Legislature, urging it to follow the example of the Virginia House of Burgesses in petitioning the Crown

41. Difficulties in North Carolina.

---

[1] Mifflin, *Defence against Aspersions*, 3–9.

[2] *Ibid.*, 11–27. See also § 106.

[3] Weeks, *Southern Quakers and Slavery*, 206–207.

against the slave-trade.[1]   For the next five years the process of emancipation went on rapidly, apparently without regard to the law, which, like that of Virginia, limited manumissions to cases of meritorious service and required a license from the county court.[2]   In 1777, however, a new law was enacted, and many of the freedmen were reduced to slavery by the authority of the county courts.   An appeal to the superior court resulted in a refusal to sanction the retroaction of the new law, but the title to the slaves was confirmed by the General Assembly in 1779, and at least one hundred and thirty-four negroes were returned to bondage.[3]   Petitions to the Assembly for a less stringent law resulted only in increasing rigor, and the Society could only protest against being deprived of the right to act in accordance with the dictates of conscience.[4]

Within a century of the Germantown Protest, the abolition of slavery among the Quakers had been practically accomplished.   It was accomplished without great strife or schism or bitterness of feeling, by a policy of gentle but persistent pressure, in which the zeal of individuals was supplemented by organized efforts well directed and steadily applied.   Individual Quakers, though lovers of peace, were tremendously in earnest and devoted their lives to the cause.   The official organizations, though cautious in taking up the work and desirous of unanimity, never gave

42. Results of the anti-slavery movement among the Quakers.

---

[1] Weeks, *Southern Quakers and Slavery*, 207–208.

[2] *Ibid.*, 205–206; *Laws of North Carolina*, Iredell, 95.   Passed in 1741.

[3] Weeks, *Southern Quakers and Slavery*, 209–210; *Laws of North Carolina*, Iredell, 288, 371; Address from the Committee of the Yearly Meeting to a Committee of Congress and other Documents, in Parrish, *Remarks on the Slavery of the Black People*, Appendix, 52–65.

[4] Weeks, *Southern Quakers and Slavery*, 210, 217–224.   The struggle resulted in a unique system of slave-holding by the Society itself, which, in 1808, undertook the charge of slaves freed by individual members, the ownership being nominally transferred.   The slaves thus received were removed from the State at the expense of the Society.   Many hundreds were thus sent to Pennsylvania and the Northwest, and some to Hayti and Liberia.   Slave-owners outside the Society began to transfer ownership to it on the same conditions, and the limitations of the movement seem to have been due largely to the expense of removal, the reluctance of the free States to increase their colored population, and the difficulty of making suitable provision for the freedmen after manumission.   Weeks, *Southern Quakers and Slavery*, 224–234; Bassett, *Slavery in North Carolina*, 67–68; Freeman, *Yaradee; A Plea for Africa*, Appendix, 357, note.

up a point they had once insisted on, and all worked together
for their common end.

Having freed their own consciences of slavery, the Friends
next applied themselves to influencing those outside their own
sect. After the Revolutionary War they joined in
the political movements for the suppression of the
slave-trade and for emancipation by law. They were also the
founders and the leaders of many of the early abolition societies,
and continued to hold a place in the literature by which public
opinion was educated to anti-slavery views. In these matters,
however, they appear not as members of a religious sect but
as members of the body politic, and play a subordinate though
an important part. Their later work will therefore be included
in subsequent chapters.

43. Later work.

In other religious denominations there was no organized opposition to slavery until near the close of the Revolutionary War.
During that period, however, some of the New England clergy used their individual influence for the
manumission of negroes. An unusually earnest
champion of universal liberty was Rev. Samuel
Hopkins of Newport, Rhode Island, who began preaching
against slavery about 1770, and whose church, in the very
centre of the slave-trade, voted in 1784, "that the slave-trade
and the slavery of the Africans, as it has taken place among
us, is a gross violation of the righteousness and benevolence
which are so much inculcated in the gospel; and therefore
we will not tolerate it in this church." [1] Connecticut is simi-
larly represented by Rev. Ezra Stiles, the President of Yale
College. Less conspicuous instances are Rev. Samuel Webster
of Salisbury, Rev. Nathaniel Niles, and Dr. William Gordon,
the pastor of the Third Church in Roxbury.[2] The lack of organized effort in the New England churches may be partly
accounted for by the fact that there was no such machinery
for the purpose as existed in the Society of Friends; the
tendency here was strongly toward individualism, and the influence of individual pastors over the individual members of
their own congregations was the natural method. The organ-

44. Other religious denominations. The Congre-gationalists.

---

[1] Park, *Memoir of Samuel Hopkins*, in Hopkins, *Works*, I, 116, 140, 160
and note. Text of resolution, *ibid.*, 157.

[2] Moore, *Notes on Slavery in Massachusetts*, 177.

ized effort necessary for the completion of the work came through political measures which were well suited to the Puritan conception of the relation between church and state. The combined influence of the Congregational ministers, however, is seen in a petition to the General Court of Massachusetts by Dr. Belknap and others, which contributed to the passage of the act prohibiting the slave-trade (1788)[1] and in a similar petition by the clergy of Connecticut, the same year, in which Dr. Jonathan Edwards and Dr. Levi Hart were among the leaders.[2]

The Methodist Conference at Baltimore, in 1780, under the combined influences of John Wesley and the American Revolution, declared that slavery was "contrary to the laws of God, man, and nature," visited its disapprobation on all members who kept slaves, advised manumission and even required it in the case of travelling preachers. At this time there was a temporary schism in the Conference, so that Virginia members were not present. In 1784 the Conference voted to suspend both local and travelling preachers in Maryland, Delaware, Pennsylvania, and New Jersey who failed to meet the requirement, but to give the local preachers of Virginia another year's trial. Regulations were also adopted for the discipline of slave-holding members, requiring the execution of deeds for the manumission of all slaves within a brief term of years, the children of such slaves to be free at birth. The right of communion was to be withheld until the execution of the deed, and recalcitrants were offered a final alternative of voluntary withdrawal or exclusion from the church. These measures were to apply only so far as consistent with the laws of the various States, but any one who bought or sold slaves was to be immediately expelled unless he had bought them in order to free them.

45. The Methodists.

This is the high-water mark of American Methodism in its early relation to slavery. The rules were zealously upheld by Bishop Coke, who had been ordained by Wesley to take charge of the church in America, and by his associate Bishop Asbury. Unfortunate legal obstructions to manumission in

---

[1] Belknap, Reply to *Queries respecting Slavery*, in 1 *Mass. Hist. Soc. Coll.*, IV, 204–205; Deane, *The Connection of Massachusetts with Slavery and the Slave-Trade*, 32 and note.

[2] Park, *Memoir of Samuel Hopkins*, in Hopkins, *Works*, I, 123, 125–126.

the Southern States, and violent opposition by many of the
Southern members led to a gradual decline in the movement.
The rules were suspended the following year, and when re-
enacted in 1796 show a considerable weakening. Children
of slaves undergoing manumission were now to be freed only at
twenty-one or twenty-five years of age, according to their sex.
Purchasers of slaves, instead of being immediately expelled,
were to hold them only for a term of years, the time to be
determined at the Quarterly Meeting. Preachers were to consider the subject " with *deep attention*," and to communicate to
the Conference " *any important thoughts upon the subject* " which
might occur to them.

Some efforts to obtain more favorable legislation were made
in Virginia and North Carolina. In the latter State the request
was for the permission to manumit slaves, in the former for
immediate or gradual emancipation by the State legislature.
It is said also that hundreds of manumissions took place at
about this time. In 1800 the Methodist regulations as to slave-
holding were again revised. Travelling preachers were now
required to manumit their slaves if practicable. The Con-
ferences were to draw up addresses to the State legislatures
urging laws for gradual emancipation, and petitions to this effect
were to be circulated through the officers of the church.
Energy in this work was exhausted by 1804, and the States south
of Virginia were now exempted from the rules. The denomi-
national effort for emancipation was finally abandoned in 1808
as interfering with the progress of spiritual salvation.[1] The
Methodists, however, continued to be regarded as friendly to
emancipation, and this view contributed to their popularity
and influence among the negroes.[2]

Anti-slavery sentiment among the Baptists flourished and
declined, as among the Methodists. The French traveller, La
Rochefoucauld-Liancourt, mentions them with honor-
46. The Baptists. able distinction in company with the Quakers (1795–
1797): in New Paltz, on the Hudson, he says, the Quakers

---

[1] The early relation of the Methodist Church to slavery is described by
Lucius C. Matlack, in *The History of American Slavery and Methodism*,
14–34. A briefer account is McTyeire, *A History of Methodism*, 377–389.
See also George Smith, *History of Wesleyan Methodism*, Appendix G, 703.

[2] T. Flint, *Recollections of the Last Ten Years*, 345.

and the Anabaptists keep no slaves, though others do.[1] Even
so far south as Georgia, the Baptists gained some notoriety in
this respect, as they are alluded to in one of the early debates
in Congress on account of their "interference."[2] The Philadelphia Association of Baptist Churches, at the instance of the
church in Baltimore, had already (about 1789) expressed its
approval of the societies for the gradual abolition of slavery
which were then forming, and recommended the co-operation of the churches.[3] The Ketocton Association of Baptist
Churches in Virginia, including Fairfax, Loudoun, and other
counties, in 1787 appointed a committee to bring in a plan for
gradual emancipation, but the opposition proved too strong for
them.[4] Two years later the General Committee of the Virginia
churches, including delegates from the seven Associations,
adopted a resolution denouncing slavery, and praying that the
Legislature might be able to accomplish emancipation.[5] The
Salem Association, on the upper waters of the James River,
lost several members by failing to give a definite answer to the
query, put by one of the churches: "Is it lawful in the sight
of God for a member of Christ's Church to keep his fellow-
creature in perpetual slavery?"[6]

In Kentucky, as was natural in a pioneer State, the agitation
against slavery was for some time of considerable importance.
Among the Baptists the most zealous advocated immediate abolition and the refusal of fellowship to slave-holders. Moderate
reformers preferred the gradual emancipation of those already
in bondage, and the immediate freedom of all born after a
certain date. Still another class objected to the confusion of
political and religious questions by bringing this discussion into
the churches.[7] The majority of church-members regarded slave-
holding as a sin, but did not wish to make it a cause for exclusion from the church;[8] but the more radical minority included

---

[1] La Rochefoucauld-Liancourt, *Travels through the United States*, II, 233.
[2] Speech by Mr. Jackson of Georgia, in *Annals of Congress*, 1 Cong.,
2 sess., 1416.
[3] Spencer, *The Early Baptists of Philadelphia*, 146.
[4] Semple, *History of Baptists in Virginia*, 303-304.
[5] *Ibid.*, 79.
[6] Brown, *Political Beginnings of Kentucky*, 225. Reference to Spencer,
History of Kentucky Baptists, I, 184.
[7] Brown, *Political Beginnings of Kentucky*, 225-226.
[8] Birney, *James G. Birney and his Times*, 19.

some preachers of extraordinary zeal, notably Joshua Carman, Carter Tarrant, and David Barrow. The first church to be established on a distinctly abolitionist basis was organized in 1791 by John Sutton and Carter Tarrant, and called the New Hope Church.[1] The question of slavery was considered in connection with the formation of a State constitution in 1792, and the opposition to it received the support of the clergy of various denominations.[2] Though the movement for emancipation by political means failed, many manumissions were executed for religious reasons; it is said that between 1800 and 1810 the number of freedmen was increased 150 per cent as compared with the previous decade, and that the anti-slavery influence was largely due to the Baptists.[3] A crisis occurred in 1805, and the emancipating Baptists seceded from the general association and formed a distinct organization.[4] They called themselves Friends of Humanity, but did not object to the name of Emancipators;[5] they numbered twelve churches, and the distinctive feature was the refusal of Christian fellowship to slaveholders.[6] A similar position was taken some years earlier by the Miami Association of Baptists in Ohio (1797) under the influence of Joshua Carman.[7]

The Presbyterians took up the slavery question at about the same time as the Methodists and Baptists. The Synod of New York and Philadelphia, in 1787, recommended in somewhat cautious language that members give their slaves "such good education as to prepare them for a better enjoyment of freedom," that those who are worthy be given an opportunity to procure their liberty "at a moderate rate," and that "the most prudent measures" be taken "to procure eventually the final abolition of slavery in America."[8] The follow-

47. The Presbyterians.

---

[1] Brown, *Political Beginnings of Kentucky*, 226, note.

[2] *Ibid.*, 227.

[3] Birney, *James G. Birney and his Times*, 23, 21.

[4] Benedict, *General History of the Baptist Denomination*, II, 231–232.

[5] *Ibid.*, 245; Benedict, *Abridgment of the General History*, 398–399.

[6] Birney, *James G. Birney and his Times*, 23; Brown, *Political Beginnings of Kentucky*, 225–226.

[7] Birney, *James G. Birney and his Times*, 18; Dunlevy, *History of the Miami Baptist Association*, 133, 37.

[8] Baird, *A Collection of the Acts*, etc., *of the Supreme Judicatory of the Presbyterian Church*, 818.

ing year they repeated the recommendation for the abolition of slavery.[1] An explicit statement against slave-holding appears in the catechism a few years later (1794),[2] and the question of excluding slave-holders from church membership was brought up in 1795. By this time the movement had apparently reached its limit. The General Assembly of the Church, which was the national organization, now began to point with pride to its previous utterances on the subject, and apparently considered these sufficient to satisfy the most zealous reformer; but although it professed to "view, with the deepest concern, any vestiges of slavery which may exist in our country," it continued to retain the slave-holders in Christian fellowship.[3]

Except in the case of the Quakers, then, the organized efforts of religious societies must be regarded as a failure. Whatever was accomplished among the latter was effected through the strong personal influence of a few individuals, and was partial, local, or incomplete through the lack of a substantial basis of public opinion. "If the agitation had been wholly left to the churches," says Professor Von Holst, "it would have been long before men could have rightly spoken of 'a slavery question.'"[4] Among the Quakers, however, the abolition of slavery had been universal and complete, so far as the local legislation permitted; and this brief summary should serve to show that if the churches had been filled with the spirit that pervaded the Friends' Meeting, there need hardly have been any slavery question at all.

48. Results.

[1] Baird, *Collection of Acts*, 818; *American Museum*, III, 592.

[2] Bourne, *Man-Stealing and Slavery denounced by the Presbyterian and Methodist Churches*, 2.

[3] Baird, *Collection of Acts*, 818. An exception to this policy was made by the Reformed Presbyterian Church in 1800, under the influence of Dr. Alexander McLeod, who, having received a call to a church in Orange County, New York, and finding some slave-holders in the congregation, would not accept the call until the presbytery had condemned the practice. Extracts from *The National Standard*, *The Banner of the Covenant*, and *The New York Evening Post*, in McLeod, *Negro Slavery Unjustifiable*. Dr. McLeod preached a sermon against slavery in 1802.

[4] Von Holst, *Constitutional and Political History of the United States*, I, 279.

CHAPTER II

THE PHILOSOPHICAL MOVEMENT OF THE
REVOLUTIONARY PERIOD, 1761–1783

IN the preceding chapter one slender stream of anti-slavery sentiment was traced from the early settlement of Pennsylvania all the way down through colonial history to its practical

49. Summary of the religious movement. issue in the complete or nearly complete abolition of slavery throughout a whole religious sect. There was comparatively little anti-slavery sentiment, however, outside the Society of Friends, and what there was did not produce any important results. There were also local limitations: the headquarters of the movement were in Pennsylvania, and other colonies had a comparatively small share in it.

In the period of the American Revolution anti-slavery sentiment assumed a new phase. The doctrine of the natural and

50. Influence of the American Revolution. inalienable rights of man, taken up by the colonists in justification of their own cause, was applied by the most logical or the most benevolent without distinction of race, color, or condition of servitude. By many this application was made only in theory: Patrick Henry, for instance, deplored the inconsistency of slave-holding among a people who proclaimed the principles of liberty and equality, realizing, too, the economic disadvantages and seeing before him " a gloomy perspective to future times," but he could not make up his mind to the personal sacrifice which a change would involve.[1] John Adams, however, had so strong an antipathy to slavery that he never owned a negro, although he believed that the employment of free labor cost him thousands of dollars which might have been saved by the purchase of slaves.[2]

---

[1] Henry, *Life of Patrick Henry*, I, 152, 114–116. See also Bayard, *Voyage dans l'Intérieur des Etats-Unis*, 92–93; Chastellux, *Travels in North America*, II, 197 f.

[2] John Adams, *Works* (1856), X, 380.

Thomas Jefferson, too, declared himself ready for the personal sacrifice,[1] and his early manhood was distinguished by several efforts in behalf of the oppressed race; but he objected to their incorporation into the State on account of "the real distinctions which nature has made," though at the same time hesitating to "degrade a whole race of men from the rank in the scale of beings which their Creater may perhaps have given them."[2] Later, as the glow of revolutionary enthusiasm faded away and was succeeded by the cold caution of advancing years, he shrank from appearing in so unpopular a cause, or perhaps honestly believed that the effort would be premature and would only retard real progress; and he finally retired from the combat, feebly hoping that the victory might yet be won by a younger generation.[3]

Washington, like Jefferson, believed that only the extinction of slavery could assure the existence of the Union,[4] and sincerely wished for some practicable plan of emancipation by legislation,[5] but he thought it "dangerous to strike too vigorously at a prejudice which had begun to diminish." Hence, believing "that time, patience, and information would not fail to vanquish it,"[6] he never made any active effort toward either national or State emancipation, and he kept and occasionally, with reluctance, bought and sold slaves.[7] The practical difficulties were too great to be overcome by abstract theories. Nevertheless anti-slavery sentiment received an enormous impetus from the principles of the Revolution; and where the difficulties were moderate or the philosophy of the Revolution was strongly reinforced by other influences, doctrinarianism was transformed into determined purpose, and the results were such as to make

---

[1] Jefferson, *Writings* (Taylor and Maury, 1853), II, 357, VII, 58. References to Jefferson's Writings are to this edition unless otherwise indicated.

[2] *Ibid.*, VIII, 380–386.

[3] *Ibid.* (Ford's Edition), IV, 184–185 (June 22, 1786); Letter to Edward Coles, Aug. 25, 1814, in Washburne, *Sketch of Edward Coles*, 24–28.

[4] Bernard, *Retrospections of America*, 90–91.

[5] Washington, *Writings* (Ford), XI, 25, 30.

[6] Brissot, *New Travels in America*, I, 245–246.

[7] Washington, *Writings*, II, 211–212, XI, 62 and note. A letter to Washington from Edward Rushton, a Liverpool philanthropist, in 1796, arraigning him in vigorous terms for inconsistency, was returned without reply. Rushton, *Expostulatory Letter to George Washington* and Preface.

it seem probable that the institution of slavery was doomed to an early end.

In this period the movement was not confined to any sect or locality. Pennsylvania still maintained an honorable position and the fullest and most vigorous expression of sentiment is found in New England. But the philosophy of Locke and Montesquieu was studied in Virginia as well as in Massachusetts, and philosophers and patriots North and South were in sympathy on the slavery question. Nor was the movement confined to any class of men, although it was led by the scholars and thinkers. The preacher was conspicuous against slavery in New England where his influence was still great, and the growing opposition to slavery among the clergy was notable in Pennsylvania.[1] In all sections of the country a leading part was played by the lawyers. In Pennsylvania two men of science, Dr. Rush and Benjamin Franklin, occupied an important place. Those who led in the Revolution led also in the anti-slavery movement; but, at least in New England, the ranks were not far behind the leaders, and orators and essayists were supported by juries and town-meetings.

51. Extent of the movement.

The principles of the American Revolution were not particularly American nor particularly new. They had been in the air at least ever since the English revolutions against the Stuarts and their exposition by John Locke. The same principles had already been applied to the discussion of slavery by Montesquieu,[2] and Montesquieu was much read in America. The Bishop of Gloucester, in 1766, declaimed against holding property in rational beings in language which shows that the doctrine of natural liberty still flourished on British soil;[3]

52. Precedents.

---

[1] Rush, Letter to Granville Sharp, in Stuart, *Memoir of Granville Sharp*, 21.

[2] Montesquieu, *Esprit des Lois*, Book XV, chapter v, *Œuvres Complètes* (Paris, 1875), IV, 185.

[3] "Gracious God! to talk (as in herds of cattle) of property in rational creatures! creatures endowed with all our faculties, possessing all our qualities but that of colour; our brethren both by nature and grace, shocks all our feelings of humanity, and the dictates of common sense. . . . *Nature created man free, and grace invites him to assert his freedom*." Extract from a Sermon preached by the Bishop of Gloucester before the Society for the Propagation of the Gospel, Feb. 21, 1766. In Benezet, *Potent Enemies*

and Scottish philosophy and law were brought to bear against slavery and the slave-trade distinctly on the ground of the original right of every man to his own liberty.[1] In America, however, the ideas of liberty and equality took root and flourished with peculiar vigor, and it is in America that they produced their fairest fruit. It is therefore with special interest that one looks for their effect on the condition of the slave.

The herald of the new era was James Otis, and it is a significant fact that the man who sounded the key-note of the Revolution pleaded at the same moment the cause of the slave. Otis's argument against the Writs 53. James Otis. of Assistance (1761), based on the rights of men to life, liberty, and property, included the rights of the black men, which were set forth in vigorous terms and caused even the stout-hearted John Adams to shudder at the conclusions that might be drawn from such premises.[2] The terms used in the imperfectly reported speech were doubtless similar in nature to some remarks of Otis on the slavery of the Africans which soon afterward appeared in print. " The Colonists," says Otis, " are by the law of nature free born, as indeed all men are, white or black. No better reasons can be given, for enslaving those of any colour, than such as baron Montesquieu has humorously given, as the foundation of that cruel slavery exercised over the poor Ethiopians ; which threatens one day to reduce both Europe and America to the ignorance and barbarity of the darkest ages. Does it follow that it is right to enslave a man because he is black? Will short curled hair, like wool, instead of Christian hair, as it is called by those whose hearts are as hard as the nether millstone, help the argument? Can any logical inference in favour of slavery, be drawn from a flat nose, a long or a short face?"[3]

---

of America, 80–83, and *Views of American Slavery taken a Century Ago*, Appendix, 107–108.

[1] Wallis, *System of the Principles of the Law of Scotland;* Hutcheson, *System of Moral Philosophy.* Quoted in Benezet, *A Short Account of that Part of Africa inhabited by Negroes*, 30–34, and *Potent Enemies of America*, 74–78. Wallis regards the right of liberty as inalienable. Hutcheson says the owner is bound to prove that liberty has been forfeited.

[2] John Adams, *Works*, X, 315. An abstract of Otis's speech made by Adams is in F. Moore, *American Eloquence*, I, 4–7.

[3] Otis, *Rights of British Colonies*, 43–44.

Though it had not yet occurred to the ordinary mind that the slavery of the Africans was in any way unjust or immoral,[1] **54. Minor influences.** the seed fell on ground not wholly unprepared. The moral influence of the Quakers had been supplemented by the economic arguments of Benjamin Franklin, who pointed out in his *Observations concerning the Increase of Mankind*, in 1751, the evil effects of slavery upon population, industry, and the production and distribution of wealth.[2] William Vassall, in the Massachusetts-Bay Province, was at about this time troubled by conscientious scruples with regard to his West India plantation.[3] Petitions were presented to the General Court of Massachusetts Bay between 1755 and 1766, praying that the importation of slaves might be prohibited, and it is probable that the conscience of the Calvinist as well as of the Quaker was awakened by the horrors and dangers of the French and Indian War.[4]

It is not, however, until after the passage of the Stamp Act that anti-slavery literature begins to appear to any extent. **55. Anti-slavery literature, 1767-1776. "Lee's Add."** Among the first to be heard is a voice from Virginia, in 1767, attacking the institution of slavery on religious and moral, political and economic grounds, and dwelling with special emphasis on the fact that "as freedom is unquestionably the birthright of all mankind, Africans as well as Europeans, to keep the former in a state of slavery is a constant violation of that right, and therefore of justice."[5]

Not long afterward appears an *Earnest Address* by Samuel Webster, of Salisbury, Massachusetts (1769), urging immediate **56. Samuel Webster and "A British Bostonian."** emancipation, in a voice that rings with the coming Revolution. "What then is to be done?" he says. "Done! for God's sake break every yoke and let these oppressed ones go free without delay — let them taste the sweets of that liberty, which we so highly prize, and are so

---

[1] Noah Webster, *Effects of Slavery on Morals and Industry*, 33, note.

[2] Franklin, *Complete Works* (Putnam, 1897), II, 226–229.

[3] Deane, *Letters and Documents relating to Slavery in Massachusetts*, in 5 *Mass. Hist. Soc. Coll.*, III, 385.

[4] *Cf.* § 36, above.

[5] Quoted from *The Virginia Gazette*, March 19, 1767, in *Views of American Slavery taken a Century Ago*, 109–112, and, under the title *Lee's Add.*, in Benezet, *Potent Enemies of America*, 78–79.

earnestly supplicating God and man to grant us: nay, which we claim as the natural right of every man."[1] A Thanksgiving *Oration on the Beauties of Liberty*, delivered by "A British Bostonian," in 1772, was not considered complete without a special plea for the rights and liberties of the Africans, which was inserted in a reprint of the original edition "by particular Desire."[2] The printer of this pamphlet, "determined, even at the hazard of his life," to maintain the liberty of the press, grants a refuge in the appendix to an utterance against the slave-trade which had been refused by the newspapers.[3] "Much has been wrote" on this subject, says the "British Bostonian," and "many begin to listen to the laws of humanity, and the force of the argument."[4]

At about this time appeared a pamphlet against the slave-trade by James Swan, a Boston merchant, a native of Great Britain, but none the less, he declares, a friend of liberty.[5] Hardly had he arrived in America and seen the slaves before he wanted to do something to relieve them, and this pamphlet is "intended to be a mean of abolishing one great part of *Slavery* here."[6] He appeals to the humanity and love of liberty "with which every true *Englishman* is or ought to be possessed of," urging his readers to declare themselves "*well-wishers of the British Empire, and consequently enemies to slavery*," and reminding them that "no country can be called free where there is one Slave."[7] A revised edition of this pamphlet was published "at the earnest desire of the Negroes in Boston," in order that a copy might be sent to each town of the Province with a view to the instruction of the representatives in the General Court.[8] The new edition was dedicated to the Governor and Legislature, and was pre-

57. Swan's Dissuasion from the Slave-Trade.

---

[1] Samuel Webster, *Earnest Address to my Country on Slavery*, extract in Coffin, *Sketch of the History of Newbury*, 338. *Cf.* A Sermon preached before the General Court by Samuel Webster, D.D., of Salisbury, May 28, 1777, pp. 22, 37–38.

[2] A British Bostonian, *Oration on the Beauties of Liberty*, Third Edition (1773), Title-page. Remarks on the Africans, pp. 73–75.

[3] *Ibid.*, 75; Article signed "Conscience," 76–78.

[4] *Ibid.*, 75.

[5] Swan, *Dissuasion from the Slave-Trade* (177-), Dedication, vi.

[6] *Ibid.*, Preface, ix; Dedication, vi.

[7] *Ibid.*, viii.

[8] *Ibid.* (1773), Preface, ix–x.

sented to them at the same time with a petition from the negroes.[1]

In Pennsylvania the awakening was probably as general as in Massachusetts, and the neighboring colonies shared in the movement to some degree. Dr. Benjamin Rush apologizes for his *Address on Slavery*, in 1773, because so much has already been said on the subject,[2] and writes to Granville Sharp, the same year, of the rapid progress of anti-slavery sentiment in Pennsylvania and other colonies. " Anthony Benezet," he says, " stood alone a few years ago, in opposing negro slavery in Philadelphia; and now three-fourths of the province, as well as of the city, cry out against it." [3]

58. Rush's Address on Slavery.

Even South Carolina, always the stronghold of slavery, is at last affected. Henry Laurens feels in 1776 that those who have refused liberty to others can hardly hope for the security of their own; he believes that the prejudices of former days are giving way, and hopes that the time for a general manumission is at hand. " You know, my dear son," he writes, in 1776, "I abhor slavery. I was born in a country where slavery had been established by British kings and parliaments, as well as by the laws of that country ages before my existence. I nevertheless disliked it. In former days there was no combating the prejudices of men supported by interest; the day I hope is approaching when, from principles of gratitude as well as justice, every man will strive to be foremost in showing his readiness to comply with the golden rule. . . . I am devising means for manumitting many of them, and for cutting off the entail of slavery. . . . I am not one of those who dare trust in Providence for defence and security of their own liberty while they enslave and wish to continue in slavery thousands who are as well entitled to freedom as themselves." [4] The issue indeed could not be evaded. The charge

59. Letter of Henry Laurens.

---

[1] A British Bostonian, *Oration on the Beauties of Liberty*, 78.

[2] Rush, *Address to the Inhabitants of the British Settlements, on the Slavery of the Negroes in America*, i.

[3] Stuart, *Memoir of Granville Sharp*, 21. See also Letters from Franklin to Dean Woodward (April 10, 1773) and Anthony Benezet (1772–1773), in Franklin, *Complete Works*, IV, 507–508, V, 128, 200; see also Nisbet, *Slavery not forbidden by Scripture*, i.

[4] Laurens, *A South Carolina Protest against Slavery*, 20–21. See also a letter from Laurens in *Pa. Mag. Hist. and Biog.*, XVI, 381.

of inconsistency, made by the loyalists in derision [1] and by the patriots in earnest appeals for reform,[2] was one which must be fairly faced. On the ground which the colonists had taken, slavery could not be justified; and there seems at this time to have been hardly an attempt to justify it.

In a forensic disputation which formed a part of the Commencement exercises of Harvard College in July, 1773, the anti-slavery advocate takes his stand on the natural rights of man with the air of one who knows his audience is with him on that ground. He is aston- ished "that in this enlightened age and land, where the principles of natural and civil Liberty, and consequently the natural rights of mankind are so generally understood, the case of these unhappy *Africans* should gain no more attention; — that those, who are so readily disposed to urge the principles of natural equality in defence of their own Liberties should, with so little reluctance, continue to exert a power, by the operation of which they are so flagrantly contradicted." [3] His opponent, with an apologetic air, entreats that even the feelings of humanity may be suspended while we calmly attend to the voice of reason. He joins in the "benevolent wish" that the Africans, whom he too is willing to call his brethren, might enjoy the blessings of liberty equally with the European races, but takes his stand on the greatest good of the whole, arguing that the subordination of some is a necessary condition of society, and that the negroes are better off in a state of limited subjection in America than they would be in a state of freedom in Africa.[4] As the advocate of the natural right to liberty now leaves his original position to contend with his opponent on this ground,[5] the latter is able to close the argument by remarking that his principle has been admitted, and he leaves the audience to judge of the facts.[6] The rights of man are thus neatly shifted into the background, but they are evidently an important feature in the thought of the time.

60. Forensic dispute at Harvard.

[1] Quotations in Moore, *Notes on Slavery in Massachusetts*, 145.
[2] *Ibid.*, 144–147, 176; Extract from *The Pennsylvania Chronicle*, Nov. 21, 1768, in *The Anti-Slavery Examiner*, 1838, No. 5, p. 27.
[3] *A Forensic Dispute on the Legality of Enslaving the Africans*, 4.
[4] *Ibid.*, 7–16, 23–31.
[5] *Ibid.*, 31–48.
[6] *Ibid.*, 48.

The idea of mutual benefit and especially of the advantage
to the negro from contact with Christian civilization was a

61. Anti-slavery arguments. Mutual benefit. favorite pro-slavery argument and a favorite object
of attack by the opposite party.[1] It was now more
vigorously dealt with than in earlier days. Dr.
Rush, in his *Address on Slavery*, compares the argument from
the evangelizing of the negro to the justification of highway
robbery on the ground that part of the money acquired is to
be devoted to some religious use.[2] He declares also that the
masters are opposed to the religious instruction of the negroes,
and that they set them an example which is not likely to
prejudice them in favor of Christianity.[3] But whatever the
very doubtful benefit which the negroes may receive in consequence of their importation, whatever the motive of " those
philanthropists who engage in the traffic "[4] and the attitude
with regard to their material and moral welfare of those who
keep them as slaves, the injustice of the system is now regarded
as the main point. " By the greatest humanity we can show
them," says Dr. Rush, in words which mark the advance of
anti-slavery sentiment within the century, " we only lessen, but
do not remove the crime, for the injustice of it continues the
same. . . . All the money you save, or acquire by their labour
is stolen from them; and . . . be assured that your crime
stands registered in the court of Heaven as a breach of the
eighth commandment."[5] Thomas Jefferson indulges in specu-
lation as to the consequences of the doctrine of reciprocal rights,
suggesting to the slave-holder the question " whether the religious precepts against the violation of property were not
framed for him as well as his slave? And whether the slave

---

[1] Among the earlier discussions of this point are those of A Native of
America, in Hepburn, *American Defence of the Christian Golden Rule*
27–30; *The Athenian Oracle*, 4 ; Appleton, *Considerations on Slavery*, 9 ;
Woolman, *Works*, I, 57–58. The most important discussions in the Revo-
lutionary period are *A Forensic Dispute*, 23–48; [Franklin], *Essay on the
Slave-Trade*, 7–12; Rush, *Address on Slavery*, 15–20.

[2] *Ibid.*, 16.

[3] *Ibid.*, 17. See also [Franklin], *Essay on the Slave-Trade*, 9–10. Dr.
Rush lost part of his medical practice for a time by accepting a pew in a
negro church in Philadelphia, in the erection of which he had been interested. *The Anti-Slavery Record*, II, 151; Letter of Dr. Rush to John
Nicholson in *Pa. Mag. Hist. and Biog.*, VI, 113.

[4] *Essay on the Slave-Trade*, 7.　　[5] Rush, *Address on Slavery*, 19–21.

may not as justifiably take a little from one who has taken all from him, as he would slay one who would slay him?"[1]

The fundamental connection between slavery and the slave-trade is another favorite anti-slavery argument, especially, as was natural, in the commercial colonies. The Rev. Samuel Hopkins, of Newport, Rhode Island, makes this argument a prominent feature of his *Dialogue concerning the Slavery of the Africans* which he addressed to the Second Continental Congress in 1776. After premising that the slave-trade is now generally admitted to be unjustifiable, he argues that slave-holding is equally so, and that it is inconsistent to admit one wrong and endeavor to put a stop to it, while continuing the other.[2]

62. Connection of slavery and the slave-trade.

Arguments drawn from the Scriptures, which were very prominent during the earlier period, now assume a subordinate position. Dr. Rush, though claiming that the Old Testament does not necessarily sanction slavery and that the New is directly opposed to it, goes so far as to say, "If it could be proved that no testimony was to be found in the Bible against a practice so pregnant with evils of the most destructive tendency to society, it would be sufficient to overthrow its divine Original."[3] On the whole, more emphasis is now laid on the inconsistency of slavery with the general spirit of Christianity, and less on individual texts and precedents.

63. Scriptural arguments.

On the other hand, since the doctrine of natural rights was intimately associated with that of natural equality, a great deal of attention was given to the confutation of arguments based on physical distinctions. This subject, as has already been noticed, proved to be too much for Jefferson's philosophy.[4] In more northern latitudes, where the political situation was less critical, or where the negroes were living under more favorable conditions, consistency was less difficult; physical distinctions were even treated with derision, after the manner of Montesquieu.[5] In this era of the advancement of

64. Natural equality.

---

[1] Jefferson, *Writings*, VIII, 385.

[2] Hopkins, *Dialogue concerning the Slavery of the Africans*, in Hopkins, *Works*, II, 556–562.

[3] Rush, *Address on Slavery*, 9.

[4] See above, § 50. Jefferson, *Writings*, VIII, 380–386.

[5] Otis, *Rights of British Colonies*, 43–44; [Franklin], parody of Shylock, in *Essay on the Slave-Trade*, 5.

science, too, the color of the African came to be regarded as the natural effect of a tropical sun, — as not a curse but a blessing;[1] and thus the favorite pro-slavery argument from the "curse of Canaan" fell to the ground. In the same way the mental and moral deficiencies of the negro were considered to be merely the effects of slavery. The condition of the African in his native land was sometimes regarded as one of ideal innocence and happiness, like that of Adam and Eve before the Fall, and the debasing influence of slavery was held responsible for the change. "Slavery," says Dr. Rush, "is so foreign to the human mind, that the moral faculties, as well as those of the understanding are debased, and rendered torpid by it. All the vices which are charged upon the Negroes in the southern colonies and the West Indies, such as Idleness, Treachery, Theft, and the like, are the genuine offspring of slavery, and serve as an argument to prove that they were not intended, by Providence for it."[2] Thus the very facts which had been used against emancipation were now turned against slavery itself. But more effective than the picture of the innocent joys of the primitive African was the work of Anthony Benezet.[3] His timely philanthropy proved, better than any *a priori* reasoning, not original equality, physical, mental, or moral, but the capacity of the negro for improvement and the possibility of his becoming a useful citizen in a free country. If slavery was not entirely responsible for the ignorance and vice of the enslaved blacks, it was at least proved that their ignorance and vice could be remedied, like that of other human beings, by suitable education and training, and that the same incentives to industry and virtue could be applied.

[1] *A Forensic Dispute at Harvard*, 5; Rush, *Address on Slavery*, 4.

[2] *Ibid.*, 2–3. See also Appleton, *Considerations on Slavery*, 9. The writers of a century before had labored to prove that the negro as a human being had a right to salvation through the Gospel and to religious instruction with a view to that end. The humanity of the negro now meant a right to personal liberty and to happiness now and here, not merely hereafter. For the earlier view, see Morgan Godwyn, *The Negro's and Indians Advocate*, 9, 68–72; Tryon, *Advice to Planters*, 90, 109–116, 214, 220; and among the colonists John Eliot and Cotton Mather, *Cf.* § 10, above.

[3] See §§ 27, 190. A further argument was the literary prowess of Phyllis Wheatley, a negro poetess, whose productions may at least be said to compare favorably with those of her white contemporaries. She is referred to in Rush, *Address on Slave-Keeping*, 2, note. *Cf.* § 190, below.

The moral effects of slavery were regarded as among the strongest arguments against an institution under which such conditions were produced among the oppressed. **65. Moral arguments.** The effects upon the oppressor were also touched upon, if not with the scathing satire of Hepburn and Lay, yet with no less earnestness of feeling than theirs. These effects are painted by no one more vividly than by Jefferson: "There must doubtless be an unhappy influence on the manners of our people produced by the existence of slavery among us. The whole commerce between master and slave is a perpetual exercise of the most boisterous passions, the most unremitting despotism on the one part, and degrading submissions on the other. Our children see this, and learn to imitate it. . . . The man must be a prodigy who can retain his manners and morals undepraved by such circumstances."[1] The effect of slavery upon the condition of the laboring whites was another subject for comment.[2]

The first to discuss the slavery question from a purely economic standpoint was probably Benjamin Franklin; and his observations, which had considerable influence both at home and abroad, were followed by more extended arguments along the same lines. **66. Economic arguments.** Franklin remarked the comparative dearness of slave-labor, which must handicap the colonies in competing under that system with British manufacturers. He considered that the economic disadvantages were met to some extent by the fact that slaves could be held at will while the free laborer was likely to leave his master and set up for himself, but he regarded slavery as retarding the increase of population and industry in the colonies.[3] The depreciation of lands in the slave States, the decline of industry, and the blighting effects of slavery upon the arts and sciences were subjects of comment among the Virginian writers.[4] The

---

[1] Jefferson, *Notes on Virginia*, in Jefferson, *Writings*, VIII, 403. See also Franklin, *Observations concerning the Increase of Mankind, Works*, II, 228–229, and [Franklin], *Essay on the Slave-Trade*, 7–10.

[2] Franklin, *Works*, II, 228; Hopkins, *Dialogue concerning Slavery, Works*, II, 559, note.

[3] See above, § 54. Franklin, *Observations concerning the Increase of Mankind, Works*, II, 226–229.

[4] Henry, *Life of Patrick Henry*, I, 114; *Lee's Add.*, in *Views of American Slavery taken a Century Ago*, 109; Jefferson, *Writings*, VIII, 404.

problem of the distribution of wealth was already presenting itself, and Dr. Rush and Dr. Hopkins noted the advantages of small farms owned by the cultivators and of a system of free labor under which the general productiveness would be greater and the distribution more nearly equal. The country would thus, it was thought, be filled with virtuous, happy families instead of comparatively few, " many of which are a burden to the earth, and a disgrace to human nature."[1]

Franklin doubted the necessity and even the advantage of applying slave labor to the production of sugar.[2] Dr. Rush, though he advocates free labor on economic grounds, refuses to regard the question as purely economic. " No manufactory," he says, " can ever be of consequence enough to society, to admit the least violation of the Laws of justice or humanity."[3] Dr. Hopkins solves the difficulty by declaring that the regions in which only the blacks can labor should be left to their possession. " The whites," he says, " should abandon the places where they cannot live unless it be on the blood of others as good as themselves, and renounce the business which is carried on in the exercise of so much unrighteousness and cruelty. If the blacks only can labor there, the lands are theirs by right, and they ought to be allowed to possess them as free men, and enjoy the fruit of their labour."[4]

As the political situation became more complicated, the political aspect of the slavery question became correspondingly

67. Political arguments. important. To other colonies besides South Carolina slavery was now a terror. Even New York had felt the foe at her heart, and her experience as well as that of the Southern colonies was used to point a moral.[5] The philosophy of the day emphasized free principles of government as well as individual liberty, and slavery was looked upon as a menace to the free institutions so highly prized. " The plant of liberty is of so tender a Nature," says Dr. Rush, " that it cannot thrive

[1] Hopkins, *Dialogue concerning Slavery, Works*, II, 559, note.
[2] [Franklin], *Essay on the Slave-Trade*, 12–13.
[3] Rush, *Address upon Slave-Keeping*, 5.
[4] Hopkins, *Dialogue concerning Slavery, Works*, II, 559, note.
[5] Appleton, *Considerations on Slavery*, 13. See also the article by " Conscience," in A British Bostonian, *Oration on the Beauties of Liberty*, Appendix. For the practical effects of this feeling, see Pennsylvania, *Statutes at Large* (1896), II, 433.

long in the neighbourhood of slavery."[1] This point is emphasized by representative writers from every section of the country. No one is more eloquent on the subject than Thomas
Jefferson. "And with what execration should the statesman
be loaded," he says, "who, permitting one half the citizens thus
to trample on the rights of the other, transforms those into
despots and these into enemies, destroys the morals of the one
part, and the *amor patriæ* of the other. For if a slave can
have a country in this world, it must be any other in preference
to that in which he is born to live and labor for another. . . .
And can the liberties of a nation be thought secure when we
have removed their only firm basis, a conviction in the minds
of the people that these liberties are the gift of God? That
they are not to be violated but with his wrath? Indeed I
tremble for my country when I reflect that God is just."[2]

The anti-slavery conscience at this time was greatly stimulated
by the critical situation of the colonies. "Remember that
national crimes require national punishments," says
Dr. Rush, in 1773. "This evil . . . cannot pass
with impunity, unless God shall cease to be just or
merciful."[3] In the New England colonies, as was natural, the
belief that slavery was "a God-provoking and wrath-procuring
sin"[4] was emphatically expressed. It seemed that the situation
of the colonists had been specially designed to make clear to
them the crime of which they were guilty.[5] "God gave us liberty, and we have enslaved our fellow-men," says Rev. Nathaniel
Niles, in a sermon on Liberty preached at Newbury, Massa-

68. Effect of
the political
crisis.

---

[1] Rush, *Address on Slavery*, 28.

[2] Jefferson, *Notes on Virginia*, *Writings*, VIII, 403–404. See also *Lee's Add.*, in *Views of American Slavery taken a Century Ago*, 109; Hopkins, *Dialogue concerning Slavery*, *Works*, II, 559, note; Rush, *Address on Slavery*, 27–28.

[3] *Ibid.*, 30.

[4] Coffin, *Sketch of the History of Newbury*, 339. Extract from an Essay by B. Colman, in *The Essex Journal*, July 20, 1774.

[5] Coffin, *Sketch of the History of Newbury*, 340–346; Hopkins, *Dialogue concerning Slavery*, *Works*, II, 549–588. "Fifty years," says Belinda, an African slave, in a petition to the General Court of Massachusetts, February, 1782, "her faithful hands have been compelled to ignoble servitude for the benefit of an Isaac Royall, until, as if nations must be agitated, and the world convulsed, for the preservation of that freedom, which the Almighty Father intended for all the human race, the present war commenced." *Petition of an African slave*, in *The American Museum*, I, 463–465.

chusetts, in 1774. " May we not fear that the law of retaliation is about to be executed on us? . . . What reason can we urge why our oppression shall not be repaid in kind? . . . Would we enjoy liberty? Then we must grant it to others. For shame, let us either cease to enslave our fellow-men, or else let us cease to complain of those that would enslave us. Let us either wash our hands from blood, or never hope to escape the avenger." [1]

From the same point of view, the Boston Port Bill was regarded as a divine visitation upon the city for having been, as it was said, the first slave-port.[2] The early successes of the war were looked upon as a reward for the non-importation resolutions and the suppression of the slave-trade.[3] Like the feeling among the abolitionists during the Civil War was the belief that nothing short of general emancipation could appease an angry God and bring the war to a successful issue.[4] This idea is a prominent motive in the most important anti-slavery effort of the period, Hopkins's *Dialogue concerning the Slavery of the Africans* (1776), which urges upon the Second Continental Congress measures for the total and immediate abolition of slavery. The influence of some of the clergy was probably effective in securing individual manumissions. It is said that Mr. Niles's sermon on Liberty induced one of his hearers to free his slave on the following day,[5] and private manumissions become common at this time, particularly in New England.[6]

After the successful issue of the war the stimulus to emancipation was removed. As the principle of equality before the law for all white men was no longer in contention, the feeling for

---

[1] Niles, *Two Discourses on Liberty*, I, 37–38. An extract is given in Coffin, *Sketch of the History of Newbury*, 340. See also an extract from *The Norwich Packet*, July 7, 1774, in Steiner, *History of Slavery in Connecticut*, IV, 22–23.

[2] Colman, in Coffin, *Sketch of the History of Newbury*, 342.

[3] *Ibid.*, 343; Hopkins, *Dialogue concerning Slavery, Works*, II, 587.

[4] *Ibid.*, II, 550–552, 572, 584–588.

[5] Coffin, *Sketch of the History of Newbury*, 340.

[6] Felt, *Annals of Salem*, II, 417. Another sermon against slavery was preached in 1774, at Farmington, Connecticut, before the Corporation and Freemen, by Rev. Levi Hart. Steiner, *History of Slavery in Connecticut*, 28. An interesting case of manumission is that of Newport Gardner. Park, *Memoir of S. Hopkins*, 155. See also Steiner, *History of Slavery in Connecticut*, 22–23, 68.

the common rights of all men became less intense.[1] There were still, however, some whose sense of moral obligation was as strong as ever, and who felt keenly the inconsistency of the American position. A clergyman had been the leading expositor of the principles of 1776, a lawyer had uttered the words which marked the opening of the contest, and " A Farmer" interprets the situation at its close. *A Serious Address to the Rulers of America,* published in 1783, is supposed to have been written by John Dickinson, and the words come with better grace from one who had been among the foremost in the constitutional struggle for liberty, who had entered with reluctance upon the contest for independence, and when that contest became inevitable served his country faithfully in field and council.[2] It was the claims of universal liberty, he reminds his readers, that were asserted in justification of the war. Now is the time to prove that America was sincere in her professions. " Ye rulers of America beware ! " he says. " Let it appear to future ages, from the records of this day, that you not only professed to be advocates for freedom, but really were inspired by the love of mankind, and wished to secure the invaluable blessing to all; that, as you disdained to submit to the unlimited control of others, you equally abhorred the crying crime of holding your fellow men, as much entitled to freedom as yourselves, the subjects of your undisputed will and pleasure." [3]

The treatment of the colonies by the British government, which had been regarded as a sufficient cause for revolution, he thinks " is no more to be equalled, with ours to the negroes, than a barley corn is to the globe we inhabit "; and the attitude of America toward Great Britain he compares to that of " an atrocious pirate, setting in all the solemn pomp of a judge, passing sentence of death on a petty thief." [4] In a series of parallels he compares the two cases, quoting the declarations of the American Congress in one column and in the opposite column adapting them to the case of the negroes.[5] No words could have been more forcible than those of the Revolutionary

69. Sentiment after the war. "A Farmer's" Address.

[1] Luther Martin, *Address to the Legislature of Maryland on the Federal Convention,* in F. Moore, *American Eloquence,* I, 391.

[2] Stillé, *Life and Times of John Dickinson.*

[3] A Farmer, *Serious Address to the Rulers of America,* 7.

[4] *Ibid.,* 7–8.   [5] *Ibid.,* 8–15.

documents now turned against their authors. There was little need for comment. The statement of the self-evident truths proclaimed as the principles of the infant nation as its justification in taking arms left only two courses: the emancipation of the slaves, or a retreat from the principles on which the government was founded. The words of "A Farmer" made the situation perfectly clear, and his pamphlet had a wide circulation.[1]

The movement toward emancipation by law had its beginnings in this period. *The Pennsylvania Chronicle* as early

70. Beginnings of emancipation by law. as 1768 called for the emancipation of *post-nati* or even of the whole race.[2] Dr. Rush, in 1773, urged that petitions against the slave-trade be sent to King and Parliament, and that slave-traders be shunned as the greatest enemies of their country; also that the young blacks be fitted to support themselves, and that laws be made "to limit the time of their servitude and to entitle them to all the privileges of free-born British subjects," suggesting, however, that the infirm and vicious remain the property of those with whom they became so.[3] The Revolutionists, as their new government took shape, naturally looked to it for action, and, as naturally, the tendency was toward State rather than national action. Rev. William Gordon, in 1776, published plans for gradual abolition by State legislation, limiting servitude to a brief term of years, regarding the descendants of Africans born within the State as free-born, and placing them wholly at their own disposal at the age of twenty-one.[4] The development of these ideas to a practical outcome in the abolition of slavery in all States north of Mason and Dixon's Line will be described in a subsequent chapter.

National action was more difficult. It went no further than the suppression of the slave-trade in 1776, which was accomplished

71. Efforts for national action. with the co-operation of the State legislatures.[5] Two of the strongest anti-slavery documents of the time, however, were expressly directed toward emancipation by national act, and their attitude deserves attention.

[1] A copy of this pamphlet, which belonged to George Washington's library, is now in the possession of the Boston Athenæum.

[2] Extract from *The Pennsylvania Chronicle* for Nov. 21, 1768, in *The Anti-Slavery Examiner*, No. 5, p. 27.

[3] Rush, *Address on Slavery*, 19–20.

[4] Letter of Dr. William Gordon, quoted in Moore, *Notes on Slavery in Massachusetts*, 176–177.   [5] See below, § 82.

The obstacles to universal emancipation, says "A Farmer," are of our own creating. "Must the innocent continue to suffer," he asks, "because we have involved ourselves in difficulties?"[1] These obstacles are discussed in detail by Dr. Hopkins in his *Dialogue concerning the Slavery of the Africans.* The chief points considered are the question of property rights, the problem of the free blacks, and the special difficulties involved in taking so momentous a step in the midst of the dangers which already surrounded the infant republic. To the claims of property rights he refuses the least regard. "Must they be forever deprived of their right, which is worth more to them than all you possess," he asks, "because you have been so foolish and wicked as to buy them. . . . He who refuses to free his negroes, that he may save his money and lay it up for his children, and retains his slaves for them to tyrannize over, leaves them but a miserable inheritance — infinitely worse than nothing."[2] He presents a dilemma to the effect that the slaves have already more than paid for themselves and therefore have a better right to a part of the estate than the children have; or else they are hardly worth keeping, and in that case may easily be parted with. The problem of the free blacks was met with equally relentless logic. If it be regarded as a justification of slavery that the manumitted blacks would be worse off than ever and would have to be maintained, it would follow, he argues, that all vicious and helpless persons should be enslaved. The solution of the problem he believes will be found in subjecting them to the same laws and restraints with other freemen, in helping those who need help, supporting the helpless, and giving reasonable wages to those who earn them. To the plea that the times are not convenient he replies that the times make it a necessity. Only thus, he thinks, can the nation avoid the judgment of God and gain his favor. Moreover, as slaves are now unprofitable on account of the lack of business during the war, they can be more readily dispensed with; and it is questionable, he adds, whether those who make this objection to freeing their slaves without delay would free them if the times

72. Discussion of obstacles to emancipation. Hopkins's *Dialogue.*

---

[1] A Farmer, *Serious Address*, 17.
[2] Hopkins, *Dialogue concerning Slavery, Works*, II, 576.

should change and slave-labor become more profitable.[1] Time
was to prove the truth of his forebodings. The revival of the
slave-trade with that of other business after the war showed that
self-interest was stronger than sentiment, and fastened the
institution upon the country more firmly than ever.

A Farmer's *Serious Address to the Rulers of America*, though
no less bold than Hopkins's *Dialogue*, has the more gloomy
73. Appeal of tone of one who sees the great opportunity passing
"A Farmer."   and the great work still undone. The author regrets
that recommendations were not made to the State legislatures,
in 1776, that no blacks imported and none born in America
after that date should be held as slaves.[2] For nearly ten years,
he says, restraints on legislation have been removed and the
country has been free to act, and still nothing has been done, a
gloomy presage for America.[3] At the time he wrote, Vermont
and Pennsylvania had provided for emancipation, but the action
of individual States gives him little satisfaction. "When a griev-
ance is general," he says, in words which mark him as a forerunner of Joshua R. Giddings and Charles Sumner, " it is but
trifling to employ partial means; it is like attempting to destroy a great tree by nibbling at its branches. It is only the
supreme power, which pervades the whole, that can take it up
by the roots."[4] He therefore makes an urgent appeal to Congress, as the head of the new republic, to put into practice the
principles that they professed in the days of their own oppression. " If neither the voice of *justice*," he writes, in paraphrase
of the words of the First Continental Congress, in 1774, "the
dictates of *humanity*, the *rights* of *human nature*, and establishment of *impartial liberty now in your power*, the good of your
country, nor the fear of an *avenging God*, can restrain your
hand from this *impious practice* of holding your fellow-men in
slavery ; making traffick of . . . *your brethren* possessed of immortal souls equal with yourselves; then let *justice, humanity,
advocates for liberty*, and the sacred name of *Christians*, cease
to be the *boast* of *American rulers*."[5]

---

[1] Hopkins, *Dialogue concerning Slavery, Works*, II, 576–577, 580–584.
[2] A Farmer, *Serious Address*, 17–18.
[3] *Ibid.*, 23–24.
[4] *Ibid.*, 18–19.
[5] *Ibid.*, 24.

Congress, even if it had wished to do so, was no longer in a position to deal effectively with the slavery question. The Continental Congress with its revolutionary powers ₇₄. Situation might have accomplished something; the Congress in 1783. of the Confederation, under the Articles which served as a constitution from 1781 to 1789, could not even interfere with the slave-trade when it revived after the close of the war. The time for national emancipation had not yet come. Throughout the country, however, the right to personal liberty for blacks as well as whites had been at least discussed, and had been advocated by prominent men. The arguments in its favor had developed very considerably, especially on the economic and political sides, and their force had been greatly intensified by the attitude of the colonists toward Great Britain. Efforts for State and national emancipation had begun; and though the principles of 1776 had failed of universal application, yet the ardent professions of Jefferson, the earnest exhortations of Hopkins, and the solemn warning of Dickinson were not altogether without avail. "Slavery," says John Parrish, in 1806, "has become less excusable since the Revolution. The rights of men were then investigated and the light was set upon the candlestick that all who were in the house (the United States) might behold things in their proper colours."[1] After this period the self-evident truths of the Declaration of Independence are quoted by anti-slavery writers even more often than the Golden Rule. Slavery is not only regarded as unjust, impolitic, and unchristian. It is inconsistent with the principles and professions of the republic. It is a monument of hypocrisy, and disgraces the nation in the eyes of the world.[2] The next step must be for those who most felt its injustice and gained least from its practice to use their political power toward its abolition.

[1] Parrish, *Remarks on the Slavery of the Black People*, 40.
[2] J. Hector St. John de Crèvecœur, *Letters from an American Farmer*, 1782, in *The American Museum*, I, 209–211. See also a Letter by Lieutenant Reeves of the Pennsylvania Line from Williamsburgh, North Carolina, March 21, 1782, on seeing a slave auction, in *Pa. Mag. Hist. and Biog.*, XXI, 388 f. *Cf.* § 189, below.

CHAPTER III

THE POLITICAL MOVEMENT IN THE REVOLUTIONARY PERIOD, 1761–1783

IT was not merely in literature or in abstract theories that the opposition to slavery showed itself during the Revolution-
75. Practical side of the philosophical movement. ary period. The philosophical movement as well as the religious had a distinctly practical side. Like that also it was directed partly against importation and partly against slavery as already existing. The Quakers, with their scruples against magistracy, had trusted to the efforts of their own organization and to appeals to the individual conscience. The Revolutionists, believing as they did that government exists for the good of the governed, endeavored to make use of its machinery in this cause; and the result was that great political agitation which, though it failed to extinguish slavery, made its continued existence a question only of time. Until the close of the war, in 1783, the practical aspect of the movement is less conspicuous than the theoretical, and the events of the period are interesting not so much on account of any widespread or continuous progress in the actual enfranchisement of the African race as because they illustrate the working of the principles of the Revolution and give evidence of the gradual development of anti-slavery sentiment. Nevertheless, important beginnings were made both in the suppression of the African slave-trade and in the emancipation of slaves within the States, and it is these beginnings that will form the subject of the present chapter.

In early colonial history there had been hardly an attempt at the abolition of slavery by political means. The only conspicu-
76. Early colonial legislation. ous efforts are the instructions of the Boston Town-Meeting, May 26, 1701, to its representatives in the General Court, which were issued soon after the publication of Sewall's *Selling of Joseph;*[1] a petition, "relating to

---

[1] See above, § 13. *Boston Town Records*, May 26, 1701.

the Enlargement of Negroes," addressed to the Pennsylvania Assembly in 1712 by William Southby, who had written against slavery in 1696;[1] and another petition, " signed by many of the Inhabitants of this Province, praying the Prohibition of Negroes," which appeared before the Pennsylvania Assembly at the same time with Southby's and led to a bill imposing a prohibitive duty.[2] The acts to limit or suppress importation which are frequently found in colonial history were generally prompted by other than humanitarian motives. In the South, as has been noticed in the case of South Carolina, they were due to fear of insurrection,[3] a fear which appears occasionally in the middle colonies and New England.[4] In the northern and middle colonies, however, the motives were mainly economic: many duty acts, especially in New York, were passed for the purpose of revenue; and some were the result of a preference for white laborers and of the feeling that slavery discouraged industry and prevented immigration.[5] The New England colonies made some attempts to prevent the introduction of slaves; though a system of draw-backs, as has been noticed by Professor DuBois, shows that there was no intention of prohibiting the trade with other colonies.[6] Pennsylvania was the first colony which passed an act to prevent the importation of negroes (June 7, 1712);[7] although at the same time that this measure was brought forward, the Assembly, in response to Southby's petition, announced that it was of the opinion that

---

[1] Bettle, *Notices of Negro Slavery*, in *Pa. Hist. Soc. Mem.*, I, 387 and note; *Votes and Proceedings of the House of Representatives of the Province of Pennsylvania*, II, 110.

[2] *Ibid.*

[3] See above, § 4.

[4] DuBois, *Suppression of the Slave-Trade*, 22, 206; *Statutes at Large of Pennsylvania*, Mitchell and Flanders, 1896, II, 433 (June 7, 1712); *Acts and Resolves of the Province of the Massachusetts Bay*, I, 698 (Aug. 23, 1712); *Conn. Col. Rec.*, V, 516, 534-535 (July 8, October, 1715).

[5] *Documents relating to the Colonial History of New York*, V, 379-380, 551, VI, 33-38; *Colonial Laws of New York* (Albany, 1896), *passim*; *Documents relating to the Colonial History of New Jersey*, IV, 196, IX, 345-348; *Acts of the General Assembly of New Jersey Province*, Allinson, ch. 494, p. 315 (Nov. 16, 1769); *Acts and Resolves of the Province of the Massachusetts Bay*, I, 634, 698 (Feb. 26, 170⅞, and Aug. 23, 1712); DuBois, *Suppression of the Slave-Trade*, chapter iii.

[6] *Ibid.*, 31, 35-36, and Appendix A.

[7] *Ibid.*, 22, 206; *Statutes at Large of Pennsylvania*, II, 433-436.

" it is neither just nor convenient to set them at Liberty." [1]   In Virginia the policy began to be restrictive as early as 1710, and although no distinct moral protest appeared before 1772, successive duties were laid with obviously restrictive intention.[2] The arraignment of the British Government by Jefferson in the *Proposed Instructions to Delegates* in 1774 and in the original draft of the Declaration of Independence in 1776, the similar charges of the Virginia Constitutional Convention, unanimously adopted June 29, 1776, and the terms of the response to Lord Dunmore's proclamation freeing negroes capable of bearing arms, all indicate a belief that the previous legislation against the slave-trade in Virginia had been influenced by moral sentiment.[3]

With the beginning of the Revolutionary War the humanitarian sentiment behind slave-trade legislation became more

77. Efforts for legislation, 1765–1774. conspicuous, and there was from that time a close connection with the idea of abolition. It is significant that the movement toward the facilitation of manumission which began in Virginia in 1769 was inaugurated by Thomas Jefferson.[4]   The change was especially marked in Massachusetts.   In the very year of the Stamp Act the town of Worcester instructed its representative " That he should use his influence to obtain a law *to put an end to that unchristian and impolitic practice of making slaves of the human species,* and that he give his vote to none to serve in his Majesty's Council, who will use his influence against such a law." [5]   Boston, the following year (May 26, 1766), issued similar instructions with a view to " the total abolishing of slavery." [6]   The result was a bill (March 13, 1767) " to prevent the unwarrantable and unusual Practice or Custom of inslaving Mankind in this

---

[1] *Votes and Proceedings of the House of Representatives of the Province of Pennsylvania*, II, 110.

[2] DuBois, *Suppression of the Slave-Trade*, 13–14.

[3] Jefferson, *Writings*, Taylor and Maury, 1853, I, 135, 23 ; *Statutes at Large of Virginia*, Hening, IX, 112–113; Force, *American Archives*, 4th Series, III, 1387.

[4] Randall, *Life of Jefferson*, I, 58.

[5] Extract from *The Boston News-Letter* of June 4, 1765, in Buckingham, *Specimens of Newspaper Literature*, I, 31 ; also in Moore, *Notes on Slavery in Massachusetts*, I, 124.   *Cf.* Resolutions of June 14, 1775, in Lincoln, *History of Worcester*, 110.

[6] *Boston Town Records, 1758-1769, p. 183.*

Province, and the importation of Slaves into the same." This bill failed to pass beyond the third reading (March 16); and a bill laying a duty on slaves which was substituted for it failed to obtain the concurrence of both houses (March 20).[1] The Boston Town-Meeting, however (March 16), on the question whether the town should adhere to this clause in its instructions, voted "in the Affirmative, Nem. Con."[2] In 1771 a bill to prevent importation was passed (April 24), but failed to secure the approval of the Governor.[3] Two years later, a still more vigorous effort was made. On this occasion the towns of Salem,[4] Sandwich,[5] Medford,[6] and Leicester[7] framed instructions against the importation of slaves. Sandwich and Leicester also instructed their representatives to endeavor to procure a gradual emancipation act, and Leicester proposed that all negro children born after a certain date should be maintained by the town or province until they became of age.[8]

At about the same time several petitions from negroes were presented to the General Court praying for emancipation. One of these petitions ventures only an expression of the sympathy of the blacks with the struggle for liberty in which the Legislature is engaged, and a gentle allusion to the "great things" which they expect "from men who have made such a noble stand against the designs of their *fellow-men* to enslave them." For the rest, they urge the Legislature to "have the same grand object, . . . civil and religious *Liberty*," in view in their next session, and accompany their letter with a

78. Negro petitions.

---

[1] *Journal of the House of Representatives of His Majesty's Province of the Massachusetts-Bay*, 1766–1767, pp. 353, 358, 387, 390, 393, 408–411, 420; *General Court Records*, 1765–1767, p. 485; Deane, *Letters and Documents relating to Slavery in Massachusetts*, in 5 *Mass. Hist. Soc. Coll.*, III, 385.

[2] *Boston Town Records*, 1758–1769, p. 200.

[3] *Journal of the House of Representatives*, 1770–1771, pp. 228, 234, 236, 240, 242–243; Moore, *Notes on Slavery in Massachusetts*, 130–132.

[4] Felt, *Annals of Salem*, II, 416–417.

[5] Freeman, *History of Cape Cod*, II, 114.

[6] Swan, *Dissuasion from the Slave-Trade* (1773), x.

[7] Washburn, *Historical Sketches of Leicester*, 442–443. The instructions of Salem, Sandwich, and Leicester are found also in Moore, *Notes on Slavery in Massachusetts*, 133–134.

[8] Washburn, *Leicester*, 443. A similar resolution was passed, Dec. 12, 1774, by the Town-Meeting of Danbury, Connecticut. Steiner, *History of Slavery in Connecticut*, 30.

copy of Swan's *Dissuasion from the Slave-Trade*.[1] Other petitioners claim that "they have in comon with other men a natural right to be free and without molestation to injoy such Property as thay may acquire by their industry."[2] A petition from Felix Holbrook and others, June 25, 1773, prays that the subscribers be freed from bondage and made freemen of the commonwealth, and also that a portion of the unimproved lands of the province be given them for settlement.[3] Although the tone of these petitions varies considerably, their number and opportuneness, in connection with the instructions from the towns, lead one to suspect a guiding hand behind the scenes, — perhaps that of no less a person than that prince of wire-pullers, Samuel Adams. In fact, Adams is found taking an active interest in the cause of the petitioners, and is evidently looked upon by them as a mediator or champion.[4]

Meanwhile, in the General Court, efforts were made to prevent the importation and purchase of slaves, though but little was attempted in the direction of emancipation.

79. Bills to prevent importation. Two bills were introduced in 1773, one of which passed the Council and the other the House.[5] The bill in response to Felix Holbrook's petition, originating (March 2, 1774) in a committee of which Samuel Adams was a member, passed both houses, but like that of 1771 failed to receive Governor Hutchinson's approval, and a similar bill passed in June encountered the same fate.[6] Governor Hutchinson probably regarded these measures as a political movement

---

[1] This petition is dated Boston, April 20, 1773. It is printed in "A British Bostonian," *Oration on the Beauties of Liberty*, Third Edition, Appendix, p. 78. A negro petition had already appeared, January 8. *Journal of the House of Representatives*, 1772–1773, p. 195.

[2] Deane, *Letters and Documents relating to Slavery in Massachusetts*, in 5 *Mass. Hist. Soc. Coll.*, III, 395–396, note, 432.

[3] *Ibid.*, 387–388, 434–435; Moore, *Notes on Slavery in Massachusetts*, 135; *Journal of the House of Representatives*, 1773–1774, pp. 85, 94, 104. Another negro petition is that of Lancaster Hill and others, in 1777. See below, § 86.

[4] Letter of S. Adams to John Pickering, Jr., Jan. 8, 1774, in Moore, *Notes on Slavery in Massachusetts*, 136; Appointment of Adams and Pickering on committee, in *House Journal*, January 26, p. 104.

[5] *House Journal*, 1772–1773, pp. 195, 203, 204, 208, 225, 252, 259, 287.

[6] *Ibid.*, 1773–1774, pp. 221, 224, 226, 237, 243 (March 2–8), and *Ibid.*, 1774, pp. 27, 41 (June 10–16); *Gen. Court Rec.*, XXX, 248, 264, 322; Moore, *Notes on Slavery in Massachusetts*, 137–139.

directed against the government,[1] and it has been remarked that
the General Court must have expected a veto, and that if their
anti-slavery sentiment had been sincere they would have adopted
measures against the slavery already existing.[2]   On this point we
have the testimony of Samuel Dexter, a member of the General
Court who was active in support of the bills.   He says that the
members of the Legislature did expect the veto of the Governor,
but wished nevertheless to do their duty so far as they could.[3]
The objections to the further introduction of slaves were doubtless stronger than the opposition to the slavery already existing, and it may well be supposed that in Massachusetts as in
Virginia it was considered useless to attempt general emancipation so long as importation remained unprohibited.   Political
considerations, however, undoubtedly had some weight, and
the suspicions of Governor Hutchinson were not altogether
unfounded.

The efforts in New Jersey (1773–1774) and Delaware (1775)
to prevent importation failed in the same manner as in Massachusetts; but Pennsylvania, both persistent and skilful in her
policy, succeeded in establishing and maintaining a prohibitive
duty (1761–1773).   Rhode Island (1774) and Connecticut (1774),
the only colonies with legislative independence, were the only
colonies besides Pennsylvania to succeed in passing prohibitory
acts.[4]

The statute enacted by the Legislature of Rhode Island was
far from satisfactory in some of its features, as it provided that
an importer should give bonds of £100 for the re-   80. Legisla-
moval of each negro imported within one year, and   tion in Rhode
laid heavy penalties for importing negroes in order   Island, 1774.
to free them.   But it was preceded by events which show genuine anti-slavery sentiment.   Jacob Shoemaker, of Providence,
had died intestate without heirs, and his property, including
several negroes, accordingly fell to the town.   It was therefore
voted in town-meeting "that it is unbecoming the character

[1] Letter to Lord Hillsborough, in Moore, *Notes on Slavery in Massachusetts*, 131–132.
[2] *Ibid.*, 132.
[3] Deane, *Letters and Documents relating to Slavery*, in 5 *Mass. Hist.
Soc. Coll.*, III, 395.
[4] DuBois, *Suppression of the Slave-Trade*, chapters iii, iv, and Appendix
A; *Conn. Col. Rec.*, XIV, 329; *R. I. Col. Rec.*, VII, 251–253.

of freemen to enslave the said negroes, and they do hereby, give up all claim of right or property in them." The same meeting passed a resolution that " Whereas, the inhabitants of America are engaged in the preservation of their rights and liberties, and as personal liberty is an essential part of the natural rights of mankind," their deputies should endeavor to obtain an act prohibiting the importation of slaves into the colony and freeing *post-nati* at a certain age.[1] The act passed by the Assembly in the following month (June, 1774), was introduced by a preamble similar to that of the Providence Town-Meeting, but the provision with regard to emancipation was omitted. In 1779, however, an act was passed prohibiting the sale and removal of slaves from the State as tending to " aggravate the Condition of Slavery, which this General Assembly is disposed rather to alleviate, till some favorable Occasion may offer for its total Abolition." [2]

The slave-trade clause in the general Articles of Association adopted by the First Continental Congress in 1774 was adopted in many of the colonies chiefly from political or economic motives.[3] In the resolutions of some of the counties of Virginia, for instance, slavery was regarded as obstructing the immigration of industrious foreigners, preventing manufactures, and turning the balance of trade against the colony.[4] The Fairfax and Hanover County resolutions protested against the slave-trade on moral grounds, but nothing was said against slavery itself.[5] In one of the colonies, however, is expressed the intention of making this measure a preliminary step toward the abolition of slavery. The inhabitants of Darien County in Georgia explicitly declare their " disapprobation and abhorrence of the unnatural practice of Slavery in *America*," and desire to prove the sincerity of their love for liberty by taking steps toward manumission as soon as may be practicable.[6] The motives of this resolution are somewhat obscure, and there is no reason to suppose that it

81. The Articles of Association, 1774.

---

[1] *R. I. Col. Rec.*, VII, 280; Staples, *Annals of Providence*, 236.

[2] *Laws of Rhode Island*, Bennett Wheeler, October, 1779, pp. 6–7.

[3] An analysis of the action of Congress and of the individual colonies is given in DuBois, *Suppression of the Slave-Trade*, 41–48.

[4] Force, *American Archives*, 4th Series, I, 494, 523, 530, 641.

[5] *Ibid.*, 600, 616.

[6] *Ibid.*, 1136.

led to any practical results; but the actuating influence of a genuine anti-slavery sentiment is at least probable, and it may be remembered that when the slavery question was agitating Georgia, thirty-five years earlier, it was the Scottish immigrants of Darien who entered a protest against the institution on the ground of justice and humanity.[1]

The action of the First Continental Congress was supplemented by that of the Second, which, assuming the commercial powers previously vested in the Crown, now (April 6, 1776) resolved "That no slaves be imported into any of the Thirteen United Colonies."[2] This measure was accepted without opposition by the colonies; but since the demand for slaves was then at a minimum on account of the war, no extraordinary credit is due them for acquiescence. Supplementary action, however, was taken by States which vainly struggled to rid themselves of the institution altogether. Delaware and Virginia were now added to the number of States prohibiting importation, the former by an article in her Constitution (1776) and the latter by statute (1778). Maryland followed the example of Virginia in 1783. The Constitution of Delaware asserted that "no person hereafter imported into this State from Africa ought to be held in slavery under any pretence whatever; and no negro, Indian, or mulatto slave ought to be brought into this State, for sale, from any part of the world."[3] Virginia (1778, 1785) and Maryland (1783, 1796) provided that no negro thereafter imported should be held in slavery.[4] Farther south, no action was taken by State legislatures until after the war, but the economic conditions were such as to make it unnecessary at the time. The slave-trade was now more nearly extinct than at any other time before the Civil War, but the combination of opposing forces had a strength which could be only temporary.

82. Suppression of the slave-trade, 1774-1783.

[1] See above, § 6. The resolutions of Darien were adopted two weeks later by the Provincial Congress of Georgia. Weeks, *Anti-Slavery Sentiment in the South*, 92.

[2] Force, *American Archives*, 4th Series, V, 1660; *Journals of Congress*, II, 122.

[3] Poore, *Federal and State Constitutions*, I, 277.

[4] *Statutes at Large of Virginia*, Hening, IX, 471, XII, 182; *Laws of Maryland*, Kilty, April to June, 1783, ch. 23; 1796, ch. 67, § 5; DuBois, *Suppression of the Slave-Trade*, 224-226.

The efforts for emancipation, though sometimes futile, are more significant. To accomplish this object four methods

83 Beginnings of emancipation.
were adopted: (*a*) the facilitation of voluntary manumission, intended as a preliminary measure, (*b*) gradual emancipation by act of legislature, (*c*) direct constitutional provision, and (*d*) the application of the general principles of the state constitution to the case of the negroes through judicial decisions.

Of these methods, the most gentle was the facilitation of voluntary manumission by the owners, which had been rigorously restricted in the Southern States. The dif-

84. Facilitation of manumission.
ficulties experienced by the Society of Friends in North Carolina[1] illustrate the necessity for such a measure, while the fact that such careful restrictions existed shows how gradual and cautious a policy must be which, with any prospect of success, should encounter the general public sentiment. It is a significant fact that in Virginia, where all four methods were attempted or at least considered, and which nevertheless remained a slave State until 1865, the campaign was begun along this line. The movement was appropriately inaugurated by Thomas Jefferson, in his first session as a member of the Virginia Assembly in 1769.[2] There was, however, a natural feeling that importation must be stopped before effective measures could be taken for emancipation;[3] and Virginia showed herself ready to prohibit the slave-trade as soon as opportunity was granted.[4] After that there was still the problem of the free blacks, and this seemed to the Virginians so serious a difficulty that although the leading patriots were interested in abolishing slavery and the Quakers were trying to manumit their own slaves and were urgent in their appeals for favorable legislation,[5] it was not until 1782 that an act was passed permitting voluntary manumission, which had hitherto been allowed only in cases of meritorious service and by a

---

[1] See above, § 41.

[2] Randall, *Jefferson*, I, 58.

[3] Jefferson, *Writings*, I, 135.

[4] See above, §§ 76, 82; Jefferson, *Writings*, VIII, 334; Tucker, in Deane, *Letters and Documents relating to Slavery*, 5 *Mass. Hist. Soc. Coll*, III, 380.

[5] Brackett, *Status of the Slave*, in Jameson, *Essays in Constitutional History*, 303–304; Mifflin, *Defence against Aspersions*, 17–18.

special license from the county court.[1] In Maryland manumission by will was forbidden (1752), but slaves under fifty years of age, if sound in mind and body and capable of self-support, could be manumitted by deed.[2] In Delaware an act passed in 1767 permitted manumission by will or otherwise, provided the owner gave surety for maintenance.[3]

In Virginia the chief obstacles to manumission were the supposed danger of letting the negroes loose upon society and the feeling that it was impossible to incorporate them as members of the commonwealth.[4] In New England, where slaves were comparatively few and where there was greater difficulty in obtaining a subsistence, the chief problem was the maintenance of the free blacks. Early laws had provided that no one should free his slaves without becoming liable to maintain them in case they should fail to support themselves.[5] The prudent and thrifty owners shrank from manumitting their slaves on such conditions. But as Virginia, after the practical close of the Revolutionary War with the surrender of Cornwallis, took courage to grapple with her chief domestic problem, so Connecticut in the very month that marks the relief of New England by the surrender of Burgoyne at Saratoga, passed an act under which the owner could obtain permission to manumit able-bodied slaves without becoming responsible for their subsequent maintenance.[6]

The next step in these States must be an attempt to supplement voluntary manumission by legislative emancipation. In Connecticut such an attempt was made in 1780. A bill providing for gradual emancipation was framed, but disappeared after passing the Upper House.[7] In Virginia a plan for gradual emancipation had been prepared by a committee appointed to revise the laws of the

85. Efforts for gradual emancipation. Connecticut and Virginia.

---

[1] *Statutes at Large of Virginia*, Hening, XI, 39–40; Laws passed in 1723 and 1748, *Ibid.*, IV. 132, VI, 112.

[2] *Abridgment and Collection of the Acts of Assembly of the Province of Maryland*, Bisset, 282–285; Pinkney, *Speech in the House of Delegates*, 5.

[3] *Laws of the State of Delaware*, 1797, I, 436.

[4] Jefferson, *Writings*, VIII, 380–387.

[5] *Acts and Resolves of the Province of Massachusetts Bay*, I, 519 (July 31, 1703); *Conn. Col. Rec.*, IV, 375–376 (May, 1702), V, 233 (May, 1711); *R. I. Col. Rec.*, IV, 415–416 (February, 172$\frac{8}{9}$).

[6] Steiner, *History of Slavery in Connecticut*, 24–25; Brackett, *Status of the Slave*, in Jameson, *Essays*, 296.   [7] *Ibid.*

State (1776-1779). Of this committee Jefferson was a member, and the other members, George Wythe and Edmund Pendleton, were also inclined toward abolition. According to their plan all persons born after a certain date were to be free; the children were to remain with their parents until a certain age and then to receive a practical education at the public expense, after which they were to be colonized under the protection of the United States. This plan was to have been brought forward as an amendment to the revised legislation on slavery prepared by the committee, but was finally withheld on the supposition that the public mind was not yet prepared for it.[1]

The efforts for emancipation by direct act of legislature were more important than those for the facilitation of voluntary manumission. In the Northern States there was a considerable public sentiment which was not inclined to stop short of the more radical measure, while in the far South nothing was likely to be accomplished in either direction. In this movement all the New England States had a share. Rhode Island promptly followed her prohibition of importation by an attempt at a gradual emancipation act in 1775.[2] In 1779, though an act was passed prohibiting the sale of slaves from the State in anticipation of their emancipation,[3] here, as in Connecticut, the complete triumph of anti-slavery sentiment was postponed until after the close of the war. In Massachusetts and New Hampshire, also, the movement was incomplete. In the former a petition to the General Court by Lancaster Hill and other negroes, introduced March 18, 1777,[4] gave rise to a bill (June 9, 1777)

86. Rhode Island, Massachusetts, and New Hampshire.

---

[1] *Cf.* § 206, below; Jefferson, *Writings*, I, 48-49, VIII, 380; Madison, *Letters*, I, 200.

[2] See above, § 80. Brackett, in Jameson, *Essays*, 293; Force, *American Archives*, 4th Series, III, 453. For correspondence between Rev. Samuel Hopkins and Moses Brown on the subject of slavery, see Park, *Memoir of Samuel Hopkins*, 119-128.

[3] See above, § 80.

[4] " The Petition of a great number of Negroes who are detained in a state of Slavery, in the Bowels of a free & Christian Country — Humbly Shewing — That your Petitioners apprehend that they have, in common with all other Men, a natural & unalienable right to that freedom, which the great Parent of the Universe hath bestowed equally on all Mankind, & which they have never forfeited by any compact or agreement whatever. . . . In imitation

"for preventing the Practice of holding Persons in Slavery." [1] There was an attempt in connection with this matter to send an application to the Continental Congress on the subject, and a letter was prepared and reported, but the majority were not ready to go so far and the report was ordered to lie.[2] A petition to the Legislature of New Hampshire, November 12, 1779, was signed by twenty slaves and prayed for the enactment of a law giving them their freedom. The petition was considered and was argued by counsel for the petitioners, but the House decided that it was "not ripe for a determination." [3]

So also in New Jersey the Assembly refused to consider a recommendation from Governor Livingston, on the ground that the times were "too critical." [4] To Pennsylvania, therefore, was left the honor of being the first of the thirteen States to set a term to human slavery (March 1, 1780).[5] In that State no times were ever too critical for the discussion of the slavery question: in season and out of season there was always some friend of the negro to keep the subject alive. Two petitions for the abolition of slavery, from residents of Philadelphia, were presented to

87. Gradual emancipation in New Jersey and Pennsylvania.

of the laudable example of the good People of these States, your Petitioners have long & patiently waited the event of Petition after Petition, by them presented to the Legislative Body of this State, & can not but with grief reflect that their success has been but too similar — They can not but express their astonishment, that it has never been considered, that every principle from which America has acted in the course of her unhappy difficulties with Great-Britain, pleads stronger than a thousand arguments in favor of your Petitioners." — They therefore beg that their petition be considered and that an act of the Legislature be passed "whereby they may be restored to the enjoyment of that freedom which is the natural right of all Men — & their Children (who were born in this land of Liberty) may not be held as Slaves after they arrive at the age of twenty-one Years — So may the Inhabitants of this State (no longer chargeable with the inconsistency of acting, themselves, the part which they condemn & oppose in others) be prospered in their present glorious struggles for Liberty." Signed by Lancaster Hill, Prince Hall, etc. The names of Judge Sergeant and others are inscribed below. Dated Jan. 13, 1777. *Massachusetts MS. Archives*, vol 212, p. 132. Cited in part in Moore, *Notes on Slavery in Massachusetts*, 180–181.

[1] *Journal of the House of Representatives*, 1777, p. 19.

[2] *Ibid.*, 25.

[3] Hammond, *Slavery in New Hampshire*, in *The Granite Monthly*, IV, 108–110.

[4] Cooley, *A Study of Slavery in New Jersey*, 23.

[5] *Laws of the Commonwealth of Pennsylvania*, Carey and Bioren, II, 246–251.

the Assembly in 1776.[1] The following year a bill was suggested to the Assembly by the Council,[2] and the subject was
urged upon them again in 1778 and 1779. " In divesting the
State of Slaves," says George Bryan, then vice-president of the
Council, in a message to the Assembly, November 9, 1778,
"you will equally serve the cause of humanity & policy, &
offer to God one of the most proper & best returns of Gratitude for his great deliverance of us & our posterity from
Thraldom. You will also set up y^r character for Justice &
Benevolence in a true point of view to all Europe, who are
astonished to see a people eager for Liberty holding Negroes
in Bondage." [3] " Honored will that State be in the Annals of
History," adds President Reed, in a message to the Assembly,
February 5, 1779, " which shall first abolish this violation of
the rights of mankind." [4] The bill, which seems to have been
largely the work of George Bryan,[5] encountered some difficulties in its passage. The members of the Assembly were
apparently agreed that the abolition of slavery was just and
desirable, but twenty-one out of fifty-five considered the measure imprudent and premature.[6] The Quakers were so unpopular during the war that any organized effort on their part was
likely to do more harm than good, but individuals were warmly
interested in the bill,[7] and Anthony Benezet is said to have
interviewed every member of the Assembly and to have had
considerable influence in securing its passage.[8]

While other States still hesitated to follow the example of
Pennsylvania, the third means of accomplishing the object, by
88. Attempts direct constitutional provision, had also begun to
at emancipa- work. This method was used chiefly in the new States
tion by con-
stitutional afterward formed from the Northwest Territory, but
provision. it had its beginnings in the Revolutionary period
and shows most clearly the Revolutionary spirit. The Bills of

---

[1] Brackett, *Status of the Slave*, in Jameson, *Essays*, 287.

[2] *Ibid.*

[3] *Pennsylvania Archives*, VII, 79 ; *Pa. Col. Rec.*, XI, 618; Bettle,
Notices of Negro Slavery, Appendix, in *Pa. Hist. Soc. Mem.*, I, 405–406.

[4] *Pa. Col. Rec.*, XI, 688 ; *Pa. Hist. Soc. Mem.*, I, 406.

[5] *Ibid.*, I, 406–410.

[6] Needles, *Hist Mem Pa. Soc.*, 23–25 ; Brackett, *Status of the Slave*, in
Jameson, *Essays*, 288.

[7] Needles, *Hist. Mem. Pa. Soc.*, 16–17.

[8] Vaux, *Memoirs of Benezet*, 103.

Rights of the various States usually enunciated the principles of natural liberty, but these principles were variously interpreted when they came to be applied to the negroes. The construction of the clause, "All men are born equally free and independent," in the Virginia Bill of Rights has already been mentioned.[1] In Pennsylvania the same expression furnished a few years later a basis for anti-slavery agitation in the hope of substituting universal and immediate emancipation for the too tardy process under the Act of 1780,[2] but the question does not seem to have come up when the Constitution was adopted. In Massachusetts, however, the clause "All men are born free and equal," adopted in 1780, soon accomplished through the courts what the legislature had failed to effect, and was applied ultimately to blacks as well as whites.[3]

In New York, Virginia, and Massachusetts attempts were made for a direct constitutional provision. In the New York Constituent Convention (1777) the attempt was defeated by members from the Hudson River counties.[4] In Virginia a plan was prepared by Jefferson, in anticipation of a constitutional convention, in accordance with which the General Assembly was not to have power to permit the further importation of slaves into the State or the continuance of slavery beyond the generation existing on the thirty-first day of December, 1800; all persons born after that day being declared free by the Constitution. The convention, however, was never called, and Jefferson's plan did not undergo the test of a popular vote.[5] In the Constitution proposed for Massachusetts, in 1778, a clause excepting negroes, Indians, and mulattoes from the franchise was severely criticised for its injustice and inconsistency, and gave an opportunity for the expression of anti-slavery sentiments which was accepted in both the eastern and the western parts of the State.[6] When this Constitution failed of ratification

---

[1] Introduction, p. 2.
[2] See below, § 138.
[3] See below, §§ 90, 91.
[4] Brackett, in Jameson, *Essays*, 297.
[5] Jefferson, *Writings*, VIII, 445-446.
[6] Letter of Rev. William Gordon to the Freemen of the Massachusetts Bay, dated April 2, 1778, published April 9 in *The Continental Journal and Weekly Advertiser;* [T. Parsons], *Result of the Convention of Delegates holden at Ipswich in the County of Essex*, 29; Letter from John Bacon of Stockbridge, enclosing the *Substance of a speech delivered in the late*

and a new one was contemplated, some effort was made to introduce a clause providing directly for emancipation. The town of Pittsfield adopted in its instructions to its representatives the declaration "that no man can be deprived of liberty, and subjected to perpetual bondage and servitude, unless he has forfeited his liberty as a malefactor."[1] No such provision was adopted, but it is said that the clause, "All men are born free and equal," was inserted with a special view to the liberty of the negro, and was generally so understood, though some doubted if it was definite enough.[2]

In Vermont, alone, a State which was not yet a member of the Union, the proposition that all men are born equally free and independent and have certain inalienable rights was carried to its logical conclusion. "Therefore," runs the first article of the Vermont Bill of Rights (1777), "no male person, born in this country, or brought from over sea, ought to be holden by law, to serve any person, as servant, slave or apprentice, after he arrives to the age of twenty-one years, nor female, in like manner, after she arrives to the age of eighteen years, unless they are bound by their own consent, after they arrive to such age, or bound by law, for the payment of debts, damages, fines, costs, or the like."[3]

89. Abolition of slavery in Vermont, 1777.

The accomplishment of emancipation by judicial process supplementary to the constitution is the distinctive honor of Massachusetts. In that State freedom suits had been the fashion ever since 1766. There was one or more nearly every year from that time until 1775,[4]

90. Emancipation by judicial process.

Convention, published in *The Independent Chronicle and Universal Advertiser*, Sept. 23, 1779.

[1] J. E. A. Smith, *History of Pittsfield*, 366, 368. It is thought that Stockbridge and perhaps other towns adopted similar instructions. *Ibid.*

[2] Belknap, Reply to *Queries respecting the Slavery and Emancipation of Negroes in Massachusetts*, 1 *Mass. Hist. Soc. Coll.*, IV, 203; Barry, *History of Massachusetts*, III, 189. The Constitution of 1780 in the original draft reads, "All men are born equally free and independent." *Report of a Constitution for Massachusetts*, 7. For a fuller account of this subject, see Moore, *Notes on Slavery in Massachusetts*, 185–194; F. E. Haynes, *The Struggle for a Constitution in Massachusetts*, 236–241.

[3] Poore, *Federal and State Constitutions*, II, 1859. The census enumerators in 1790 reported 17 slaves and 255 free colored persons. *Statistical View of the Population of the United States*, 1790–1830, pp. 36–37.

[4] For cases in 1766 and 1768, see John Adams, *Works*, II, 200, 213; in 1769, 1 *Mass. Hist. Soc. Coll.*, IV, 202, and 4 *Ibid.*, IV, 334–335; about

and it was seldom that a jury declared against the negro.[1] The master himself seems to have been somewhat indifferent, " for such was the temper of the times, that a restless, discontented slave was worth little,"[2] and the economic conditions of New England were such that he may not have been sorry sometimes to have this opportunity for manumitting his slaves without thereby incurring the liability to maintain them afterwards.[3]

In a second series of cases, which arose after the adoption of the Bill of Rights in 1780, the clause " All men are born free and equal" was regarded as a literal and authoritative expression of the law of nature, superior to any law or custom to the contrary.[4] Mr. Nathaniel Jennison, the owner of a slave named Quork Walker, was the victim, in this instance, of the cause of liberty; and the series of cases in which he was involved is regarded as finally accomplishing the abolition of slavery in Massachusetts. Mr. Jennison lost one suit against his neighbors the Caldwells, for enticing away his slave on the assurance that he was free under the new Constitution; and he was cast in another suit for damages for assault, brought by Quork Walker himself. He then appealed to the General Court, stating that he had been deprived of ten negroes by judgment of the supreme judicial court, and praying that if that judgment should be approved, he might be freed from his obligation to support them (June 18, 1782).[5]

91. Case of Quork Walker vs. Nathaniel Jennison.

1770, Lyman, *Free Negroes and Mulattoes*, 11–12; Deane, *Letters and Documents*, in 5 *Mass. Hist. Soc. Coll.*, III, 392; 1773, Coffin, *Newbury*, 241, 339; 1774, *etc.*, Moore, *Notes on Slavery in Massachusetts*, 112–120.

[1] Letter of John Adams in Deane, *Letters and Documents*, 5 *Mass. Hist. Soc. Coll.*, III, 401–402. A case brought before the General Court fared no better than before an ordinary jury. Joseph Prout, of Scarborough, petitioned this body on account of his two negroes who had been told by Mr. William Vaughan that by an Act of Court all negroes were made free. The petition was read and dismissed. *Journal of the House of Representatives*, 1777, p. 86; Moore, *Notes on Slavery in Massachusetts*, 185.

[2] Discussion of Chief-Justice Parsons, Winchendon *vs.* Hatfield, *Mass. Rep.*, IV, 127. See also Letter of John Adams in Deane, *Letters and Documents*, 5 *Mass. Hist. Soc. Coll.*, III, 402.

[3] Dane, *General Abridgment and Digest of American Laws*, II, 426–427.

[4] Brief of Levi Lincoln in 5 *Mass. Hist. Soc. Coll.*, III, 438–442, and *Mass. Hist. Soc. Proc.*, 1857, pp. 197–201.

[5] Washburn, *Extinction of Slavery in Massachusetts*, in 4 *Mass. Hist. Soc. Coll.*, IV, 336–339; Moore, *Notes on Slavery in Massachusetts*, 211–219; *MS. Journal of the House of Representatives*, III, 99. For other cases, see Moore, *Notes on Slavery*, 210–211; Jones, *Stockbridge*, 239–241.

The House referred the memorial to a committee, and a few days later (June 21) a bill was introduced with the object of repealing the Act of 1703 which required manumittors to give bonds for the future maintenance of the freedmen.[1] This bill was referred to the next session,[2] when a committee, February 8, 1783, was ordered to bring in a bill declaring that there had never been legal slaves in Massachusetts, but indemnifying masters who now held slaves and making suitable provision for the support of the negroes.[3] This bill failed to pass the Senate,[4] but the courts had by this time practically settled the question of slavery and legislation was no longer necessary. Most of the slaves were already free: some had been granted their liberty by their masters; some had left their masters and were not recalled; and some towns had voted to have no slaves among them and had released the former owners from the obligation to maintain the aged and infirm.[5]

In the New Jersey Supreme Court, between 1775 and 1793, a considerable number of freedom suits was brought. Of these, twenty were decided in favor of the negro and two against him.[6]

Side by side with the movement for the emancipation of all the slaves in a State, was at work a practice which set free a class and thus weakened the whole system. The policy of enlisting negroes in the Revolutionary army with a provision for emancipation in return for service is an important feature of the period, though its significance in connection with anti-slavery sentiment has perhaps been somewhat overrated. The enlistment of slaves as such was forbidden by the Committee of Safety in Massachusetts in 1775, as inconsistent with the principles of liberty,[7] and the same idea prevailed in most of the other colonies. In Virginia

92. Enlistment of negroes.

---

[1] MS. Journal of the House of Representatives, III, 118.

[2] Ibid.

[3] Ibid., 436, 444, 529, 537.

[4] Senate Journal, III, 413.

[5] Letter of Thomas Pemberton in Deane, Letters and Documents, 5 Mass. Hist. Soc. Coll., III, 393. No slaves are enumerated in the census of 1790, and 6,001 free colored persons. Statistical View of the Population of the United States, 1790–1830, pp. 24–25.

[6] Cases Adjudged in the Supreme Court of New Jersey.

[7] Brackett, Status of the Slave, in Jameson, Essays, 290; Force, American Archives, 4th Series, II, 762.

slaves were sometimes enlisted as substitutes for free persons under the supposition that they were themselves free, and those who had performed military service were declared free by act of legislature in 1783.[1] In Maryland slaves are said to have been received and set free as recruits.[2] In Rhode Island the policy of freeing the negroes on enlistment and compensating the masters was begun in February, 1778, but was continued only until June, and less than ninety slaves were so purchased.[3] A similar measure failed to pass the Massachusetts General Court, but negro soldiers were placed in the same regiments with the whites.[4] In Connecticut also a bill failed to pass, designed to permit negroes to enlist provided they could arrange to buy their own freedom; but some slaves were freed for enlistment by individual owners.[5] In New Hampshire negroes who enlisted for three years were entitled to the same bounty as the whites; this was given to the masters as the price of their liberty, and the slaves were then manumitted.[6] In New York an act was passed, March 20, 1781, arranging for a grant of unappropriated lands to masters who would offer able-bodied slaves for enlistment, the slaves to be allowed their freedom after service.[7] In short, there was in nearly all the States a tendency to enlist negroes and to grant them liberty in return for their service.[8] Several leading patriots were in favor of a

---

[1] Brackett, in Jameson, *Essays*, 304–305.

[2] *Ibid.*, 303.

[3] Rider, *Historical Tracts; The Black Regiments of the Revolution*, 9–20; Rhode Island Resolve, February, 1778, in *Massachusetts MS. Archives of the Revolution*, vol. 199, pp. 82–83. For subsequent maintenance of negroes who had enlisted, see *Laws of Rhode Island*, February, 1785, p. 16.

[4] Livermore, *Historical Research*, 159–162. Thomas Kench, who proposed to enlist negroes as separate troops and to give them their freedom in return for service, writes, April 7, 1778, that it is justifiable " that Negroes Should have their freedom and None amongst us Be held as Slaves, as freedom and liberty is the grand Controversay that we are contending for." *Mass. MS. Arch.*, vol. 199 pp. 80–81, 84.

[5] Brackett, *Status of the Slave*, in Jameson, *Essays*, 296; Steiner, *History of Slavery in Connecticut*, 25 ; Fowler, *Historical Status of the Negro in Connecticut*, 134.

[6] Belknap, Reply to *Queries respecting the Slavery and Emancipation of Negroes in Massachusetts*, in 1 *Mass. Hist. Soc. Coll.*, IV, 203.

[7] *Laws of the State of New York* (1886), I, 351 ; *Ibid.*, printed by Hugh Gaines, I, 64–65; Brackett, in Jameson, *Essays*, 297.

[8] Livermore, *Historical Research*, 164; Moore, *Historical Notes on the Employment of Negroes in the Army of the Revolution*, 5–22.

more general enfranchisement for this purpose, and Congress in 1779 recommended enlistments in South Carolina and Georgia and offered compensation to the owners; but it proved impossible to carry out the project.[1]

Another vexatious question arose out of the capture of negroes by one side or the other during the war. In the Southern States the negroes taken from confiscated Tory estates were generally sold,[2] and the same policy was evidently pursued to some extent at the North, the proceeds, as " A Farmer " sarcastically says, being used " for the defense of American liberty." [3] In the North, however, there are instances of effective opposition to the sale of captured or confiscated negroes. In Massachusetts the capture and advertised sale of two negroes aroused such indignation that the sale was forbidden by a resolution of the General Court (September 14, 1776), although with the omission of a proposed clause arraigning slavery as a violation of natural rights.[4] Later in the war some fugitives from South Carolina were carried off by the British and recaptured by Massachusetts vessels; the General Court resolved to return them to their owners on payment of the cost of maintenance; but the Judiciary, to whom Governor Hancock referred the matter, caused them to be freed, — " a specimen of Puritanism," says Governor Guerard of South Carolina, " I should not have expected from gentlemen of my Profession," [5] but one which is quite in keeping with their action on other occasions. Another instance of a similar sentiment is connected with the capture at Stony Point of three negroes whom General Wayne and his officers agreed in wishing to set free.[6]

93. Captured or confiscated negroes.

---

[1] Moore, *Historical Notes on the Employment of Negroes in the Army of the Revolution*, 8–16; Livermore, *Historical Research*, 167–180; Letter of Hamilton to Jay (March 19, 1779), in Hamilton, *History of the Republic*, I, 530–531; Letter of Madison to Joseph Jones, Nov. 28, 1780, in *The Madison Papers*, I, 68; Letters of Washington to Col. John Laurens, in Washington, *Writings* VII, 371, VIII, 48.

[2] Brackett, *Status of the Slave*, in Jameson, *Essays*, 305, 310.

[3] A Farmer, *Serious Address*, 16.

[4] Moore, *Notes on Slavery in Massachusetts*, 148–153; *General Court Records*, March 13 to Sept. 18, 1776, pp. 581–582.

[5] Moore, *Notes on Slavery in Massachusetts*, 163–174.

[6] *Ibid.*, 159–160; Dawson, *Assault on Stony Point*, 111, 118.

The confiscation of Tory estates in New England gave rise to some interesting petitions in the name of the negroes attached to them. The slaves of such an estate in Connecticut ventured to petition the legislature for freedom, urging that they were free-born in their own country and had done nothing to forfeit their liberty. They suggested that " *the free State of Connecticut*, engaged in a war with tyranny," ought not to sell good honest Whigs and friends of the freedom and independence of America, like themselves, in order to support the war, " because the Whigs ought to be *free ;* and the *Tories* should be sold." [1] Another petition is that of Belinda, the slave of Colonel Isaac Royall, a Massachusetts Tory (dated February, 1782): Belinda's master has now fled to " a land where lawless dominion sits enthroned, pouring blood and vengeance on all who dare to be free"; and Belinda petitions the General Court not for liberty, which is taken for granted, but for a maintenance from the Royall estate, " a part whereof hath been accumulated by her own industry, and the whole augmented by her servitude." [2]

94. Negro petitions.

In New York the slaves on confiscated estates, if unable to support themselves, were to be maintained by the commissioners out of the revenues of the estates. A later act provided that they should be manumitted and in case of infirmity should be provided for at the public expense.[3]

The years immediately following the Revolutionary War were years of hope and promise to some of the emancipationists, of gloom and disappointment to others. There was an expectation that the slave-trade would in due time be permanently abolished,[4] and the prospect of emancipation by one State after another seemed to the more sanguine not far distant.[5] The crisis through which the coun-

95. Conditions after the war.

---

[1] Livermore, *Historical Research*, 149–150; Steiner, *History of Slavery in Connecticut*, 27–28.

[2] *Petition of an African slave*, in *The American Museum*, I, 463–465. The house of Colonel Royall, with the neighboring slave-quarters still standing, is in Medford, Mass., and is now in the care of the Sarah Bradlee Fulton chapter of the Daughters of the American Revolution.

[3] *Laws of the State of New York* (1886), II, 316, 9th sess., ch. 58; *Ibid.*, printed by Hugh Gaines, I, 174, 325 (May 19, 1784, May 1, 1786).

[4] DuBois, *Suppression of the Slave-Trade*, 50–52.

[5] *Ibid.* ; Campbell, Oration in Philadelphia, July 4, 1787, in *The American Museum*, III, 21.

try had just passed might well have prevented further progress during the years of the conflict, and time had not yet proved the truth of Dr. Hopkins's warnings.[1] The principles of the Revolution were still an active force, and prosperity had not yet dulled the sense of natural rights. How strong was the feeling that the Revolution was antagonistic to slavery may be seen from a celebration of the close of the war, July 4, 1783, at Woodbridge, New Jersey. On this occasion Dr. Bloomfield, afterwards president of the New Jersey Abolition Society, mounted the platform, followed by his fourteen slaves. " As a nation," he said, " we are free and independent — all men are created equal, and why should these, my fellow-citizens — my equals, be held in bondage? From this day they are emancipated, and I here declare them free and absolved from all servitude to me, or my posterity." [2]

On the other hand there was the spirit of procrastination, the desire to put off the act of emancipation till a more convenient season. The war was followed by hard times, and as neither the legislators nor their constituents could make up their minds to part with their property, they contented themselves, even in those sections where anti-slavery principles were most prevalent, with acts which left slavery to linger on for more than half a century. The States south of Virginia had made no effort toward emancipation and had shown no disposition to do so. Thus anti-slavery sentiment at the close of the war had become distinctly sectional. National emancipation under the Articles of Confederation was impossible to accomplish, and the increased demand for slaves which accompanied the revival of industry after the war gave little occasion for the hope that slavery would die a natural death at the South.[3]

This condition was well described by Thomas Jefferson, at this time the leading Southern opponent of slavery. In acknowledging the receipt of a pamphlet on slavery by Dr. Price, an English philanthropist, Jefferson writes, in 1785:

[1] See above, § 72.
[2] Quoted from *The Newark Eagle* in *The American Anti-Slavery Almanac* for 1844, p. 34. Biographical note, *Ibid.* Dr. Bloomfield's son, as Attorney-General, also distinguished himself in the cause of the slave. See below, § 102.
[3] DuBois, *Suppression of the Slave-Trade*, 49–50.

" Southward of the Chesapeake it will find but few readers con-
curring with it in sentiment, on the subject of slavery. From
the mouth to the head of the Chesapeake, the bulk of the
people will approve it in theory, and it will find a respectable
minority ready to adopt it in practice; a minority, which, for
weight and worth of character, preponderates against the
greater number, who have not the courage to divest their families of a property, which, however, keeps their consciences
unquiet. Northward of the Chesapeake, you may find here and
there an opponent to your doctrine as you may find here and
there a robber and murderer; but in no greater number." [1]

Nevertheless, although the policy of national emancipation
had failed of adoption, although State emancipation was partial and incomplete, freedom had secured a foothold in the
country which it was never to lose. Sectionalism gave occasion
for strife and disruption, but the continual friction served to
keep warm the sentiment which had been kindled by the
national struggle for liberty. It was Pennsylvania, the State
nearest the border, that was to preserve its anti-slavery spirit
when others became indifferent. In the same way the policy of
gradual emancipation acts left slavery to linger on, even in some
Northern States, far into the next century; but the very necessity for continued effort in order to get rid of it at last served
to keep alive the organizations which had been formed to hasten
the process and to protect the freedman and the slave.

[1] Jefferson, *Writings*, I, 376–378.

CHAPTER IV

ABOLITIONISTS AND ABOLITION SOCIETIES, 1783–1808

IN early colonial history opposition to the slave-trade did not necessarily or even generally signify antipathy to slavery or a desire for emancipation. The early years of the Revolutionary period were characterized by a double movement, directed partly against the slave-trade and partly toward emancipation. In the period following the Revolutionary War (1783–1808), there is a conscious effort to distinguish between the two; but even when there is no direct connection, the attacks upon the slave-trade are prompted to a great extent by anti-slavery motives. The attempt to suppress the slave-trade after its revival at the close of the war becomes an essential part of the history of the anti-slavery movement; not because opposition to the slave-trade always meant opposition to slavery, but because the opponents of slavery often found their most hopeful course in the direction of attacks upon the trade. In this period, also, with the development of national consciousness, there is an increasing tendency to appeal to the general government, and the action of the national legislature becomes an important element in the problem. Enfranchisement by the States goes on along the lines laid down in the Revolutionary period; but a national domain comes into existence, and the contest between slavery and freedom for the possession of that soil begins to be one of the great national issues. Localization of anti-slavery sentiment becomes more apparent, and sectional bitterness as its natural consequence; but to the end of the period slavery is still almost universally regarded as an evil or a misfortune which all would gladly shake off if circumstances permitted.

The period from 1783 to 1808 appears in three aspects: (*a*) emancipation by State legislation and by national regulation of the Territories (chapters v, vii); (*b*) attempts at the suppression of the slave-trade by the States and by the nation, culminating in the prohibition of the African trade in 1807 (chapter vi); (*c*) what may be called the out-of-door sentiment, which was not in court or council-hall, but was behind them, and may be studied in the literature of the period (chapter viii). In the practical work of this epoch, which will be considered under the first two heads, three agencies may be distinguished: the State governments of the North and of the South, and the national government, swayed by both. The Northern States in the course of a few years embarked upon a policy of emancipation; the South, after more or less vigorous efforts on the part of the Border States, relapsed into the old policy, and became more and more conservative. Congress, meanwhile, wavered between the two; in the case of the slave-trade a combination of the North and a part of the South produced a result favorable to the anti-slavery cause, while on the question of the national territory the South gained a decided advantage.

97 Analysis.

In the progress of emancipation during the years after the Revolutionary War, which is an important feature of this period, the means of arousing public sentiment, as well as the agencies employed to give that sentiment practical effect, became more numerous and more complex than in the earlier period. The work of individuals was supplemented by that of organized Abolition Societies, and the societies themselves combined their efforts by means of National Conventions. By petitions or memorials to the State and national legislatures, by printed appeals to the public, by orations delivered under their auspices, and by correspondence among themselves and with persons of authority, the early Abolition Societies accomplished a vast amount of work, intensifying, extending, and perpetuating the anti-slavery sentiment which without their aid might have died out after the influence of the Revolution had spent its strength, or would have lingered only in the hearts of a few individuals.

98. Means of arousing public sentiment.

By this time the efforts of Thomas Jefferson against slavery were practically over, and no one else so conspicuous in national affairs took an equal interest in the work of emancipation. Still there were a few prominent Virginians who had personal objections to slavery, and who were willing

99. Influence of individuals.

to use their influence at least to mitigate the evil.[1] To the northward in almost every State there were individuals conspicuous for either political or literary activity in the anti-slavery cause, — men whose fame is less world-wide than those of Revolutionary times, but who were equally far-sighted and earnest.

Dr. Samuel Hopkins continued to use his pen and his personal influence in this work until the close of the century,[2] and

100. Theologians. Ezra Stiles, the President of Yale College (1778–1795), did in Connecticut a work similar to that of Dr. Hopkins in Rhode Island.[3] Other prominent theologians were Dr. Jonathan Edwards, of New Haven, the famous son of a more famous father; and Dr. Jeremy Belknap, of Boston.[4] Some of the Presbyterian and Baptist clergy also exerted an important influence. The anti-slavery attitude of Dr. McLeod has already been mentioned.[5] James Gilliland, pastor of a Presbyterian church in South Carolina, also preached against slavery to his congregation, and on being required by the synod to content himself with private efforts in behalf of the negro, finally gave up his charge and went to Ohio (1804–1805), where he became a leader among the abolitionists of that day.[6] There was also Rev. David Rice, who removed from Virginia to Kentucky in 1783, is said to have organized there the first grammar-school in the West, and was noted as a preacher of abolition and especially for his speech in the Constitutional Convention in Kentucky in 1792.[7] The Emancipating Baptists of Kentucky were led by Joshua Carman and David Barrow, John Sutton and Carter Tarrant, and the influence of these men was largely

---

[1] Jefferson, *Writings*, Taylor and Maury, IV, 419–422, V, 563–565; Washington, *Writings*, Ford, X, 220, XI, 25, 30, XII, 113–114; George Mason in *The Madison Papers*, III, 1390–1391; Madison, *Letters*, I, 161, 322, *The Madison Papers*, III, 1427, 1429, 1430, and *Annals of Congress*, I Cong., I sess., 339–340. For St. George Tucker, see below, § 141.

[2] Park, *Memoir of the Life and Character of Samuel Hopkins*, in Hopkins, *Works*, I, 115–166.

[3] Holmes, *Life of Ezra Stiles*, 157, 249, 303–304, 311; Kingsley, *Life of Stiles*, 44, 69–70.

[4] See §§ 44, 192, 195, 198, 202; § 146, note 4.

[5] See above, p. 45, note 3.

[6] Sprague, *Annals of the American Pulpit*, IV, 137–138; Birney, *James G. Birney and his Times*, 433–434.

[7] Brown, *Political Beginnings of Kentucky*, 226.

responsible for the schism in the church which has been mentioned in a previous chapter.[1]

Dr. Stiles, as President of Yale College, must have had at least an indirect influence in cultivating an anti-slavery sentiment among his students. Another college president of this period, Samuel Stanhope Smith, of Princeton, **101. Educators.** is said to have taught that slavery was a moral wrong and a political evil, though he thought that the only remedy was in voluntary manumission.[2] Of greater value to the anti-slavery cause were the teachings of George Wythe and St. George Tucker, professors of law at William and Mary University. The former was associated with Jefferson in his plans for emancipation by law, and afterward manumitted his own slaves, furnishing them with means of support until they learned to maintain themselves.[3] The latter is noted for a *Dissertation on Slavery* which had formed a part of a course of lectures given at the University, and by means of which Judge Tucker hoped to stimulate the legislature to accomplish gradual emancipation in the State.[4] Among educators may be mentioned also William Rogers, professor of English literature in the College of Philadelphia and its successor the University of Pennsylvania, and at one time the vice-president of the Pennsylvania Abolition Society.[5] The widest influence of all was perhaps that of Rev. Jedidiah Morse, "the father of American geography," who omits no opportunity in his instructive pages to point a moral with regard to slavery. As his works for thirty years enjoyed almost a monopoly of this department of literature,[6] they must have had a wide circulation, and their maxims must have sunk deep in the minds of ingenuous youth.

In the Revolutionary period the influence of the legal profession was particularly conspicuous, not only in the contest for the independence of the white race, but also in the effort to

[1] Brown, *Political Beginnings of Kentucky*, 226; Birney, *James G. Birney*, 17–19. See above, § 46.

[2] Birney, *James G. Birney*, 26–27.

[3] Jefferson, *Writings*, I, 42, 48–49.

[4] See below, § 141 ; Tucker, *Dissertation on Slavery*, vii.

[5] *The American Museum*, VII, 255; Drake, *Dictionary of American Biography ;* Appleton, *Encyclopedia.*

[6] *Ibid.* Morse's observations on slavery are copied without acknowledgment in Winterbotham, *An Historical, Geographical, Commercial and Philosophical View of the United States.*

extend liberty to the blacks. So also in the years immediately following, the leading anti-slavery men of Virginia were nearly all of them interested in the law. In Pennsylvania, if we except the body of the Quakers, we find the greatest activity among the lawyers, not only in connection with the Emancipation Act of 1780,[1] but also in cases of fugitive slaves or the kidnapping of free negroes. Among those who gave their services in these directions are James Pemberton,[2] William Lewis,[3] William Rawle,[4] and Myers Fisher;[5] and in New Jersey the names of Joseph Bloomfield and Elias Boudinot are frequently found in connection with pleas for the negro in the freedom suits which were so numerous in that State at this time.[6] In Maryland the leading effort for the promotion of emancipation was made by William Pinkney,[7] and the attempt at a national prohibition of the slave-trade was inaugurated by a Maryland lawyer, Luther Martin.[8] Gouverneur Morris and John Jay in New York were interested in the abolition of slavery by State legislation, and desired to limit it as far as possible in national affairs.[9]

102. Lawyers.

In New England the rapid disappearance of slavery in the Northern States led to a cessation of activity, but in Connecticut, where even the children born after the passage of a general emancipation act were still to be " held in Servitude," several young lawyers co-operated with the theologians in the endeavor to hasten or complete the process of emancipation. Zephaniah Swift, afterwards Chief-Justice of Connecticut, was prominent in this anti-slavery movement; Noah Webster, the great lexicographer, at that time engaged in the practice of law, devoted some of his talent for research to the production of an important essay

---

[1] See above, § 87.
[2] Needles, *Hist. Mem. Pa. Soc.*, 35–36; *Pa. Col. Rec.*, XVI, 210.
[3] *Pa. Mag. Hist. and Biog.*, XIV, 13–14.
[4] David Paul Brown, *The Forum*, I, 511–513.
[5] Brissot de Warville, *New Travels in the United States*, I, 249.
[6] *Cases Adjudged in the Supreme Court of New Jersey.*
[7] See below, § 131.
[8] Elliot, *Debates on the Federal Constitution*, V, 457.
[9] *Pa. Mag. Hist. and Biog.*, II, 187; Roosevelt, *Gouverneur Morris*, 66–67, 157–160; *The Madison Papers*, III, 1263–1265; William Jay, *Life of John Jay*, I, 69, 229–235; John Jay, *Correspondence*, I, 136 and note, 407, III, 340–345.

on the moral and economic effects of slavery; and Theodore Dwight, also a lawyer, was one of the most uncompromising of abolitionists, a forerunner of Garrison and Phillips.[1] Massachusetts, too, though free from slavery herself, sent Rufus King and Nathan Dane to win the freedom of the Northwest.[2]

The influence of Benjamin Franklin and Dr. Rush was in this period as conspicuous as in the Revolutionary epoch. Dr. Rush succeeded Franklin as president of the Pennsylvania Abolition Society,[3] and Caspar Wistar, also a physician, succeeded Dr. Rush in that office.[4] A member of the same profession in Maryland, George Buchanan, is noted for one of the most important anti-slavery orations of this period.[5] *103. Other professions.*

In the Federal Convention and in Congress there was further opportunity for individual influence, and here a noticeably large proportion of those who favored the cause of the negro were from Pennsylvania and Massachusetts. Messrs. Wilson, Bard, Findley, Gallatin, Scott, Smilie, Swanwick, and Waln, of Pennsylvania, and Messrs. Barker, Bidwell, Dexter, Hastings, Quincy, Sedgwick, Thatcher, and Varnum, of Massachusetts, compete for the honor of the most constant and vigorous effort. The honors of the two States are pretty evenly divided; but for undaunted effort in season and out of season, for caustic language and refusal of compromise, the palm must be awarded to George Thatcher, of Massachusetts. The declining anti-slavery sentiment of Virginia was represented by Messrs. Madison, Mason, Nicholas, Page, and Parker. Delaware may glory in James A. Bayard; New Jersey in Elias Boudinot, Mr. Southard, and Mr. Sloan; and Mr. S. L. Mitchell represented the anti-slavery sentiment of New York. Connecticut sent Theodore Dwight to redeem the compromising policy of her other *104. Members of Congress.*

---

[1] See below, §§ 137, 192.

[2] See below, § 170, note.

[3] Needles, *Hist. Mem. Pa. Soc.*, 49–52; American Convention, *Minutes of Proceedings*, 1794, including *An Address to the Citizens of the United States*, prepared by Dr. Rush.

[4] Needles, *Hist. Mem. Pa. Soc.*, 62; Appleton, *Cyclopedia of American Biography*.

[5] Buchanan, *An Oration on the Moral and Political Evil of Slavery*, A copy of this oration, in the library of George Washington, is now the property of the Boston Athenæum. The literary work of this period is discussed below in chapter viii.

members; and Mr. Bradley, of Vermont, had the honor of intro-
ducing the bill for the prohibition of the African slave-trade.[1]

Several of the prominent Pennsylvanians already mentioned
as interested in the anti-slavery movement were members of the

105. The
Quakers.
Isaac Tatem
Hopper.

Society of Friends.   Other members of the society
conspicuous during this period were Isaac Tatem
Hopper and Warner Mifflin.   The former, at the age
of nine, impressed by the story of an old colored man, " made a
solemn vow to himself that he would be the friend of the
oppressed Africans during his whole life."   While serving his
apprenticeship to the tailor's trade in Philadelphia, at sixteen
or seventeen years of age, he assisted a fugitive slave; and after
becoming a member of the Abolition Society, about 1796, he
became widely known as a friend and adviser of the colored
race, teaching two or three evenings a week in Benezet's school,
and giving frequent assistance to fugitives and kidnapped negroes.   On being accused of having robbed many people of
their slaves, he once said, " Thou art mistaken.   I only prevent
Southern marauders from robbing people of their liberty." [2]

Warner Mifflin presents a different but no less characteristic
phase of the Quaker attitude.   His manumission of his own slaves

106. Warner
Mifflin.

has been described in a previous chapter.[3]   He was
one of the founders of the Delaware Abolition
Society.[4]   Like John Woolman, he travelled from State to
State preaching anti-slavery principles among the Friends, and
in the course of his life he visited all the Yearly Meetings in
America.   He also made earnest efforts for State and national
legislation against slavery.   In 1782 he appeared before the
Assembly of Virginia, and his influence is said to have helped
to secure the passage of the manumission act of that year.   In
1783 he presented a memorial to Congress with regard to the
African slave-trade, and he afterwards visited the legislatures of
Pennsylvania, Maryland, and Delaware.[5]   He had great hopes
from the national declaration, in 1776, of principles which he
had already been preaching for years;[6] and after the organiza-

---

[1] For debates on slavery see below, chapters v, vi, vii.
[2] Lydia Maria Child, *Life of Hopper*, 1–86.
[3] See above, § 40.
[4] Brissot, *New Travels in the United States*, I, 236.
[5] Appleton, *Encyclopedia;* Mifflin, *Defence against Aspersions*, 18, 20.
[6] *Ibid.*

tion of government under the Constitution his efforts to secure legislation to the utmost constitutional limit made him the *bête noir* of Southern Congressmen. The first act of Congress limiting the foreign slave-trade (1794) is drawn on lines suggested by him to a House Committee and embodied in the committee report (March 5, 1790) and, with modifications, in the ensuing resolutions of Congress.[1] This legislation, however, was so long delayed that Mifflin felt the need of another effort. A petition from him was presented, November 26, 1792, urging upon Congress some action in regard to the African slave-trade.[2] This petition was the occasion for a violent attack on the petitioner, to whom it was returned, though without expunging its entry from the Journal as was proposed by an indignant opponent.[3] To this treatment Mifflin responded with a vigorous expression of his views on the whole question. " I profess freely," he says in an *Expostulation with the Members of the House*, " and am willing my profession was known over the world, that I feel the calls of humanity as strong towards an African in America, as to an American in Algiers, both being my brethren ; especially as I am informed the Algerine treats his slave with more humanity ; and I believe the sin of oppression on the part of the American, is greatest in the sight of the Father of the family of mankind."[4]

Mifflin's opponents regarded him as a fanatic whose efforts were of a most mischievous tendency, and his petition in 1792 was not defended even by those who ordinarily stood as champions for the appeals of the Quakers.[5] Yet a contemporary wrote of him in 1790 that he was " not only distinguished by his extensive philanthropy, but by a sound judgment; and that his prudence and good temper were equal to his zeal; "[6] and Brissot de Warville wrote of him, after meeting him in

---

[1] See below, § 152. *The American Museum*, VIII, 61–65; *Annals of Congress*, 1 Cong., 2 sess., 1413–1415, 1473–1474.

[2] Mifflin, *Memorial*. Reprinted from *The Providence Gazette* of Dec. 22, 1792.

[3] *Annals of Congress*, 2 Cong., 2 sess., 728–731.

[4] Mifflin, *A Serious Expostulation with the Members of the House of Representatives*, p. 14; reprinted in a pamphlet called *Liberty*, 1837, pp. 31–33.

[5] *Annals of Congress*, 2 Cong., 2 sess., 728–731.

[6] *The American Museum*, VIII, 60.

1788: "What humanity! and what charity! It seems, that to love mankind, and to search to do them good, constitutes his only pleasure, his only existence; . . . The attachment of an angel like Warner Miflin to the sect of Quakers, is the fairest apology for that society." [1]

Though the Quakers were now frequently found acting in combination with philanthropists of other sects, they also continued their efforts as a distinct organization.

107. The Society of Friends. An occasional memorial from the Society of Friends appeared before Congress, sometimes alone, sometimes reinforcing similar appeals from the Abolition Societies.[2] The language of these memorials was temperate, and their demands were studiously moderate, and strictly within the constitutional powers of Congress. The furious antagonism which they aroused was evidently not on account of the terms of the petitions so much as because of the determined opposition to the whole institution of slavery which was known to lie behind their quiet language. Their opponents, however, were in the minority, and the petitions were uniformly received and read, and in the House were referred to a committee.[3]

In the case of the slave-trade three or four successive memorials, with terms gradually narrowed down to meet the conditions in a practical way, were among the influences which brought about the limitation of the foreign slave-trade in 1794.[4] Several years later an effort was made by the society to obtain relief for the re-enslaved freedmen of North Carolina (November 30, 1797),[5] and soon after the annexation of Louisiana the society appealed to Congress to prevent the introduction of slavery into the Western territory (January 21, 1805).[6]

---

[1] Brissot, *New Travels in the United States*, I, 157, f.

[2] Mifflin, *Defence*, 18; *Journal of the United States in Congress Assembled*, VIII, 418–419, 425; *Annals of Congress*, 1 Cong., 2 sess , 1182–1183; 3 Cong., 1 sess., 36, 249, 253; 5 Cong., 2 sess., 475, 656, 657; 8 Cong., 2 sess., 39, 996.

[3] *Ibid.*, 1 Cong., 2 sess., 1198, 1205; 3 Cong., 1 sess., 36, 253; 5 Cong., 2 sess., 475, 656–670, 945–946, 1032–1033 ; 8 Cong., 2 sess., 39, 996.

[4] See below, §§ 151–155.

[5] See above, § 41. *Annals of Congress*, 5 Cong., 2 sess., 475, 656–657.

[6] See below, § 174. *Annals of Congress*, 8 Cong., 2 sess., 39, 996. In the States the Quakers worked chiefly as members of the Abolition Societies, but here too a petition from the Society of Friends occasionally appears. See below, §§ 129–131, 134.

It has been remarked that the influence of individuals at this time was supplemented by the work of Abolition Societies. Although this title is regarded by Professor Von Holst as misleading,[1] it is the name that they themselves adopted, and abolition was their avowed object.[2] This object, according to their view, was to be accomplished by moral force rather than through a definite political program; but the failure to accomplish it was due to external conditions rather than to the character of the societies: to the undreamed of rise and growth of the slavocracy, to the overwhelming force of self-interest, the paralyzing weight of general indifference, and the slow growth of a higher public sentiment, — slow partly because of the defective means of communication then at command. That these societies under such unfavorable conditions did a great and necessary work will, it is hoped, be shown in the following pages. Though the institution of slavery rather than the opposition to slavery seems to be strengthening through the years of their existence, and though the slave-power continued to strengthen until it culminated in the Dred Scott Decision, yet in the earlier period, as well as in the later, a process of public education was going on which must in time have a decisive influence upon the issue. To these earlier societies, as to the later ones, the progress of educated public opinion was very largely due.

108. Influence of Abolition Societies.

The first Abolition Society, as might be expected, was organized in Pennsylvania (April 14, 1775). Its original object was merely the relief of free negroes unlawfully held in bondage. The manumission of slaves by the Quakers and those who came under their influence had brought into existence a large class of free negroes and of negroes whose bondage was limited to a term of years. The practice of kidnapping began almost at once, and as the efforts of benevolent individuals proved inadequate to prevent it, those most interested combined for more effective action.[3] The society at first consisted chiefly or entirely of Quakers. Its

109. The Pennsylvania Abolition Society.

---

[1] Von Holst, *Constitutional and Political History of the United States*, II, 80.

[2] American Convention, *Minutes of Proceedings*, 1794, pp. 11, 14, 22–25; Ibid., *Address to the People of the United States*, 1804, pp. 3–7.

[3] Needles, *Hist. Mem. Pa. Soc.*, 13–16.

work was suspended during the Revolutionary War, though individual members continued to be active in a quiet way, protecting the free blacks and promoting the passage of the Emancipation Act of 1780.[1] In 1784 they renewed their meetings, and the membership now included men of other religious denominations.[2]   Three years later the society was reorganized under the title of " The Pennsylvania Society for Promoting the Abolition of Slavery, the Relief of Free Negroes unlawfully held in Bondage, and for Improving the Condition of the African Race."[3]   Of this society Benjamin Franklin was elected president, and a new constitution was adopted[4] which was excellently adapted to its purpose and served as a model for the organization of other societies which soon sprang up in the neighboring States.[5]

The society at once became more vigorous and influential than in its earlier form.   It distributed copies of its constitution

110. Work of and of the Emancipation Act of Pennsylvania and
the society.   also tracts and " pictorial representations " apparently

much after the manner of the societies formed half a century later.[6]   It reprinted foreign publications of kindred nature, such as Clarkson's *Essay on the Slave-Trade* and Brissot's *Oration upon the Necessity of establishing at Paris a Society to co-operate with those of America and London.*   It entered into correspondence with other societies at home and abroad, and addressed letters to the governors of the various States and petitions to the State legislatures.[7]   In the opening year of its new existence it addressed a memorial to the Federal Convention, then in

---

[1] Needles, *Hist. Mem. Pa. Soc.*, 16–17.

[2] *Ibid.*, 26–28.

[3] *Ibid.*, 28–30. A list of the incorporators is given in Pennsylvania Society, *Constitution and Act of Incorporation*, pp. 6–8. It includes over two hundred members from Pennsylvania, about thirty from the other Middle States, Maryland, and Virginia, twelve from New England, twelve from Great Britain, and five from France.

[4] *Ibid.* Text also published in *The American Museum*, I, 388–389. Preamble in Needles, *Hist. Mem. Pa. Soc.*, 30.

[5] Constitutions of the Chestertown (Maryland) Society and of the Maryland Society in *The American Museum*, XI, Appendix II, 90*–92*, VII, Appendix II, 6–8. Pennsylvania, New Jersey, and Maryland societies, *Constitutions; Constitution of a Society for Abolishing the Slave-Trade* (the Providence Society).

[6] Needles, *Hist. Mem. Pa. Soc.*, 30, 35.

[7] *Ibid.*, 30–33, 35.

session in Philadelphia.[1]   Three years later, when the work of
the Federal Convention had been completed, Congress, then in
its first session, was addressed by the Pennsylvania Society in a
memorial which is remarkable for being one of the few attempts
to procure direct national legislation against slavery.[2]

In the mean time other abolition societies were organizing, so
that by 1791 there were as many as twelve, representing all the
States from Massachusetts to Virginia,[3] with the ex-
ception of New Jersey, where a society was formed **III. Other abolition societies.**
the following year.[4]   That of New York, formed in
1785 with John Jay as president, took the name of Manumission
Society, limiting its aims at first to promoting manumission and
protecting the free blacks.[5]   After the reorganization of the
Pennsylvania Society on a broader basis, in 1787, other societies
were organized with similar titles and objects, though with some
variations of detail.   Those of Connecticut and Rhode Island,
formed after the passage of acts for gradual emancipation, were
mainly for the purpose of preventing the slave-trade and the
deportation of negroes from the State, and of looking after the
execution of the provisions for emancipation, but aimed also at
the more remote object of general abolition.   Those of New
York and New Jersey, organized before the passage of State
emancipation acts, though primarily for the relief of free
negroes unlawfully held in bondage, also undertook to promote
emancipation by State legislation; and the societies of
Delaware, Maryland, and Virginia made efforts in the same
direction.   An important feature in all the societies was " the
relief of free negroes unlawfully held in bondage."   Pennsyl-

---

[1] See below, § 148 ; *The American Museum*, III, 404-405.

[2] See below, § 126.

[3] Memorials were presented to Congress, Dec. 8, 1791, by nine societies:
Providence, Connecticut, New York, Pennsylvania, Washington (Pa.), Maryland, Chestertown (Md.), Caroline County (Md.), and Virginia. *Memorials
presented to Congress.*   The Providence Society drew 68 of its 189 mem-
bers from Massachusetts and a few from Connecticut and Vermont.   Park,
Memoir of S. Hopkins, 126, note; Poole, *Anti-Slavery Opinions before the
Year* 1800, p. 54, note ; *The Nation*, Nov. 28, 1872, p. 349.   Other societies
existing at this time were the Delaware, Wilmington (Del.), and Choptank
(Md.) societies.   American Convention, *Minutes of Proceedings*, 1797,
Appendix containing Reports of Societies ; Needles, *Hist. Mem. Pa.
Soc.*, 34.

[4] *Ibid.*, 40.   [5] William Jay, *Life of John Jay*, I, 231.

vania especially, as a free State surrounded by slavery, was in continual difficulty on account of fugitives and kidnappers; and the society was very active in aiding individuals and in appeals to the legislature for more satisfactory laws. In Delaware, where slavery was declining without direct legislation, the conditions and the work were somewhat similar. Another common purpose of the societies was the improvement of the condition of the free blacks by mental and moral training and by teaching and helping them to support themselves. This work they regarded as a matter of justice to the negro as well as a social necessity, and they were deeply impressed with the importance of success in this direction as an encouragement to further emancipation.[1]

The favorite form of organization was that of the Pennsylvania Society. Here, besides the usual officers, including two

112. Organization of the Abolition Societies. secretaries whose duties were to promulgate the views and promote the objects of the society by correspondence with individuals and with other societies, there were four counsellors, who were to explain the State laws and constitution so far as they related to emancipation, and to urge claims to freedom, when legal, before the proper authorities. There was also an executive committee to transact business during the recess of the society, and on the activity of this committee the society depended greatly for its efficiency. As the work increased, new committees were formed for special purposes: (1) a committee of inspection, advice, and protection, (2) a committee of guardianship to look after the children and set them to trades or other occupations, (3) a committee of education to superintend school instruction, and to influence the negroes to attend the classes, and (4) a committee of employment. Special committees for various purposes were also appointed on occasion.[2] In this society and also in the Providence Society slave-holders were excluded from membership.[3] A similar restriction in the Maryland and Chestertown (Maryland) constitutions was modified

---

[1] See below, § 121.

[2] *Address to the Public* by the Pennsylvania Society, in *The American Museum*, VI, 383–385. See also Needles, *Hist. Mem. Pa. Soc.*, passim.

[3] Pennsylvania Society, *Constitution;* also printed in *The American Museum*, I, 388–389; *Constitution of a Society for abolishing the Slave-Trade*, 5.

by permitting the societies to appoint counsellors who were slave-holders.[1] In the Alexandria Society slave-holders were even admitted to membership, and this laxity was afterwards regarded as one of the causes of the failure of the society.[2]

Although the Abolition Societies were formed mainly for local purposes, their activity extended to national affairs, and for effective work in that direction it was soon found necessary to combine their efforts. The original occasion of this combination was a common effort to obtain congressional limitation of the African slave-trade, in accordance with the resolutions passed by Congress, March 23, 1790.[3] As no further action was taken in that or the following session of Congress, nine of the societies prepared petitions for such action, which were presented December 8, 1791.[4] The petitions were referred to a special committee,[5] but were heard of no more in Congress, nor was anything further accomplished toward a restriction of the slave-trade during that or the following session. In 1793, therefore, the New York Manumission Society suggested a convention of delegates from all the Abolition Societies to meet in Philadelphia to deliberate on the means of attaining their object and to unite in an address to Congress.[6] Early in 1794 the delegates came together, representing nine societies, decided upon a plan of action, prepared memorials to Congress and to some of the State legislatures and addresses to the Abolition Societies and the citizens of the United States, and instituted a system of annual meetings in general convention.[7]

The object of the American Convention was twofold. It was

113. The American Convention of Abolition Societies, 1794-1838.

[1] Maryland Society, *Constitution;* Constitutions of the Maryland and Chestertown Societies in *The American Museum*, VII, App. II, 6-8 ; XI, App. II, 90*-92*.

[2] American Convention, *Minutes of Proceedings*, 1805, p. 21. For advice of the Convention to the societies, see *Ibid.*, 1798, p. 15.

[3] See below, § 152.

[4] *Annals of Congress*, 2 Cong., 1 sess., 241 ; *Memorials presented to Congress*, published by the Pennsylvania Society, 1792.

[5] *Annals of Congress*, 2 Cong., 1 sess., 241.

[6] See below, §§ 153, 154.

[7] American Convention, *Minutes of Proceedings*, 1794 *et seq.* Meetings were omitted in 1799 and 1802. In 1806 the meetings were made triennial, and in 1818 biennial. *Ibid.*, 1806, p. 25 ; *Minutes of a Special Meeting*, 1818, and *Constitution of* 1818, Article II, § 1.

to increase the zeal and efficiency of the individual societies by its advice and encouragement, stimulating them to effort by requiring annual reports of progress and by laying out new lines of work,[1] and it was also to take upon itself the chief responsibility in regard to national affairs.[2] This did not necessarily preclude the action of individual societies, and that of Pennsylvania still felt an occasional call for its services, especially in later years, when but few societies were represented in the Convention, and the moral force of the latter was accordingly diminished.[3] But in 1794 the Convention, in the buoyancy of youth and hope, was a real force, as is shown by the success which crowned its first great effort, directed toward the national restriction of the foreign slave-trade.[4]

114. Aims.

One of the chief defects of the new association was its looseness of organization. The most distant societies were seldom represented at the meetings, though the absent societies occasionally sent reports in writing. There was no written constitution until 1801.[5] The officers were at first only a president and a secretary. Even after a treasurer was added to the list of officers [6] the funds were very inadequate [7] and the dependence was still to some extent upon individual societies.[8] A committee was appointed at each session to digest the annual reports of the various societies and to prepare a plan of action for the following year. There were also committees for preparing memorials and addresses and for their publication and distribution, but the latter work was left mainly to the societies.[9]

115. Organization.

---

[1] Addresses to the Abolition Societies and Reports of the Societies, in American Convention, *Minutes of Proceedings*, 1794–1806.

[2] *Ibid.*, Addresses to State Legislatures, Congress, etc.

[3] Needles, *Hist. Mem. Pa. Soc.*, 43–47, 60, 66, 72, 79, 80. These efforts occur in the years 1796, 1813, 1818, 1821, 1824.

[4] See below, §§ 154, 155 ; American Convention, *Minutes of Proceedings*, 1795, p. 14.

[5] Constitution in *Ibid.*, 1801, pp 34–36.

[6] *Ibid.*, art. i, § 2.

[7] American Convention, *Minutes of Proceedings*, 1801, p. 16 ; 1803, pp. 8, 10, 14, 18 ; 1804, p. 29.

[8] *Ibid.*, 1803, pp. 21–22. *Cf. Ibid.*, 1798, p. 12 ; 1800, pp. 18, 22 ; 1801, p. 8.

[9] *Ibid.*, 1794, p. 29 ; 1798, p. 18 ; 1800, pp. 15, 19–20; 1801, pp. 14, 16, 20, 45–47 ; 1803, pp. 11, 17; 1805, pp. 10–11, 13–14. *Cf.* § 117, below.

The policy of the Abolition Societies was somewhat different from that of the later anti-slavery organizations. The intention here was merely to persuade by appeals to the rea- *116. Policy* son and conscience and by the gradual education of *of the* *Abolition* public opinion, and every effort was made to avoid *Societies.* arousing suspicion or antagonism. The purpose to bring about total abolition was indeed avowed; and the delegates of the societies in their first annual convention declare their hope that " their labours will never cease, while there exists a single slave in the United States." [1] But they tried to disarm hostility by explaining that there was no intention of violating the laws or infringing on " nominal rights of property, although those rights may only be traced to our statute-books; " [2] and they were inclined to abate their efforts in the face of extreme opposition.

For the ultimate object of abolition the first step must be the education of public sentiment. With this end in view, information with regard to slavery in the various States *117. Educa-* was collected by the local societies, including copies *tion of public* of laws and minutes of judicial decisions, with the *sentiment.* intention of compiling a history of slavery in the United States.[3] By some of the societies a series of orations on slavery was undertaken. The Connecticut Society, founded in 1790, provided a series of addresses for several years, and the Rhode Island, New York, and Maryland societies instituted a similar custom.[4] Some of these orations, by Edwards, Webster, and

---

[1] Address to the People of the United States, in American Convention, *Minutes of Proceedings*, 1794, p. 25.

[2] American Convention, *Address to the People of the United States*, 1804, p. 7.

[3] Ibid., *Minutes of Proceedings*, 1795, pp. 9–10; 1796, pp. 19–22, 24–26; 1797, pp. 9–11, and Appendix; 1798, pp. 7, 9; 1800, pp. 17, 29–35; 1801, pp. 16, 46; 1803, pp. 18–19, 24; 1804, pp. 28, 34–35; 1805, p. 17; 1806, p. 22.

[4] Seven or eight addresses are reported as having been given under the auspices of the Connecticut Society. They include the orations of James Dana, D.D., 1790, Zephaniah Swift, 1791, Jonathan Edwards, 1791, Noah Webster, 1793, and Theodore Dwight, 1794. An address by William Patten, A.M., was read before the Providence Society, Feb. 14, 1793, and ordered printed. Samuel Hopkins delivered a discourse May 17, the same year. Occasional discourses are reported by the society in 1798. American Convention, *Minutes of Proceedings*, 1798, p. 8. The New York Manumission Society, 1785–1786, printed 2000 copies of Dr. Hopkins's *Dialogue concerning the Slavery of the Africans*, and sent copies to members of Congress and to the members of the State legislature. Park, *Memoir of Samuel Hop-*

Dwight in Connecticut, and by Buchanan in Maryland, are among the most valuable contributions to the anti-slavery literature of the period. The publication and distribution of anti-slavery essays and other literature on the subject was undertaken by some of the societies at the suggestion of the Convention of Delegates.[1] Addresses to the Citizens of the United States were occasionally published by the Convention. One of these addresses, intended to be published in one or more newspapers of each State (1794), stated some of the arguments against slavery and recommended exertions against the slave-trade and the formation of societies for the abolition of slavery, the relief of negroes unlawfully held in bondage, and the general improvement of the condition of the African race.[2] Another address, of which 5000 copies were sent to the societies for distribution (1801), deplored the recent insurrection in Virginia, explained the attitude of the societies, and urged gradual emancipation.[3] A third, published in pamphlet form (1804), soon after the open renewal of the slave-trade by South Carolina, called attention to the fact that slavery was increasing instead of diminishing, and urged the co-operation of every friend of justice and lover of his country, especially in the effort to prevent kidnapping and the clandestine slave-trade.[4]

A more direct influence than that of orations and pamphlets was exerted by the societies through their applications to court

kins, 117. In 1787 they offered a gold medal for the best Commencement oration "on the injustice and cruelty of the slave-trade, and the fatal effects of slavery." Brissot, *New Travels in the United States*, I, 248–249, note. In 1797 and 1798 addresses were delivered under the auspices of the society by Samuel Miller and Elihu H. Smith. An Address by George Buchanan, M.D., was delivered at a public meeting of the Maryland Society, July 4, 1791. The New York and Maryland societies as well as that of Connecticut report the institution of periodical discourses. American Convention, *Minutes of Proceedings*, 1796, pp. 19, 21–22; 1797, p. 42. The Pennsylvania Society reported in 1797 that such a custom was not needed in that State. *Ibid.* The New Jersey Society regards such orations as unnecessary in West Jersey and unpopular in East Jersey. *Ibid.*, 1798, p. 9. The Delaware Society reports an oration in 1805, but has difficulty in finding suitable persons to deliver such addresses. *Ibid.*, 1805, p. 19.

[1] *Ibid.*, 1797, p. 42; 1804, pp. 11–12; 1805, pp. 10–11, 14, 18.

[2] *Ibid.*, 1794, pp. 22–25.

[3] *Ibid.*, 1801, pp. 37–41, 47.

[4] American Convention, *Address to the People of the United States*, 1804.

and legislature. Efforts to influence State legislatures were most vigorous and extensive in the early years of the Convention. In 1794 and 1795 addresses were sent to all States which had not prohibited importation or had not abolished domestic slavery.[1] States which had already begun the process of emancipation were urged to carry the work still further.[2] The Southern States were addressed chiefly on the subject of the slave-trade, foreign and domestic, as a necessary preliminary to the extirpation of slavery.[3] Next in importance was the alleviation of the condition of the slaves. "Until a radical abolition of slavery," it was urged, " by exploding the general opinion, that the colour of a man is evidence of his deprivation of the rights of man," it may reasonably be expected that the negroes shall receive protection through special prohibitions and penalties.[4] The necessity for education, in order to prepare them "for that state in society upon which depends our political happiness," was also emphasized.[5] The encouragement of voluntary manumission with a view to gradual emancipation is suggested, and the hope expressed that the freedmen may participate in civil rights and privileges as fast as they are qualified by education.[6]

118. Petitions and memorials to State legislatures.

[1] American Convention, *Minutes of Proceedings*, 1794, pp. 8, 11–18, 29 ; 1795, pp. 17–19, 20–22, 24–25, 31–32 ; 1796, pp. 9–11.

[2] *Ibid.*, 1794, pp. 8, 16–17; 1795, p. 17.

[3] *Ibid.*, 1794, pp. 11–13; 1795, pp. 20–25.

[4] *Ibid.*, 1794, pp. 14–15.

[5] *Ibid.*, 1795, p. 21.

[6] *Ibid.*, 1794, pp. 15–16. These memorials were probably not even presented in South Carolina and Georgia. *Ibid.*, 1795, p. 18 ; 1796, p. 11. Those sent to North Carolina probably met the same fate, but an act to prevent the importation of slaves was passed at about the same time. *Ibid.*, 10–11. See also § 147, note. In 1803 and 1804 committees appointed to prepare similar memorials for North Carolina reported that public sentiment in that State was so hostile to emancipation that it seemed best not to attempt the work. American Convention, *Minutes of Proceedings*, 1803, pp. 22, 27–28 ; 1804, pp. 18–19, 25. In Maryland and Virginia the addresses were not presented, but the Virginia Abolition Society in 1795-1796 sent in a memorial signed by citizens of the State. *Ibid.*, 1796, p. 10. See § 141. A similar course was pursued in New York. American Convention, *Minutes of Proceedings*, 1796, p. 9. In Delaware the addresses were presented but not acted on, and the efforts of the Abolition Society were continued by means of petitions and memorials signed by citizens. *Ibid.*, 1795, p. 17 ; 1796, p. 10 ; 1805, pp. 18–19 ; 1806, p. 16. In New Jersey a bill for gradual abolition was lost by one vote. *Ibid.*, 1796, p. 9. See below, § 134.

The custom of petitioning Congress, inaugurated by the Pennsylvania Abolition Society in 1790 and confirmed by the action of eight other societies in 1791,[1] was, after the establishment of the American Convention of Delegates, left almost entirely to that organization, although a petition from a single society occasionally appears.[2] During this period the energy of the Convention was directed chiefly toward securing restrictive legislation on the foreign slave-trade; and this was accomplished in 1794 to such an extent that the act, when considered by the Convention with a view to its amendment, was thought to go as far as the Constitution permitted.[3] The societies, however, watched over the execution of the law, complained of evasions,[4] and finally petitioned Congress for further legislation.[5] Another opportunity for national legislation had meanwhile arisen in the purchase of Louisiana Territory, and the American Convention rose to the occasion in a memorial to Congress urging the exclusion of slavery from this territory (January 23, 1804),[6] which may be regarded as the first step in the Free-Soil movement.

119, Addresses to Congress.

A third method by which the Abolition Societies endeavored to extend liberty to the negro was through application to the courts. This work was necessarily confined to the States where favorable legislation had already been obtained, and included the enforcement and amendment of emancipation and manumission acts and the prevention of kidnapping and sale from a free to a slave State. It also included the prosecution of offenders against State or national laws restricting or prohibiting the slave-trade. The latter work was especially urged upon the societies by the Convention of Delegates in 1797, and information against offenders was sought

120. Suits in courts of law.

---

[1] See below, §§ 126, 153.

[2] Memorial of the Abolition Society of Massachusetts and Rhode Island, presented Feb. 23, 1793, in *Annals of Congress*, 2 Cong., 2 sess., 888, 889; Memorial of the Providence Society for the Abolition of the Slave-Trade, presented Jan. 28, 1794, in *Annals of Congress*, 3 Cong., 1 sess., 349.

[3] American Convention, *Minutes of Proceedings*, 1795, pp. 22–23.

[4] *Ibid.*, 1797, pp. 18–20; 1805, pp. 35–36, 39–40.

[5] *Annals of Congress*, 9 Cong., 2 sess., Appendix, 992–993 (Feb. 13, 1806).

[6] Text in *Ibid.*, 8 Cong., 2 sess., Appendix, 1596–1597, and in American Convention, *Minutes of Proceedings*, 1804, pp. 40–42.

from the Governor of Sierra Leone. Efforts in this direction were continued throughout the period.[1] A Rhode Island slave-trader was successfully prosecuted by the New York Manumission Society,[2] and prosecutions were reported by the societies of New Jersey and Pennsylvania.[3] The relief of negroes unlawfully held in bondage, which was the primary object of the individual societies, was during these most critical years of the process of gradual emancipation carried on with considerable vigor. This work was the subject of special reports from the Abolition Societies to the Convention of Delegates in 1797. The New York Society reported 90 complaints, 36 persons freed, 21 cases still in suit, and 19 under consideration. From New Jersey the report was not definite, and Pennsylvania simply reported the liberation of " many hundreds." Through the agency of the Wilmington (Delaware) Society 80 had been liberated. The Choptank (Maryland) Society reported more than 60 liberations and only 1 failure in court. The Alexandria Society had received 26 complaints, 6 persons had been liberated, 5 more releases were probable, and suits were still pending for the rest, two of these at the society's expense. The Virginia Society had suits for 20 or 30 persons still pending.[4] Additional cases were reported from year to year.[5]

In addition to the ultimate object of the abolition of slavery and the immediate one of liberation of negroes unlawfully held in bondage, the Abolition Societies had a third object which throughout this period of gradual emancipation remained their constant care. This was the improvement of the condition of the free blacks by attention to their material welfare, by systematic education, and by urging and aiding them to self-support, self-respect, and usefulness in the community. The local societies were expected to report to the Convention of Delegates on the number of free blacks in their

121. Care of the free blacks.

---

[1] American Convention, *Minutes of Proceedings*, 1798, pp. 12-15, 19; 1800, pp. 15, 21-22; 1801, pp. 5-6, 40-41; 1803, pp. 8, 13, 33; 1804, pp. 8, 24, 38, 46; 1805, pp. 35-36, 39-40.

[2] *Ibid.*, 1806, p. 6.

[3] *Ibid.*, 1804, p. 8; 1806, p. 14. See also Humanitas, *Reflections on Slavery*, 18-24.

[4] American Convention, *Minutes of Proceedings*, 1797, pp. 38-39.

[5] *Ibid.*, 1798, pp. 8, 10; 1800, pp. 9-10, 15; 1801, pp. 5, 10, 22, 30-31; 1803, pp. 10, 17; 1804, pp. 5, 7, 14; 1805, pp. 5-20; 1806, pp. 5-18.

State, and on their property, employment, and conduct.[1]   Addresses to these people were issued by the Convention from time to time, advising them with regard to religion and morality, education and industry, and the acquisition and use of property, and especially urging them to good conduct as the best aid they could give toward the liberation of their brethren in bondage.[2]   In one instance, the Pennsylvania Society took charge of 126 negroes on board vessels arrested for illegal slave-trade, gave them assistance and protection and found them employment.[3]   Education was regarded as of great importance, especially in Philadelphia, where the large number of negroes who took refuge there strained the powers of the enterprising Abolition Society to the utmost.[4]   Seven schools are reported there in 1797,[5] and the educational work continued to flourish under the society until at their suggestion in 1820 the education of the colored children became a part of the public school system.[6]   The New York Society had several flourishing schools,[7] an " academy " was established by the Maryland Society,[8] and some efforts for education were made in Rhode Island,[9] Delaware,[10] New Jersey,[11] and Virginia.[12]   In addition to

[1] American Convention, *Minutes of Proceedings*, 1795, p. 28 ; 1796, pp. 21–22 ; 1797, pp. 39–40.

[2] Address to Free Africans, in *Ibid.*, 1796, pp. 12-15, reprinted in Paul Cuffe, *An Account of Sierra Leone*, Appendix.   Address in 1804 in *Minutes of Proceedings*, pp. 30–33 ; Address in 1805, *Ibid.*, pp. 36–39.   Addresses were also issued by the Pennsylvania Society.   Needles, *Hist. Mem. Pa. Soc.*, 47.

[3] *Ibid.*, 46–47.

[4] Address of the Pennsylvania Society to the American Convention, 1809, in Needles, *Hist. Mem. Pa. Soc.*, 56–57.

[5] An account of the educational work in Pennsylvania is given in American Convention, *Minutes of Proceedings*, 1797, pp. 31–34, 41.   See also *Ibid.*, 1800, p. 7 ; 1801, p. 18 ; 1803, p. 13.

[6] Needles, *Hist. Mem. Pa. Soc.*, 70.

[7] American Convention, *Minutes of Proceedings*, 1797, pp. 29–31, 41 ; 1798, p. 8 ; 1800, pp. 13–14 ; 1801, pp. 6–7 ; 1803, pp. 6–7 ; 1805, pp. 6–7 ; 1806, pp. 6–7.

[8] *Ibid.*, 1796, p. 22.

[9] *Ibid.*, 1798, p. 8 ; 1806, p. 22.

[10] American Convention, *Address to the People of the United States*, 1804, p. 16 ; Ibid., *Minutes of Proceedings*, 1801, p. 20 ; 1803, p. 17 ; 1806, pp. 16-17.

[11] *Ibid.*, 1797, p. 41 ; 1798, p. 9 ; 1801, pp. 11–12 ; 1803, p. 11 ; 1805, p. 9.

[12] See above, § 40 ; American Convention, *Minutes of Proceedings*, 1797, pp. 34–36, 41 ; 1798, p. 10 ; 1801, p. 32 ; 1805, p. 23.

this educational work was the supervisory work of the committees of inspection and advice, guardianship and employment, which had been organized by the Pennsylvania Society in 1789 and later by other societies.[1] Under such supervision the negroes were reported to have shown themselves as capable of improvement as the whites, and an argument against slavery was drawn from the difference between those who were under the care of the society and those who were not.[2]

It is noticeable that the Abolition Societies of Connecticut and Rhode Island played but a small part in the work outlined by the American Convention of Delegates in their Minutes of Proceedings. At the annual meetings from 1794 to 1796 one or both of these societies were represented, but after 1798 neither sent delegates. The Providence Society reported in 1805 that slavery was so nearly extinct in that locality that it had but little to do, and excused itself from attendance on account of the length of the journey and the inclemency of the season.[3]

122. Decline of the Abolition Societies.

The Southern societies had also fallen away by 1803 so that the only ones represented at the later meetings of this period were those of New York, New Jersey, Pennsylvania, and Delaware. The lack of zeal in the New England societies was at least partly due to the local conditions which made diligent effort at home no longer necessary, and to the apparent impracticability of any interference with slavery in the Southern States. The decline of those in the Southern States was largely due to the difficulties encountered in carrying on their work: the early successes of these societies had aroused an opposition which tended to discourage further effort. The Maryland Society, for instance, was at one time so powerful that it was said to be useless to defend a suit which it brought; but its activity excited so much hostility that it narrowly escaped a vote of censure from the State legislature and considered it expedient to suspend its efforts.[4] In Virginia the activity of the society was seriously checked by a statute imposing a penalty

[1] See above, § 112.
[2] American Convention, *Minutes of Proceedings*, 1806, p. 13.
[3] *Ibid.*, 1805, p. 43.
[4] Brackett, *The Negro in Maryland*, 54–55. The society, however, retained a large membership for some time, reporting 231 members in 1797. American Convention, *Minutes of Proceedings*, 1797, p. 38.

of one hundred dollars on any person who assisted a slave in asserting a claim to freedom, provided he should fail to establish the claim;[1] another legislative provision, that no member of an abolition society should serve as a juror in a freedom suit,[2] made the prospect of establishing such a claim far from brilliant. Under such conditions it is not surprising that the society relaxed its efforts in the courts, and its failure to obtain more favorable legislation left it without any resource except the persistent aggressiveness of a Garrison or an ignominious death.[3]

A few years after the insurrection of Gabriel, in 1800, the Alexandria Society is reported dissolved,[4] and the Maryland and Virginia societies, which were still apparently flourishing in 1797, are not even heard from. A committee appointed by the Convention of Delegates in 1804 to draw up a plan for the gradual abolition of slavery in the United States confesses itself inadequate to the task.[5] Even the Pennsylvania Society, always the mainstay of the movement, becomes for once weak and discouraged, and inquires whether any material injury would arise from a temporary suspension of its functions.[6] The Convention, although it preserves a courageous attitude in its addresses, decides upon triennial instead of annual meetings (1806).[7]

The local work of the societies in the Middle States was still continued; after the second absorbing contest with England was over, the work of the Convention, which, although never abandoned, had become comparatively unimportant, was renewed with a vigor equal to that of earlier years and continued without interruption until the administration of Andrew Jackson; and although in that

123. Revival of activity in the Convention, 1817–1829.

---

[1] American Convention, *Minutes of Proceedings*, 1805, pp. 21–22; *Statutes at Large of Virginia*, 2d Series, I, 364.   Passed Dec. 25, 1795.

[2] *Ibid.*, II, 77.   Passed Jan. 25, 1798.

[3] A large number of Quakers and some others who were unable to reconcile themselves to life in a slave State emigrated to the Northwest Territory. Weeks, *Southern Quakers and Slavery*, 1–2, 243 ff.   One of the most conspicuous instances is Edward Coles, who was Governor of Illinois at the time of the struggle to preserve the free-state constitution in 1823–1824. Washburne, *Sketch of Edward Coles*, 19–212.   See § 170, note.

[4] American Convention, *Minutes of Proceedings*, 1805, p. 21.

[5] *Ibid.*, p. 31.

[6] *Ibid.*, 1806, p. 12.   [7] *Ibid.*, p. 25.

darkest period before the dawn the Pennsylvania Society noted with discouragement the falling away of its companions, there was still a steadfast band to extend the hand of welcome to the new societies [1] as they sprang into existence under the inspiration of William Lloyd Garrison. The younger societies, in the awful magnitude of the task before them, recognized but faintly that anything had as yet been accomplished; nevertheless, the soil had been prepared for them by the quiet but persistent labors of their predecessors, the chief points of attack had been noted, the chief lines of action marked out, precedents had been set, arguments and examples furnished, conditions ameliorated, and public opinion considerably educated.

[1] American Convention, *Minutes of Proceedings*, 1818–1828; Letters from the Pennsylvania Society to the New Haven Anti-Slavery Society, in Needles, *Hist. Mem. Pa. Soc.*, 90–91; Birney, *James G. Birney and his Times*, Appendix C, pp. 414 f.

CHAPTER V

GRADUAL EMANCIPATION IN THE STATES, 1783–1808

T HE political movement toward the abolition of slavery which had begun during the Revolutionary era will be considered in the period from 1783 to 1808 under three distinct aspects according to the specific objects which its promoters had in view: gradual emancipation by State legislation (chapter v); the suppression of the African slave-trade by State and national action (chapter vi); and the attempt to prevent slavery from extending itself into the Territories of the United States (chapter vii). Of these three movements, the first and second, which had made a promising beginning before the close of the Revolutionary War, were practically completed during this period, and, though not entirely successful, left no very threatening prospect of disaster. The third, on the contrary, beginning at the close of the Revolutionary War with the existence of a national domain, was so far unsuccessful that it left an opening for the growth of slavery which threatened to lead to the destruction of both liberty and union.

124. Phases of the political movement, 1783-1808.

The principal means for arousing public sentiment have been described in the preceding chapter, and an account has been given of some of the methods which were employed to stimulate it to action. It is necessary next to consider in what directions anti-slavery effort, from whatever source, could be applied with most efficiency. The persuasion of individual slave-owners to manumit their own slaves was a slow and toilsome process of achieving the liberation of a race. The action of organized religious bodies, with the exception of the Society of Friends, was very limited, partial, or abortive; and in the case of the Methodists its continuation was regarded as threatening the spiritual efficiency of the sect.[1] Abolition societies to be of any real value must exclude slave-

125. Opportunities for effective action.

[1] See above. §§ 44–47.

holders from membership, and could gain numbers and power only where the local conditions were fairly favorable to their growth. The only organizations through which really important results could now be reached were: (*a*) the constitutional conventions held for the formation of new States calling for admission to the Union; (*b*) the State legislatures; and (*c*) the national Congress.

Of these the constitutional conventions might provide for the total prohibition of slavery, as had been done in the Revolutionary period by Vermont;[1] or they might state a general principle which the courts could interpret in such a way as to accomplish the same result, as was done in Massachusetts.[2] They might provide for gradual emancipation by pronouncing free all persons born after a certain date, as had been proposed by Jefferson in Virginia;[3] or they might give expression to the general principle, enjoining upon the legislature to find the most suitable method of carrying it out, as was proposed in Kentucky by Rev. David Rice.[4] To a constitutional convention all things were possible, and it was here that the hope for the Border States of the West would chiefly lie. Then too the Federal Convention, on whose decisions hung the very existence of the infant nation, provided an opportunity for the zealous abolitionist. Not for general and immediate or even gradual emancipation; local interests and institutions were now too sacred for that thought to enter the mind of any but the most ardent radical; but the suppression of the African slave-trade, it was thought, might surely be made a subject for their deliberations, and thus facilitate the gradual extinction of slavery itself.[5]

(a) Constitutional conventions.

In the older States, where constitutions had already been adopted and would not be easily changed, the only hope was in the State legislatures or the courts of law. Here was the opportunity for interpreting liberally the broad principles of the State Bills of Rights either by judicial decision or, failing there, by declaratory statute; and the precedent set by Massachusetts might inspire hope for such an enterprise. There was still, after the Revolutionary War, the

(b) State legislatures.

---

[1] See above, § 89.
[2] See above, §§ 88 *inf.*, 91.
[3] See above, § 88.
[4] See below, § 128.
[5] See below, § 148.

necessity for guarding against the revival of the slave-trade, or
for the suppression of it when revived.   There was ample occasion in most of the States for more liberal provisions with
regard to manumission; and at the beginning of this period
only one State legislature, that of Pennsylvania, had passed a
gradual emancipation act.[1]

As for Congress, the feeble legislative body of the Confederation could hardly be expected to accomplish much, and
(c) Con-   perhaps no one but the ever active Quaker would
gress.   attempt to urge it.   Yet the Congress of the Union,
with its wider sphere of action, could limit, regulate, and in
time suppress the foreign slave-trade; it could regulate commerce among the several States, and that would include the
domestic slave-trade; it could, as even the Congress of the
Confederation did in part,[2] prohibit slavery in the national
domain; it could "hold up to public view, a continual avowal
of sentiment"[3] which might modify without directly interfering
with local legislation.

The results of anti-slavery agitation with regard to the slave-
trade and the national domain will be related in the following
126. Efforts   chapters.   Emancipation in the States, the present
for emanci-   subject for consideration, was attempted almost ex-
pation by   clusively within the States themselves.   The direct
Congress,
1790, 1800.   interference of Congress with the existence of slavery
in the States was, however, twice solicited.   It is interesting to
find that the first instance, occurring in the very first year after
the Constitution went into operation (February 3, 1790), was
authorized by one of the members of the Federal Convention,
— no less a person than Benjamin Franklin, at that time
president of the Pennsylvania Abolition Society, which presented the memorial to Congress.   The application is based
upon the preamble of the Constitution.   Certain powers, declare the memorialists, were vested in Congress " for ' promoting the welfare and securing the blessings of liberty to the
people of the United States ; ' and as they conceive that these
blessings ought rightfully to be administered, without distinc-

---

[1] See above, § 87.

[2] See below, § 170.

[3] *Queries of Warner Mifflin, addressed to a Committee of Congress*, in
The American Museum, VIII, 61.

tion of color, to all descriptions of people, so they indulge themselves in the pleasing expectation, that nothing which can be done for the relief of the unhappy objects of their care will be either omitted or delayed." They therefore urge that Congress will turn its attention to the subject of slavery, that it " will be pleased to countenance the restoration of liberty to these unhappy men," and that it " will devise means for removing this inconsistency from the character of the American people."[1] Congress, after an excited discussion, referred the memorial to a committee[2] which reported on this point that Congress had no authority to interfere in the internal regulations of particular States (March 5, 1790).[3]

The subject, however, was brought up again ten years later, when Absalom Jones and others, free blacks of Philadelphia, in petitioning for the revision of the laws concerning the slave-trade and fugitives from justice, begged also for the adoption of measures leading to the gradual emancipation of their race.[4] This clause of the petition provoked violent opposition in the House.[5] During the debate significant allusions were made to "the several plans which had been proposed"[6] and to "a certain society" (evidently the Society of Friends) which had been in the habit of presenting petitions every year and was expected to keep on doing so.[7] A Southern Congressman became much excited over the spread of the "new-fangled French philosophy of liberty and equality" among the blacks, and talked of " entering wedges," and of the necessity of yielding the slave-trade as "a peace-offering" to the " philanthropists."[8] In vain did a representative from Massachusetts endeavor to propitiate the slave-holders by declaring that the aspect of a certain petition was very dangerous and unpleasant, and that "those who did not possess this species of property

---

[1] Text of the memorial in *Annals of Congress*, 1 Cong., 2 sess., 1197–1198. Presented Feb. 12, 1790.

[2] *Ibid.*, 1198–1205.

[3] Text of the report in *Ibid.*, 1414–1415; Report of Committee of the Whole House, 1474.

[4] *Ibid.*, 6 Cong., 1 sess., 229–230, 235.

[5] *Ibid.*, 230–245.

[6] Speech of Mr. Thatcher of Massachusetts, *Ibid.*, 240.

[7] Speeches of Mr. Christie of Maryland and Mr. Harper of South Carolina, *Ibid.*, 234.

[8] *Ibid.*, 230, 241–242, 689. Speeches of Mr. Rutledge of South Carolina.

had better leave the regulation of it to those who were cursed with it." [1] The member from South Carolina gives warning that "there is one alternative . . . that is, that we are able to take care of ourselves, and if driven to it, we will take care of ourselves." [2]

One stanch champion, Mr. Thatcher of Massachusetts, rose to defend the obnoxious clause, declaring that slavery was "a cancer of immense magnitude that would some time destroy the body politic except a proper legislation should prevent the evil," and suggesting that slavery might be abolished without injury to the slave-owners and that an appropriation should be made for the purpose. [3] The House, however, though referring the rest of the petition to a committee, voted 85 to 1 that this section "ought to receive no encouragement or countenance from this House." [4] Emancipation, therefore, was left to the States, and so far as accomplished at all was the work of constitutional conventions and State legislatures.

Abolition by State constitution, attempted in New York, accomplished in Vermont, and finally effective in Massachusetts, [5] was applied in only one other State of the original thirteen. In New Hampshire it is not certain that there was a direct intention of abolishing slavery by this means. The Bill of Rights, like that of Pennsylvania, states simply that "all men are born equally free and independent." [6] The logical application of the principle is not directly stated as in Vermont; but the activity of public opinion, added to the influence of conditions in the neighboring States, was such that slavery disappeared without direct legislation or judicial action. [7] After the adoption of the Constitution a few negroes were still held as slaves, and although the legislature in 1789 struck off "male and female servants"

127 Abolition by constitution. New Hampshire and Ohio.

---

[1] *Annals of Congress*, 6 Cong., 1 sess., 231. Speech of Mr. Harrison Gray Otis of Massachusetts.

[2] *Ibid.*, 242. Speech of Mr. Rutledge.

[3] *Ibid.*, 232, 240.

[4] *Ibid.*, 245-246.

[5] See above, §§ 88, 89, 91.

[6] *New Hampshire State Papers*, IX, 896; Poore, *Federal and State Constitutions*, II, 1280.

[7] *New Hampshire State Papers*, IX, 896–898, Note by Editor; Hurd, *Law of Freedom and Bondage*, II, 35; Walker, *A History of the New Hampshire Convention*, vii and note.

from the list of taxable property,[1] the obligation to maintain the aged and infirm still rested with the masters.[2] Many, however, remained with their former masters in the capacity of servants; there were no sales of slaves, and if any one chose to leave his master the public authority was not used for his recovery. Negroes who remained with their masters were treated like the other servants, and the black children went to the same schools as the white. " No better plan could be adopted," says La Rochefoucauld-Liancourt, who visited America in 1795, " by a people who stopped short of total emancipation."[3]

The most favorable opportunity to apply a constitutional restriction was when the new States began to come into the Union from the country west of the Alleghanies and the question of slavery came up in connection with the formation of each State. Here the influence of territorial conditions was decisive. Ohio, the only State formed from the Northwest Territory before 1808, adopted the prohibition contained in the Ordinance of 1787 as a part of her Constitution, not, however, incorporated in the Bill of Rights, as was done in Vermont, but in a separate article and without the significant " therefore."[4]

Kentucky and Tennessee, to which slavery had already been admitted, failed to pass any provision against it now, though there was an attempt to do so in Kentucky. At the Constitutional Convention the six clerical members are said to have been unanimously against the recognition of slavery, and a vote to expunge a clause forbidding emancipation without consent of the owners had a strong minority of 16 to 26.[5]

128. Failure in Kentucky.

The most important leader in the anti-slavery movement in Kentucky at this time was Rev. David Rice, and his address to the convention is one of the most earnest and forceful produc-

---

[1] In 1775 negroes and slaves for life were reported as numbering 657. In 1790 the number was reduced to 158, in 1800 to 8, and in 1810 none were reported. *New Hampshire State Papers*, IX, 897, note.

[2] Wadleigh, *Slavery in New Hampshire*, in *The Granite Monthly*, VI, 377-379.

[3] La Rochefoucauld-Liancourt, *Travels through the United States*, II, 191. *Cf.* § 145, below (Washington's fugitive).

[4] Poore, *Federal and State Constitutions*, II, 1461, art. viii, §§ 1, 2. *Cf.* § 89, above.

[5] Brown, *Political Beginnings of Kentucky*, 227-230; note, p. 230.

tions of the period. In this address he points to the anomaly of " a free moral agent, legally deprived of free agency, and obliged to act according to the will of another," while still accountable to the Creator for his actions, and sarcastically declares that the legislature, in order to be consistent, should make the master accountable both here and hereafter.[1] He regards liberty as inalienable by the legislature except for vicious conduct, and claims to property in slaves as invalid. " A thousand laws," he says, " can never make that innocent, which the divine law has made criminal." [2] On the question of expediency, he replies to the argument that slave-holders would be prevented from emigrating to Kentucky by saying that five useful citizens would come for every slaveholder that was lost, and that if slavery was permitted, free labor would seek other regions.[3] The alleged unfitness of the slave for freedom is met by the question whether we shall " continue to maim souls, because a maimed soul is unfit for society; " [4] but he considers that present conditions should be taken into account and that gradual emancipation is the only practicable plan. His proposal is that the Constitution shall declare against slavery as a matter of principle, leaving the legislature to find the most suitable means of abolishing it.[5] Emancipation by some means he regards as a political necessity, and he closes with a prophecy of the calamities which will attend the continuance of slavery and an earnest appeal that the new State may not be stained with this sin at its birth. " The slavery of the Negroes," he says, "began in iniquity; a curse has attended it, and a curse will follow it. National vices will be punished with national calamities. Let us avoid these vices, that we may avoid the punishment which they deserve." [6]

Kentucky failed to respond to his appeal, but a few years later (1797–1798), an attempt was made to amend the Constitution on this point. It is said that the prohibition of slavery was even probable at that time, and that it was only the reaction of political sentiment caused by the passage of the Alien and Sedition Acts at this inopportune moment that prevented

Speech of Rev. David Rice, 1792.

---

[1] Rice, *Slavery inconsistent with Justice and Good Policy*, 5–6.
[2] *Ibid.*, 3–4, 12–14.
[3] *Ibid.*, 15–16.
[4] *Ibid.*, 20–21.
[5] *Ibid.*, 22.
[6] *Ibid.*, 24.

Kentucky from becoming a free State.[1] The anti-slavery feeling continued to be strong for some time, and showed itself in the schism of the Baptist churches of Kentucky in 1805 and the formation of abolition societies.[2] Nevertheless, except the permission of voluntary manumission,[3] nothing further was accomplished south of the Ohio River.

Emancipation by act of legislature was the only remaining weapon, and it was successfully wielded in four States of the Union besides Pennsylvania. In most cases it was connected with efforts to procure the removal of restraints on manumission, which had already been provided for in Connecticut (1777) and Virginia (1782).[4] Soon after the Revolutionary War, efforts in this direction were made in every State north of the Potomac in which there was occasion for them. In Maryland and Delaware attempts at gradual emancipation acts soon gave way to the milder measure of facilitating manumission. The Quakers seem to have been the chief agents in both States. *129. Manumission acts.*

In Delaware a bill for the gradual abolition of slavery was introduced in January, 1786, and supported by a petition from 204 Friends, praying that such relief should be given to the slaves of the State as the rights of mankind and religion required; after consideration, it was replaced by a bill for furthering manumission, and this bill was postponed until the following June and finally dropped.[5] The following year, however, an act was passed permitting manumission by will or other written instrument, without security furnished by the master, in the case of slaves between eighteen and thirty-five years of age, sound in mind and body and capable of self-support (February 3, 1787).[6] Under the new law many manu- *130. Manumission in Delaware.*

---

[1] Birney, *James G. Birney and his Times*, 21–22. See also Weeks, *Anti-Slavery Sentiment in the South*, 101.

[2] See above, § 46.

[3] See below, § 132.

[4] See above, § 84.

[5] Brackett, *The Status of the Slave*, in Jameson, *Essays in the Constitutional History of the United States*, 300–301; Stillé, *Life and Times of John Dickinson*, 323; Draft of a proposed Act for gradual abolition in Delaware, from the original in the handwriting of John Dickinson, *Ibid.*, appendix viii.

[6] *Laws of the State of Delaware* (1797), II, 886.

missions were made by will;[1] and though many negroes were kidnapped, the Abolition Societies were active in procuring their liberation.[2] The number of slaves in 1790 was 8,887, in 1800, 6,153, and in 1810 had diminished to 4,177; while the number of free colored persons rose from 3,899 in 1790 to 13,136 in 1810.[3] Further efforts toward a gradual emancipation act, however, met with no success.[4]

In Maryland the question was still more sharply contested. Petitions from citizens of several counties praying for immediate or gradual abolition were presented to the House of Delegates in December, 1785. These were rejected by a vote of 32 to 22. In 1787 a petition from the Yearly Meeting of Friends in Baltimore for the emancipation of slaves was refused by a vote of 30 to 17.[5] Two years later an effort was made to facilitate voluntary manumission by owners with a view to bringing about gradual emancipation by that means. Both the Society of Friends and the Maryland Abolition Society were behind this movement, and it had a strong support in the legislature. Petitions from both societies had been addressed to the House, and a committee reported in their favor.[6]

131. Manumission in Maryland.

William Pinkney, who had already distinguished himself as a champion of this cause by a speech in the previous session, now marked the occasion by a fervid address on the rights of man and the inconsistency and impolicy of slave-holding. He attempted to grapple with the two chief arguments of the pro-slavery party, the problem of the free blacks and the rights of property. In reply to the former he declared that free negroes would be no more dangerous to society than slaves, that the blacks were no worse than the whites would be under the same conditions, and that all they needed to disprove their inferiority was an equal chance

Speech of William Pinkney, 1789.

---

[1] Mifflin, *Defence against Aspersions*, 27.

[2] See above, § 120; Mifflin, *Defence*, 23, 29; American Convention, *Minutes of Proceedings*, 1797, pp. 38–39.

[3] *Statistical View of the Population of the United States*, 1790 to 1830, pp. 52–53.

[4] American Convention, *Minutes of Proceedings*, 1805, p. 18; 1806, p. 16.

[5] Brackett, *The Negro in Maryland*, 52; *Status of the Slave*, in Jameson, *Essays*, 302.

[6] Ibid., *The Negro in Maryland*, 53.

with the more favored race.[1] To the argument in behalf of property rights he replied that the impoverishment of families was of no consequence in such a case, and that he should glory in the cause of their distress while wishing them a more honest patrimony.[2] A bill for the gradual abolition of slavery was introduced in the Senate, and the House was invited to confer but refused to do so. An attempt in the following session was equally unsuccessful. On this occasion a petition from the Maryland Abolition Society was received by the Senate and referred to the House, and by the House was referred to a committee. A vote that the committee be instructed to express disapprobation of that part of the petition which related to gradual abolition was lost by two votes, but the whole subject was allowed to drop.[3] An act simply removing restraints on manumission was finally passed in 1796. This act was similar to that of Delaware, except that the maximum age limit was forty-five years and no minimum was mentioned.[4]

Manumission acts were passed also in New Jersey (1786, 1798), New York (1785, 1788), Kentucky (1798, 1800), and Tennessee (1801). Rhode Island in 1784 included in her gradual emancipation act[5] a clause providing for voluntary manumission, and in Connecticut the process, already permitted (1777), was further facilitated in 1784 and 1792. The chief feature of these acts, as in the case of Delaware and Maryland, is the endeavor to prevent the freedmen from becoming a public charge. In Rhode Island the manumittor was still liable for maintenance unless the slave manumitted was between eighteen or twenty-one and forty years of age and otherwise capable of self-support.[6] In New Jersey (1786) the age limits were twenty-one and thirty-five

132. Manumission in other States.

---

[1] Pinkney, *Speech in the House of Delegates in Maryland*, 11–17. Both speeches of Pinkney on this subject are given in *The American Museum*, VI, 74–77 (July, 1789), and *Ibid.*, 1798, pp. 79–89.

[2] Pinkney, *Speech in the House of Delegates*, 18.

[3] Brackett, *The Negro in Maryland*, 53–54.

[4] *Laws of Maryland*, Kilty, 1796, ch. lxvii, §§ xiii, xxix; Stroud, *A Sketch of the Laws relating to Slavery*, 151–152.

[5] See below, § 134.

[6] *Laws of Rhode Island*, Bennett Wheeler, February, 1784, p. 7. See also *Public Laws of the State of Rhode Island and Providence Plantations*, 1798, p. 611.

years. Outside those limits bonds were required, but even if not manumitted according to the prescribed legal methods the slave secured his liberty, though the master was liable for his maintenance.[1] In New York, under similar conditions (1785), slaves might be manumitted without security until fifty years of age.[2] In Connecticut novel conditions were introduced: the good character of the slave, the real advantage to himself, and his own desire for emancipation.[3] Thus the liberality in the provisions for emancipation varied with the latitude, and, as might be expected, the provisions in Kentucky and Tennessee were much more stringent. In both these States a bond for maintenance was required in all cases; and in the latter, owing, as the preamble of the act stated, to the large number of petitions for permission to execute manumissions, the owner could free his slave only on the presentation of a petition to the court showing reasons which, in the opinion of two-thirds of that body, were consistent with the interest and policy of the State.[4] In the States south of Virginia the tendency was toward increasing the restrictions on manumission rather than diminishing them.

Thus North Carolina, in 1788, undertook to amend the Act of 1777. "And whereas," runs the preamble of the new act, "divers Persons, from religious Motives, in Violation of the said Law, continue to liberate their Slaves, who are now going at Large to the Terror of the People of this State: And whereas the Mode prescribed for apprehending such Slave or Slaves [by free-holders only] is found by Experience not to answer the good Purposes by the said Act intended," information with regard to illegal

133. Southern restrictions on manumission.

---

[1] *Laws of New Jersey*, cited in American Convention, *Minutes of Proceedings*, 1797, p. 50; Brackett, *Status of the Slave*, in Jameson, *Essays*, 299. The maximum age limit was afterwards changed to forty. *Laws of the State of New Jersey*, Paterson, 311–312, Statute of March 14, 1798.

[2] *Laws of the State of New York* (1886), 1785, ch. 68 (Vol. II, p. 121), 1788, ch. 40 (Vol. II, 678–679); *Ibid.*, printed by Hugh Gaines in 1789, II, 255–256.

[3] *Acts and Laws of the State of Connecticut*, Hudson and Goodwin, 1796, pp. 398, 399; *Ibid.*, Timothy Green, 234–235, 413.

[4] Stroud, *Sketch of the Laws relating to Slavery*, 149–150; *Digest of the Statute Laws of Kentucky*, Morehead and Brown, I, 608–609; *Compilation of the Statutes of Tennessee*, Caruthers and Nicholson, 277–278; *Laws of the State of Tennessee*, Scott, I, 714–715.

manumissions may now be given to the justice of the peace by any freeman, and the justice is required immediately to issue a warrant for the negro's apprehension. The act, however, still allowed manumission for meritorious service, to be adjudged by the county courts.[1] In South Carolina and Georgia the restrictions were even more severe: in the former State no manumissions could take place except by deed executed according to certain regulations, by obtaining the approval of a justice of the quorum and five free-holders (December 20, 1800). In the latter State, after 1801, manumission could be accomplished only by special legislative act, an example followed in 1820 by South Carolina.[2]

In Rhode Island the attempt to facilitate manumission, in response to a petition from the Society of Friends (1783), developed into a gradual emancipation act (1784),[3] thus reversing the process of Delaware and Maryland. Gradual emancipation in Connecticut was inaugurated the same year.[4] In New York and New Jersey there was a longer interval between the removal of restraints on manumission and an emancipation act. New York attempted such an act in 1785, but the bill was rejected by the Council of Revision on account of a provision prohibiting negro suffrage. It then passed the Senate over the veto, but failed in the House.[5] The subject came up again in 1796 in response to a petition from the Manumission Society, but action was postponed.[6] In 1798 an act was passed

134. Gradual emancipation acts. Rhode Island, Connecticut, New York, and New Jersey.

[1] *Laws of the State of North Carolina*, Iredell, 637–638 (November, 1788, ch. xx). *Cf. Ibid.*, 288 (April, 1777, ch. vi), and 371 (January, 1799, ch. xii).

[2] Stroud, *Sketch of the Laws relating to Slavery*, 145–147; *Statutes at Large of South Carolina*, Cooper and McCord, VII, 442–443, 459. The Constitution of Georgia as revised in 1798 prohibits the legislature from passing laws for the emancipation of slaves without the consent of each of their respective owners. Poore, *Federal and State Constitutions*, I, 395, art. iv, § 11. The Constitution of Kentucky, 1792, has a similar provision, but includes pecuniary compensation. *Ibid.*, I, 653, art. ix.

[3] Brackett, *Status of the Slave*, in Jameson, *Essays*, 294–295; *Public Laws of Rhode Island*, 610.

[4] *Acts and Laws of Connecticut*, 1784–1792, printed by Timothy Green, 235; *Ibid.*, Hudson and Goodwin, 1796, p. 399; Brackett, *Status of the Slave*, in Jameson, *Essays*, 297.

[5] *Ibid.*, 298.

[6] American Convention, *Minutes of Proceedings*, 1796, p. 20; 1797, p. 40.

declaring valid the previous manumissions of slaves by the Quakers even when the process had not been strictly legal, though holding the manumittor liable for maintenance in cases enjoined by the laws.[1] A gradual emancipation act was finally passed in 1799,[2] and an immediate act followed in 1817.[3]

In New Jersey the situation was complicated by the fact that the western part of the State was inhabited largely by Quakers and the eastern by the descendants of the thrifty Dutch.[4] The tendency, however, was in the direction of emancipation. In the same year that manumission was facilitated (1786), the legislature in setting free the negro Prime for services during the Revolutionary War expressed itself as " desirous of extending the Blessings of Liberty."[5] In 1788 an act preliminary to emancipation was passed, giving negroes equal rights in the criminal courts, making instruction in reading compulsory upon the masters, and forbidding the removal of the slave to another State without his own consent.[6] The State Supreme Court in numerous cases which came before it between 1775 and 1795 was almost without exception favorable to the negro.[7] A gradual emancipation act introduced in 1795 failed by one vote;[8] action was postponed in 1796 and it was not until 1804 that the New Jersey Abolition Society could triumphantly announce its success.[9]

Gradual emancipation is defined as the extinction of slavery by depriving it of its hereditary quality.[10] In distinction from the clauses in the constitutions of Vermont, Massachusetts, and New Hampshire, which directly or indirectly affected the con-

See also E. H. Smith, *Discourse delivered before the New York Manumission Society*, 26, note.

[1] *Laws of New York* (1886), IV, 168.   Passed March 9.

[2] *Ibid.*, IV, 388–389; Stroud, *Sketch of the Laws relating to Slavery*, 138. Passed March 29.

[3] See below, § 139.

[4] Brissot, *New Travels in the United States*, I, 232.

[5] *Cases Adjudged in the Supreme Court of New Jersey*, 16, note.

[6] American Convention, *Minutes of Proceedings*, 1797, p. 51; Brackett, *Status of the Slave*, in Jameson, *Essays*, 300.   These provisions appear also in 1798. *Laws of New Jersey*, Paterson, 309–311.

[7] See above, § 91, *inf.*

[8] American Convention, *Minutes of Proceedings*, 1796, p. 9.

[9] *Ibid.*, 1797, p. 40; 1805, p. 10.   For the persistent efforts of the emancipationists see Cooley, *A Study of Slavery in New Jersey*, 18–26.

[10] Stroud, *Sketch of the Laws relating to Slavery*, 142.

dition of slavery as already existing,[1] the gradual emancipation acts left this condition unchanged, and affected only the children born after the passage of the act or after a fixed date. Most of these acts followed that of Pennsylvania in providing that the children of a slave-mother should remain with her owner as servants until they reached a certain age, of from twenty-one to twenty-eight years as stated in the various enactments. In Pennsylvania, however, they were to be regarded as free. In Connecticut, on the other hand, they were to be "held in Servitude" until twenty-five years of age and after that to be free. The most liberal policy was that of Rhode Island, where the children were pronounced free but were to be supported by the town and educated in reading, writing, and arithmetic, morality and religion. The latter clauses, however, were repealed the following year, leaving the children to be supported by the owner of the mother until twenty-one years of age, and only if he abandoned his claims to the mother to become a charge of the town. In New York and New Jersey they were to remain as servants until a certain age, but were regarded as free, and liberal opportunities were given the master for the abandonment of his claims, the children in such cases to be supported at the common charge.[2]

135. Provisions for gradual emancipation.

The manumission and emancipation acts were naturally followed, as in the case of the constitutional provision in Vermont, by the attempts of some of the slave-owners to dispose of their property outside the State.[3] Amendments to the laws were found necessary,[4] and the Abolition Societies found plenty of occasion for their exertions in protecting free blacks from seizure and illegal sale and in

136. Efforts for immediate emancipation.

---

[1] See above, §§ 88–91, 127.

[2] *Laws of the Commonwealth of Pennsylvania*, Carey and Bioren, II, 246–251; *Acts and Laws of Connecticut*, Hudson and Goodwin, 1796, pp. 398–399; *Laws of Rhode Island*, February, 1784, pp. 6–7, October, 1785, p. 15; *Laws of New York* (1886), IV, 388–389; *Laws of New Jersey*, 1800 to 1811, Bloomfield, 103–104.

[3] *Cf.* §§ 146, 147, below.

[4] *Laws of Pennsylvania*, Carey and Bioren, III, 268–272 (March 29, 1788); *Acts and Laws of Connecticut*, Hudson and Goodwin, 399–401 (October, 1788, October, 1789, May, 1792); *Ibid.*, Timothy Green, 368–369, 412–413; *Public Laws of Rhode Island* (1798), 608–609; *Laws of New York* (1886), V, 548 (April 8, 1801).

looking after the execution and amendment of the laws. The process of gradual emancipation was also unsatisfactory on account of the length of time it would require, and in Pennsylvania and Connecticut attempts were made to obtain acts for immediate emancipation.

The effort in Connecticut, prepared for by a series of addresses on the subject of slavery pronounced before the Abolition Society and published by it for distribution,[1] culminated in 1794. To this undertaking Theodore Dwight contributed an oration before the Abolition Society which marks him as one of the most eager and uncompromising advocates of immediate and total abolition to be found before the days of Garrison. The orator contends that slavery is absolutely unjustifiable, and that those who defend it on the plea of political expediency are specious enemies of the freedom and happiness of mankind.[2] The claim of the slave to liberty and that of the master to compensation he declares to be distinct questions. The State should grant the former at any rate, and the latter may be dealt with separately. But he insists that "in abolishing African slavery, no injury is done to private property," because "it is impossible, in any situation, or under the authority of any laws, to acquire a property in a human being."[3] Moreover, he argues, the laws of Connecticut not only do not sanction slavery but are positively opposed to it, and even if they did authorize it no such laws could apply to the slave, since he was not a party to the original compact.[4] "On the part of the slaves," he says, "it is a question of right; and on that of the state, a question of justice."[5] It is also, he urges, a question of expediency. "Since the mighty, and majestic course of Freedom has begun, nothing but the arm of Omnipotence can prevent it from reaching the miserable Africans" and to attempt to oppose it will only bring war and devastation.[6]

A bill which was the practical expression of this effort succeeded in passing the House, but was negatived by a small

§ 137. Connecticut. Oration of Theodore Dwight.

---

[1] See above, § 117.
[2] Dwight, *Oration before the Connecticut Society*, 6–8, 21.
[3] *Ibid.*, 8–9.
[4] *Ibid.*, 9–13.
[5] *Ibid.*, 22.
[6] *Ibid.*, 23–24.

majority of the Council,[1] and nothing further was accomplished except that in 1797 the age limit until which negro children should be "held in Servitude" was lowered from twenty-five to twenty-one years.[2]

In Pennsylvania attempts to procure the total abolition of slavery were made in connection with the judicial courts as well as with the legislature, the action in both cases being based on the clause in the Bill of Rights in the State Constitution, "All men are born equally free and independent."[3]   Albert Gallatin, while a member of the legislature, in 1793, was the author of a committee report declaring that in the opinion of the committee "slavery is inconsistent with every principle of humanity, justice, and right, and repugnant to the spirit and express letter of the constitution of this Commonwealth," and submitting a resolution that slavery be abolished in the Commonwealth and that a committee be appointed to bring in a bill for the purpose.[4]   Further efforts in the same direction were made from time to time,[5] but failed to produce either a declaratory act interpreting the Constitution in their favor or an amendment of the gradual emancipation act.   The Pennsylvania Abolition Society at about the same time (1795–1802) attempted to obtain a Supreme Court decision in regard to the interpretation of the disputed clause.   The question was argued on behalf of the negro by Jared Ingersoll, William Lewis, and William Rawle; but the judges, unlike the juries of Massachusetts, unanimously decided that slavery was consistent with the Constitution.[6]   In 1801 a measure was introduced in the legislature proposing to create a fund for the purchase and liberation of slaves by a special tax on the free blacks.   Against this preposterous measure the society earnestly protested, and they succeeded in defeating it.   In 1804 a more satisfactory bill was under consideration in the Senate, and the society addressed the legislature in its favor.   But the bill

138. Pennsylvania.

---

[1] American Convention, *Minutes of Proceedings*, 1795, p. 17.

[2] *Ibid.*, 1796, p. 9; Stroud, *Sketch of the Laws relating to Slavery*, 141.

[3] Poore, *Federal and State Constitutions*, II, 1541.

[4] Adams, *Life of Gallatin*, 86.

[5] American Convention, *Minutes of Proceedings*, 1797, p. 40; Needles, *Hist. Mem. Pa. Soc.*, 46.

[6] *Ibid.*, 42 ; Stroud, *Sketch of the Laws relating to Slavery*, 143–144 and note.   Case of the Negress Flora *vs.* Joseph Graisberry.

was lost and an attempt to procure immediate and total abolition in 1820 was equally unsuccessful.[1]

New York, therefore, is the only State that followed up the granting of liberty to the yet unborn by an act which affected *ante-nati*. By the Act of 1817 children born after July 4, 1799, the date fixed by the original emancipation act, were definitely pronounced free but required to serve out the term already allotted in the capacity of servants. A briefer term, twenty-one years instead of twenty-eight and twenty-five, was allotted to those born after July 4, 1817, and all negroes born in the State before July 4, 1799, were to be free after July 4, 1827.[2]

139. New York, 1817.

It was said that at the North few masters would hesitate to manumit their slaves were it not for the obligation to maintain them if they failed to support themselves.[3] In the South the difficulties were much more serious. Even voluntary manumission was hardly to be accomplished south of Virginia. The unsuccessful efforts of the Quakers in North Carolina have already been mentioned.[4] In South Carolina and Georgia there is still less evidence of any attempt at emancipation. Addresses from the American Convention of Delegates of the Abolition Societies to the legislatures of the Southern States received no response and apparently no attention.[5] It was said that "the most elevated and liberal Carolinians abhor slavery; and will not debase themselves by attempting to vindicate it;"[6] but their voices are never heard against it unless in a deprecatory tone in the halls of Congress, and the Resolutions of Darien County,[7] Georgia, sank into oblivion without a sign.

140. Unsuccessful efforts for emancipation.

In Virginia, however, anti-slavery sentiment was not yet dead. More than ten thousand slaves are said to have been set at

---

[1] Needles, *Hist. Mem. Pa. Soc.*, 48–49, 52–53, 70–71.

[2] Stroud, *Sketch of the Laws relating to Slavery*, 139.

[3] Dana, *The African Slave-Trade*, 31.

[4] See above, § 41. An attempt to obtain redress through federal interference, in *Annals of Congress*, 4 Cong., 2 sess., 2015–2024. Memorial presented Jan. 30, 1797.

[5] See above, § 118; American Convention, *Minutes of Proceedings*, 1795, 1796.

[6] *Sketch of the character of the S. Carolinians. By the late dr. Ladd.* In *The American Museum*, V, 130–131.

[7] See above, § 81.

liberty within ten years after the Manumission Act of 1782.[1]
Laws were made giving better protection to the life and liberty
of the negro.[2] In 1785 an act was passed limiting
slavery to the slaves already within the State and the
descendants of the females of them, and this clause
was re-enacted in 1792.[3] Finally came an attempt at gradual
emancipation of which the most important feature is the *Dissertation on Slavery* by Judge Tucker. This document had
been carefully prepared after a correspondence with Dr. Jeremy
Belknap, of Massachusetts, for the purpose of learning by what
means emancipation had taken place in the sister State, in order
to profit by her experience.[4] The purpose of the author was
to take into account every possible obstacle and objection, to
eliminate, so far as possible, the opposing elements of prejudice,
timidity, and love of possession, and in short to present a plan
of emancipation as practicable as the circumstances would permit.[5] A plan less alarming could hardly have been devised.
The language is temperate and inoffensive, and the point of
view is that of the slave-holder. The scheme provided that
only the females born after a certain date were to be free;
these were to transmit freedom to their descendants, but the
latter were to be held in service until such an age as to have
paid for their rearing by their labor; the free blacks, moreover, were to be bound to compulsory service and to be incapable of owning land, holding office, or bearing arms.[6] The
process of emancipation was to be so gradual that slavery would
actually increase for thirty years, would not diminish for ten
years more, and would require more than a century for its
extinction.[7] Moreover, life was to be made so unpleasant for
the free blacks that there should be every inducement for their

(margin note: 141 Virginia. Tucker's Dissertation on Slavery.)

---

[1] Samuel J. May, *Liberty or Slavery the only Question*, 5.

[2] *Statutes at Large of Virginia*, Hening, XII, 531, 681 (Jan. 8, Nov. 21, 1788).

[3] *Ibid.*, 182; *Ibid.*, 2d Series, I, 122 (Dec. 17, 1792).

[4] *Queries respecting the Slavery and Emancipation of the Negroes in Massachusetts*, in 1 *Mass. Hist. Soc. Coll.*, IV, 191–211; Deane, *Letters and Documents relating to Slavery in Massachusetts*, in 5 *Mass. Hist. Soc. Coll.*, III, 373–442.

[5] *Ibid.*, 418–421; Tucker, *A Dissertation on Slavery*, 76–89.

[6] *Ibid.*, 91–94.

[7] *Ibid.*, 98–104; Deane, *Letters and Documents*, in 5 *Mass. Hist. Soc. Coll.*, III, 418–421.

voluntary emigration.[1]   The Dissertation was simply laid on
the table by the House of Delegates,[2] and from the Senate the
author received merely " a civil acknowledgment." [3]

The Virginia Abolition Society at about the same time prepared a memorial signed by a considerable number of citizens,
urging a gradual emancipation act which should free all males
born after that time at twenty-one years of age and females at
eighteen.   The memorial was read in the House of Delegates,
but further consideration was negatived by two votes.[4]   The
cause was now regarded as hopeless, and from this time Virginia
is found drifting farther and farther into a distinctly pro-slavery
attitude.   The problem of the free blacks was still pre-eminent.
After the insurrection of Gabriel, in 1800, schemes for colonization were discussed,[5] and it was thought that here might be an
opening for emancipation.   But these schemes dwindled away,
and the apprehensions with regard to free blacks were finally
met by a law (January 25, 1806) which forbade manumitted
negroes to remain in the State for more than one year on
penalty of re-enslavement.[6]   The unsuccessful efforts for gradual
emancipation in Maryland and Delaware have already been
mentioned in connection with manumission acts.[7]

In the year 1808, then, slavery no longer existed in Vermont, New Hampshire, Massachusetts, or Ohio; its abolition
was nearly complete in Rhode Island, Connecticut,
and Pennsylvania; its doom had been sealed in New
York and New Jersey; and its foothold in Delaware
was but slight.   In the Border States, however, notwithstanding
considerable efforts, no legislation had been secured except for
the removal of restraints on manumission.   Delaware and
Maryland, Virginia, Kentucky, and Tennessee reached their
limit in these measures; and in the far South, where a larger
black population existed, even voluntary manumission was not

142. Sum-
mary of
results.

---

[1] Tucker, *Dissertation*, 93–96.

[2] Deane, *Letters and Documents*, 5 *Mass. Hist. Soc. Coll.*, III, 426–427.

[3] *Ibid.*, 427–428.

[4] American Convention, *Minutes of Proceedings*, 1796, p. 10.

[5] *Annals of Congress*, 9 Cong., Appendix, 994–1000; Jefferson, *Writings*,
IV, 419–422.

[6] *Statutes at Large of Virginia*, Hening, 2d Series, III, 252.   Passed
Jan. 25, 1806.

[7] See above, §§ 130, 131.

permitted. Even in the Border States it was regarded as a dangerous experiment, and men sometimes felt that they had no right to indulge in private manumissions when they might thereby endanger the lives of the community. There were, perhaps, many who, like Jefferson, would have been equal to the personal sacrifice, but who felt, like him, that it was necessary to hold the tiger by the throat.

The sectional division of the country brought about by the accomplishment of emancipation at the North and its failure at the South led to the rise of another question which was destined to become one of the chief factors in bringing on the final contest. The public obligation to return fugitives, which had already been provided for in several Indian treaties (1781–1786),[1] was established in the Northwest Territory in 1787 in connection with the prohibition of slavery in that region.[2] The same provision was incorporated in the Federal Constitution, and the first Fugitive Slave Law was enacted for the execution of this provision.[3]

143. Question of fugitive slaves.

This act originated in an attempt to obtain the arrest of some kidnappers who had taken a free negro from Pennsylvania to Virginia, and included "fugitives from justice and from the service of their masters."[4] Its provisions, however, were more severe toward the negro than toward the criminal; it allowed no trial by jury, and required conviction on oral testimony of the claimant or on affidavit certified by a magistrate of the State from which the negro was alleged to have fled.[5] Though less severe than the Act of 1850 it was sufficiently so to arouse a sense of injustice, and was not accepted without a protest. The Maryland Abolition Society immediately published a letter addressed to it by the English philanthropist, Granville Sharp, in behalf of fugitive slaves, with a preface by the society protesting against the recent act.[6] A debate on the execution of the British

144. The first Fugitive Slave Law. 1793.

---

[1] McDougall, *Fugitive Slaves*, § 13.
[2] The Northwest Ordinance, in Poore, *Federal and State Constitutions*, I, 432.
[3] *Annals of Congress*, 2 Cong., 2 sess., 861.
[4] McDougall, *Fugitive Slaves*, §§ 17, 18.
[5] *Ibid.*, Appendix B; *Laws of the United States*, 2 Cong., 1 sess., ch. vii.
[6] Granville Sharp, *Letter to the Maryland Society for promoting the Abolition of Slavery*.

Treaty, in 1796, furnished occasion for some remarks from Mr. Hillhouse, of Connecticut, against the principle of surrendering fugitive slaves.[1] A more elaborate protest is that of John Parrish, a Quaker of Maryland, who argues that the act is unjust in its provisions and contrary to the scriptural law of the Old Testament and the New; that it is contrary to the principles of the Declaration of Independence and to the pledges of the Constitution as expressed in the preamble; and that it shows the inconsistency of Congress, which professed to have too much regard for the Constitution to interfere for the relief of the slave, but has been willing to pervert its purpose and mis-construe its phrases for the purposes of this law. He denies also that any service or labor can be "due" from a person deprived of his natural rights.[2]

The escape of fugitives into the free States had already been connived at. The master who attempts to recover a slave, says Brissot de Warville, in 1788, "meets little re-spect, and finds little assistance," and the optimistic French traveller thinks that this fact lessens the value of the slave, leads to milder treatment, and will finally convince people of the superiority of free labor.[3] It is said that the Quakers of Rhode Island encouraged slaves to escape over the border into Massachusetts, and became particularly odious to the slave-holders on that account.[4] After the pas-sage of the Fugitive Slave Act but little seems to have been done to execute it. Public sentiment in Massachusetts is said to have been so strong against it that it would be very rarely that a slave could not escape his master's pursuit.[5] On the first attempt to enforce the law in Boston, the constables were overthrown and the slave escaped through the opening ranks of the audience without waiting to hear the end of the speech which his counsel, Josiah Quincy, was making in his defence. An attempt at prosecution for failure to enforce the act was disregarded, and the Fugitive Slave Law was from this time practically void in Massachusetts.[6] Public sentiment in New

145. Diffi-culty of enforcing the act.

---

[1] *Annals of Congress*, 4 Cong., 1 sess., 1084–1085.
[2] Parrish, *Remarks on the Slavery of the Black People*, 12–15, 32.
[3] Brissot, *New Travels in the United States*, I, 230.
[4] La Rochefoucauld-Liancourt, *Travels through the United States*, I, 507.
[5] *Ibid.*, II, 167.   [6] McDougall, *Fugitive Slaves*, § 34.

Hampshire was equally effective; a fugitive from the estate of George Washington was found at Portsmouth in 1796, but could not be returned without danger of serious disturbance, perhaps a mob or a riot, and this the owner was unwilling to occasion.[1]

The difficulties were felt most keenly in the Border States. Here fugitives and kidnappers were both to be found, and appeals for more satisfactory laws or for a stricter execution of those already existing were made by both parties.[2] There was a certain tailor in Philadelphia who used to sit at his window with his work, and whenever he saw in the street a negro who had the appearance of a fugitive, he would rush out to offer his protection and aid him in finding employment.[3] When Philadelphia became the national capital a bill was brought forward in the Pennsylvania Assembly to enable officers of the United States to hold slaves in the State, but the Pennsylvania Abolition Society vigorously opposed it, and it was finally suppressed.[4] A Southern Congressman during this period alludes bitterly to attempts in the Quaker City to beguile servants away from their masters.[5] Ohio also had its share of fugitives, more than a thousand of whom are reported to have been forwarded to Canada before 1817.[6] The Abolition Societies, which were active in securing the liberation of free negroes unlawfully held in bondage, would be inclined to give the negro the benefit of every doubt, and the contests over fugitives and kidnapping must have served more than anything else to keep up the anti-slavery sentiment along the border.

[1] Correspondence of George Washington with Mr. Whipple, Collector of Portsmouth, New Hampshire, Nov. 28 to Dec. 22, 1796, in Charles Sumner, *Works*, III, 177-178; McDougall, *Fugitive Slaves*, § 35.

[2] Brackett, *The Negro in Maryland*, 85; Parrish, *Remarks on the Slavery of the Black People*, 11 ; *Annals of Congress*, 4 Cong., 2 sess., 1730, 1741, 1767; 5 Cong., 2 sess., 656 ff.; 6 Cong., 1 sess., 916, 1034, 1044-1045.

[3] Sutcliffe, *Travels in some Parts of North America*, 76. This tailor he found to be Thomas Harrison, who was a prominent member of the Pennsylvania Abolition Society. *Ibid.* ; Needles, *Hist. Mem. Pa. Soc.*, 28 f.

[4] *Ibid.*, 38-39.

[5] *Annals of Congress*, 1 Cong., 2 sess., 1202. Speech of Mr. Smith of South Carolina.

[6] Birney, *James G. Birney and his Times*, 435.

CHAPTER VI

THE VICTORY OVER THE SLAVE-TRADE, 1783-1808

I N the peace negotiations with Great Britain, at the close of the Revolutionary War, John Jay proposed that British subjects should not be permitted to import slaves into the United States from any part of the world, "it being the intention of the said States entirely to prohibit the importation thereof."[1]   The same year a memorial on the African slave-trade was presented to Congress by the Quakers; but although "the Christian rectitude of the concern" was generally acknowledged, the Congress of the Confederation did not consider itself competent to legislate upon it.[2] Meanwhile the revival of industry at the close of the war led to a great demand for slaves in the Southern market, and Northern traders were not slow to avail themselves of the opportunity.   The trade flourished for several years.[3]   Massachusetts, among the first to extend the blessings of liberty over her own soil, did not prohibit the slave-trade until 1788,[4] and supplementary legislation was required in

146. Condition under the Confederation, 1783-1789.

[1] DuBois, *Suppression of the African Slave-Trade*, 133; Sparks, *Diplomatic Correspondence*, X, 154.

[2] Mifflin, *Defence against Aspersions*, 18; *Journal of the United States in Congress Assembled*, 1783, pp. 418-419, 425.

[3] DuBois, *Suppression of the Slave-Trade*, 49-50.

[4] *Acts and Laws of the Commonwealth of Massachusetts*, 1787-1788, ch. 48 (March 26, 1788).   The occasion which directly led to this act was the kidnapping of three free citizens of Boston who were taken to the West Indies but were recovered through the efforts of Governor Hancock.   The congregational ministers, led by Dr. Belknap, and the negroes, led by Prince Hall, took advantage of the public sentiment aroused on this occasion, and the Act of 1788 was the result.   See above, § 44; *Queries respecting the Slavery and Emancipation of Negroes in Massachusetts*, in 1 *Mass. Hist. Soc. Coll.*, IV, 204-205.   The petition of Prince Hall is printed in *The American Museum*, III, 410-411 (May, 1788).

Pennsylvania,[1] Connecticut,[2] and Rhode Island[3] at about the same time.

Notwithstanding the inefficiency, both moral and constitutional, of the Congress of the Confederation, and the urgent demand for labor and for wealth in a community whose resources had been exhausted by war, the States were gradually falling into line on the question of the slave-trade, and there was a fair promise of its permanent cessation. New Hampshire had never had either slavery or the slave-trade to any extent.[4] New York (1785, 1788)[5] and New Jersey (1786)[6] prohibited the importation of slaves; Delaware, Maryland, and Virginia had already done so;[7] North Carolina laid a prohibitive duty (1786),[8] and South Carolina (1787, 1788) passed acts prohibiting importation for a term of years.[9] In Rhode Island, Pennsylvania, New York, and Delaware, as already in Virginia and Maryland, negroes illegally brought in were to be freed.[10] Acts to limit or prevent exportation from the State became necessary during the process

147. State legislation, 1783-1789.

[1] Passed March 29, 1788. *Laws of the Commonwealth of Pennsylvania*, Dallas, II, 586–590. *Ibid.*, Carey and Bioren, III, ch. 1334, pp. 268–272.

[2] *Acts and Laws of Connecticut*, Hudson and Goodwin, 399–401; *Queries respecting Slavery*, 1 *Mass. Hist. Soc. Coll.*, IV, 205.

[3] *Ibid.*; *Laws of Rhode Island*, October, 1787, pp. 4–5. The Quakers used their influence in Connecticut, Rhode Island, and Massachusetts as well as in Pennsylvania. Fowler, *Historical Status of the Negro in Connecticut*, 125; *Petition of the people called quakers, of New England to the general assembly of the state of Rhode-Island*, in *The American Museum*, III, 127–128; *Laws of Rhode Island*, June, 1787, p. 8; *Queries respecting Slavery*, 1 *Mass. Hist. Soc. Coll.*, IV, 205.

[4] See above, § 127.

[5] DuBois, *Suppression of the Slave-Trade*, Appendices A, B; *Laws of the State of New York*, Gaines, II, 253; *Ibid.* (1886), II, 121 (eighth session, ch. 68, April 12, 1785) and 676 (eleventh session, ch. 40, Feb. 22, 1788).

[6] *Laws of the State of New Jersey*, published in American Convention, *Minutes of Proceedings*, 1797, Appendix, p. 49.

[7] See above, § 82.

[8] *Laws of the State of North Carolina*, Iredell, 577–578. North Carolina repealed this act in 1790, but passed another in 1794. DuBois, *Suppression of the Slave-Trade*, 72 and Appendix A; Martin's *Iredell*, I, 492, II, 53.

[9] *Statutes at Large of South Carolina*, Cooper, V, 38, 91 (March 28, 1787, Nov. 4, 1788).

[10] *Public Laws of the State of Rhode Island*, 607; *Laws of the Commonwealth of Pennsylvania*, Carey and Bioren, II, 269; *Ibid.*, Dallas, II, 586; *Laws of the State of New York* (1886), II, 121, 676; *Laws of the State of Delaware*, II, 886–887, 1323.

of gradual emancipation which was now going on to the north of
Mason and Dixon's Line, and provision against such removal
was made in Rhode Island (1779), Vermont (1786), Delaware
(1787, 1789), Connecticut (1788), New York (1788), Pennsylvania (1788), and New Jersey (1788).[1] Massachusetts also provided against kidnapping (1788).[2]

Thus the tendency of State legislation during the period of
the Confederation was toward a speedy and complete suppression of the slave-trade so far as it related to importation; and in
all but the three Southern States the intention of limiting or
abolishing the institution of slavery was clearly indicated. The
only threatening features were the temporary character of the
prohibitory acts of South Carolina, and the failure of Georgia
to pass any restrictive act whatever.

Side by side with State legislation, the movement toward the
national suppression of the slave-trade had begun. The Fede-
148. The   ral Convention, in 1787, gave a possible opportunity
Federal   for the insertion of another anti-slavery wedge, and
compro-
mises, 1787. on this occasion an anti-slavery society appears for
the first time in the arena of national politics. A memorial
imploring the convention to make the subject of the slave-trade
"a part of their important deliberations" was prepared by the
Pennsylvania Abolition Society, and given to Benjamin Franklin,
the president of the society, to present. It was finally withheld,
however, on account of the expectation that the subject was to
be considered in any case, and the fear that the address might

---

[1] *Laws of Rhode Island*, October, 1779, pp. 6–7; *Statutes of the State of
Vermont* (1787), p. 105 (passed Oct. 30, 1786); *Laws of the State of Delaware*, II, 886–887, 943, 1093–1094, 1323 (Feb. 3, 1787, Feb. 3, 1789, June 14,
1793); *Acts and Laws of the State of Connecticut*, Hudson and Goodwin,
399–401 (1788, 1789, 1792); *Laws of the State of New York* (1886), II, 676;
Ibid., Gaines, II, 253; *Laws of the Commonwealth of Pennsylvania*, Carey
and Bioren, II, 269, 272, Dallas, II, 587; *Laws of the State of New Jersey*,
in American Convention, *Minutes of Proceedings*, 1797, Appendix, p. 51;
Ibid., Paterson, 311. The laws of Delaware limiting importation were tested
in the case of Joseph Sawyer, a slave belonging to Abraham Saunders of
Maryland, who was hired and brought into Delaware by a resident of the
latter State with the knowledge of the owner. In a suit brought in behalf of
the negro, the Court decided (May term, 1790) in favor of the plaintiff, in
accordance with the provision (Feb. 3, 1787) that any negro or mulatto slave
brought into the State "for sale or otherwise" was declared free. *The
American Museum*, VIII, 191–192.

[2] *Laws of the Commonwealth of Massachusetts*, March 26, 1788.

do more harm than good by exciting the suspicions of Southern members.[1] With what results the subject was considered by the convention it is hardly necessary to state here. The threats of South Carolina and Georgia, the truckling avarice of New England, the fear of a rupture at this critical moment, and the illusory hope that years would bring a more convenient season all contributed to the fatal adjustment. A committee appointed at the suggestion of Gouverneur Morris to arrange a compromise on the commercial clauses proposed that the importation of slaves should not be prohibited by Congress before 1800, and that a tax might be laid on importation. The date was changed to 1808, partly by the vote of the New England States; and the clause requiring the assent of two-thirds of the members present in each House for the passage of navigation acts was struck out, as a reward for their complaisance.[2] People flattered themselves that even by this measure slavery was doomed; it was remarked that the temporary reservation of the power of Congress was equivalent to an admission that after 1807 the power should be exercised. "The importation of slaves from any foreign country," says Tench Coxe, "is by a clear implication held up to the world as equally inconsistent with the dispositions and the duties of the people of America. A solid foundation is laid for exploding the principles of negro slavery."[3] Southern defenders of the Constitution took an essentially different view of the clause, and at the North there was enough apprehension to excite considerable opposition, especially in Massachusetts and Pennsylvania; but the urgent need for political unity finally overrode all other considerations.[4]

In Congress the attempts to limit or suppress the African slave-trade appeared in several distinct forms. (1) The simplest and most apparent mode of attack was that suggested in the Constitution, the limitation by a tax not exceeding ten dollars on each person imported. *149. Legislation by Congress.* (2) There was also a general attack, with the purpose of induc-

---

[1] Text in *The American Museum*, III, 404-405; Note by Humanitas, *Ibid.*, 404; Needles, *Hist. Mem. Pa. Soc.*, 30-31.

[2] Elliot's *Debates (The Madison Papers)*, V, 471, 477-478, 489-492.

[3] *Letters on the federal government*, in *The American Museum*, II, 387.

[4] The condition of public sentiment and the attitude of the State conventions are summed up in DuBois, *Suppression of the Slave-Trade*, 62-68.

ing Congress to take any measures against slavery which should not be inconsistent with the Constitution.   (3) The only feasible method which appeared as the outcome of this movement was the opposition to the supply of foreign ports by United States citizens or by vessels fitted out in United States ports. Later, with the organization of the Mississippi Territory and the annexation and organization of Louisiana, came (4) the attempt to prohibit importation into the Territories. Finally, when the prescribed interval had expired, Congress enacted (5) the prohibition of importation from Africa.

An attempt to limit importation by a tax on each negro imported was made before Congress had been many days in session. In the House Committee of the Whole on the Impost Bill, May 13, 1789, after "looking-glasses and brushes" had been added to the list of dutiable articles, Mr. Parker of Virginia moved that a tax of ten dollars a head should be laid on the importation of slaves.[1] The debate was a warm one. Mr. Jackson of Georgia was the only man who attempted to defend either slavery or the slave-trade;[2] but there was considerable opposition to the tax on the ground that it was partial in its operation and therefore oppressive to particular States, and that the act of taxation would give an appearance of countenancing the traffic and would degrade human beings by classing them as merchandise.[3]

150. Attempt to limit by taxation. Mr. Parker's Resolution.

The advocates of the measure argued that this degradation of human beings was the result not of the tax but of the trade;[4] the tax, they said, had been intended by the framers of the Constitution, and would now be regarded as an expression of national disapprobation and of a desire to limit the trade as far as possible. It was unfortunate that the trade had been allowed, but this act would at any rate tend to diminish it and was better than no action at all. The national character, they argued, was at stake on this question; and it was necessary to do all that was possible "to restore to human nature its inher-

---

[1] *Annals of Congress*, 1 Cong., 1 sess., 336.

[2] *Ibid.*, 336–338.

[3] *Ibid.* Speeches of Mr. Sherman of Connecticut and Mr. Ames of Massachusetts.

[4] *Ibid.*, 339. Speech of Mr. Madison of Virginia.

ent privileges," to give evidence of the sincerity of their recent professions, and to " wipe off the stigma " that rested upon the republic.[1]   The national prosperity, too, they continued, was involved in the issue; an expression of disapprobation now, by helping to destroy the trade, would save posterity from " the imbecility ever attendant on a country filled with slaves."   It would be a benefit even to the States which now opposed the tax, for every addition they received to their number of slaves tended to weaken and render them less capable of self-defence, was a means of inviting attack in foreign war and a danger to themselves and to the Union.[2]

The strongest expressions of anti-slavery sentiment came from Virginia, and the representatives of New England, although avowing a virtuous detestation of slavery, sided with their political ally in the South in opposition to the tax.   Mr. Parker's resolution was finally dropped in deference to those who had expressed their abhorrence of ranking human beings as merchandise, and Mr. Parker was placed on a committee to bring in a separate bill.[3]   The bill, however, was not brought in until late in the session, was then postponed until the next session of Congress,[4] and was never heard of again.

Anti-slavery sentiment in the national councils may next be considered in connection with the memorials presented to Congress, February 11 and 12, 1790.   Two of these memorials, from the Yearly Meetings of Friends in Philadelphia and New York, confined themselves strictly to the subject of the slave-trade.   The third, from the Pennsylvania Abolition Society, although suggesting national legislation against slavery itself, was especially directed against the slave-trade.[5]   All, however, were regarded by Southern members as attacks upon slavery and the slave States and "upon the palladium of the property of our country." [6]   The opposition was much more violent than in the case of the resolutions for an impost duty.   Mr. Jackson of Georgia de-

151. Anti-slavery memorials, 1790.

---

[1] *Annals of Congress*, 1 Cong., 1 sess., 336–337.   Speeches of Mr. Parker of Virginia.

[2] *Ibid.*, 340.   Speech of Mr. Madison.

[3] *Ibid.*, 341–342, 366.

[4] *Ibid.*, 903.

[5] *Ibid.*, 1 Cong., 2 sess., 1182–1184, 1197–1198.

[6] *Ibid.*, 1187, 1202, 1453.   Speeches of Mr. Jackson of Georgia and Mr. Smith of South Carolina.

clared that the abolition of the slave-trade by national act would show " a disposition towards a total emancipation," and undertook to defend slavery on scriptural grounds.[1] Mr. Smith of South Carolina also defended slavery at some length, asserting its necessity and depicting the evils of emancipation.[2] Both violently attacked the Quakers.

The friends as well as the opponents of the memorials were inclined to consider their broader significance. Mr. Scott of Pennsylvania said that the legislature might be able to go no further than to impose a tax of ten dollars; but if he were one of the judges of the United States, and the negroes came before him to claim their liberty, he did not know how far he might go, but was certain he should go as far as he could.[3] Mr. Boudinot of New Jersey made a vigorous anti-slavery speech, illustrating his remarks by the story of the Israelites in Egypt, and exclaiming that the Almighty Power that accomplished their deliverance is the same yesterday, to-day, and forever. He pleaded the principles of the Revolution and the genius of the government as well as the spirit and precepts of Christianity[4] Mr. Gerry of Massachusetts suggested the possibility of emancipation by the purchase of the Southern slaves from the proceeds of the Western land sales.[5]

The Memorials were committed February 12, 1790, and were reported by the committee (March 5).[6] Warner Mifflin, the Quaker philanthropist, was at that time in New York for the purpose of supporting the memorial of the Philadelphia Yearly Meeting, and the report of the committee was in accordance with suggestions offered by him.[7] By the adoption of this report (March 23, 1790), Congress declared that they had a right to regulate or interdict the African slave-trade when carried on by United States citizens for the supply of foreigners, and also that they had authority to prohibit foreigners from fitting out vessels in United States ports for transporting persons from Africa to foreign ports.[8]

152. Resolutions of Congress.

[1] *Annals of Congress*, 1 Cong., 2 sess., 1187.
[2] *Ibid.*, 1453–1464.
[3] *Ibid.*, 1199–1200.
[4] *Ibid.*, 1466–1471.
[5] *Ibid.*, 1204.
[6] *Ibid.*, 1205, 1413.
[7] See above, § 106.
[8] Report of the committee in *Annals of Congress*, 1 Cong., 2 sess., 1414–1415. Report as amended, *Ibid.*, 1474.

It was, therefore, toward the suppression of these features of the African slave-trade that the anti-slavery party next turned its attention. The results appear in the memorials of the Abolition Societies, presented December 8, 1791. These memorials were based on the resolutions on the slave-trade which had been adopted the previous year, and united in praying that Congress would exercise its powers by putting these resolutions into effect. Several of the memorialists took advantage of the opportunity to express their sentiments with regard to slavery. Nearly all of them alluded to the principles of the American Revolution and to the incongruity of slavery in a land which based her own liberty on the rights of man. The Connecticut Society also expressed the desire that Congress would do all it consistently could to check the progress of slavery and to alleviate the condition of the slaves while the institution existed.[1]

153. Memorials of Abolition Societies.

The memorials were referred to a committee (December 8, 1791) appointed by Nathaniel Macon of North Carolina, then Speaker of the House,[2] and composed of men either indifferent or hostile to the purpose of the petitioners. They were never reported by the committee, but their influence did not end here. They were published by the Pennsylvania Society in 1792, and were followed up by a second memorial from the Society of Massachusetts and Rhode Island (the Providence Society), which was laid on the table (February 22, 1793).[3] A correspondence then arose among the societies which resulted in the appointment of delegates for a convention at Philadelphia.[4] This convention met primarily for the purpose of preparing a joint address to Congress on the neglected subject of the foreign slave-trade, and though it at once announced its interest in the abolition of slavery[5] the memorial to Congress was rigidly limited to the trade to foreign ports and the equipment of foreign vessels in the ports of the United States.[6] A petition on the same subject from the New

154. Memorial of the American Convention, 1794.

---

[1] *Memorials presented to Congress by the societies instituted for promoting the abolition of slavery.*

[2] *Annals of Congress,* 2 Cong., 1 sess., 241.

[3] *Ibid.,* 2 Cong., 2 sess., 888–889.

[4] See above, § 113. [5] See above, § 116.

[6] American Convention, *Minutes of Proceedings,* 1794, pp. 26–29; *Annals of Congress,* 3 Cong., 1 sess., 38–39.

England Yearly Meeting of the Society of Friends had been coldly received in the Senate (January 21), but in the House was referred to a select committee (January 20–21). That of the Convention of Delegates from the Abolition Societies and a separate address from the Providence Society, which had not been represented at the convention, were referred to the same committee (January 28).[1]

In Congress, during these years, some of the Southern members had been greatly exasperated by the presentation of such memorials. The cautious but persistent conduct of the Abolition Societies, however, now won a more friendly response. A bill providing against the slave-trade to foreign ports and the equipment of foreign vessels for the slave-trade in United States ports was passed by the House (March 7) and subsequently by the Senate (March 19).[2]

155. Act limiting the foreign slave-trade, 1794.

The movement against the foreign slave-trade differs in several respects from the attempt to restrict importation by a tax. Both were intended to express the national disapprobation of the trade as an infringement of the rights of man and the principles of the federal government, as inconsistent and unchristian, unjust and impolitic. There are the same attempts to distinguish between slavery and the slave-trade, with occasional lapses which show how intimately the two were connected; the same suspicions on the part of the slave-holders that every attempt to limit the trade is part of a deep-laid scheme for total abolition. But the prohibition of the foreign trade, while it touched more slightly the interests or the sensibilities of the Southern element, appealed more powerfully to the sensibilities of the anti-slavery party than did the limitation by a ten-dollar tax. Those who felt or professed a reluctance to stain the national coffers with the price of human liberty could have nothing to say in favor of the sacrifice of liberty involved in the West India trade. This was a cause, too, which involved no moral compromise, and perhaps it was for this reason that Quakers and Abolition Societies ignored the right of Congress to lay a tax on importation and concentrated their efforts upon the foreign trade.

156. Character of this movement.

---

[1] *Annals of Congress*, 3 Cong., 1 sess., 36, 249–250, 253, 349.
[2] *Ibid.*, 3 Cong., Appendix, p. 1425. Approved March 22.

The attempt at limitation by a tax was therefore carried on chiefly or solely within the halls of Congress, while the movement against the foreign trade originated and developed outside that body. The latter, from beginning to end, was carried on by means of petitions and memorials addressed to Congress. The American Convention and the various societies of which it was composed, the Quakers and, a little later, the free blacks, all had a part in it. The anti-slavery men in Congress, on the other hand, seem to have had comparatively little to say on the subject. The act limiting the foreign slave-trade was apparently carried through with little difficulty, and diatribes against slavery were perhaps withheld from motives of prudence.

It was not long before a new national question loomed upon the view. This was the territorial question, more closely connected with slavery than with the slave-trade, but appearing also in connection with importation. The prohibition from importing foreign slaves directly into the Territories was regarded with special favor by South Carolina, though importation into the Territo- 157. Attempt to prevent importation into the Mississippi Territory.
ries from within the United States by way of South Carolina and Georgia was a different matter. March 26, 1798, while the bill for the organization of the Mississippi Territory was under consideration, Mr. Harper of South Carolina introduced an amendment against importing slaves from any place without the limits of the United States. Mr. Thatcher of Massachusetts moved to strike out the words " without the limits of the United States "; but his motion was not seconded, and the bill passed with Mr. Harper's amendment (March 27).[1]

Meanwhile the temporary prohibitions of South Carolina, although evaded, were renewed from time to time.[2] Georgia prohibited importation in 1793, and her Constitution, adopted in 1798, contained a provision 158. State legislation, 1789–1807.
against the further importation of slaves from places outside

---

[1] *Annals of Congress*, 5 Cong., 2 sess., 1313, 1318.

[2] DuBois, *Suppression of the Slave-Trade*, Appendix B ; *Statutes at Large of South Carolina*, Cooper and McCord, V, 204, 248, 330, 377, 380, 397, VII, 430, 431 f., 434–436, 444, 447. Mr. Lowndes of South Carolina defended the repeal of the State prohibitory act in 1803 on the ground that South Carolina had been unable to enforce the law and had had no help from Congress. *Ibid.*, 8 Cong., 1 sess., 992.

the United States.[1]   For a few years the increase of slavery by
foreign importation was apparently at an end.   By this time,
however, Virginia began to show interest in the inter-state trade.
Her opposition to the foreign trade had been for some years
open to suspicion.   By an act passed January 21, 1801, the illegally imported negro, instead of being freed, was to be removed
from the State, if possible, at the expense of the importer or of
the holder of the slave; otherwise he was to be sold to pay the
cost of his removal from the State.[2]   A few years later the law
went one step farther, the negro being forfeited to the overseers
of the poor, by whom he was to be sold, the proceeds going
to lessen the poor rates (January 25, 1806).[3]   The prohibitory
acts of other States, North and South, were continually evaded;[4]
and the annexation of Louisiana led to the reopening of the
ports of South Carolina (December 17, 1803) and the practical
nullification of the anti-slave-trade clause in the Georgia Constitution.[5]   It was now evident that the slave-trade would continue long if it were left to State legislation to suppress it.

Efforts for national action, however, were steadily continued.
The Act of 1794 was evaded; and the American Convention of
Delegates, in letters to the Secretaries of State and
of the Treasury, urged a more rigorous execution of
the law.[6]   January 2, 1800, was presented to Congress a petition on this subject, from the free blacks
of Philadelphia, praying for the revision of the laws on the
slave-trade and on fugitives.[7]   This petition aroused a discussion
even more lively than was usual on such occasions;[8] but a committee had already been appointed to consider the revision of
the Act of 1794,[9] and to this committee the part of the petition

*159. Amend-
ment of the
act limiting
the foreign
slave-trade.*

[1] DuBois, *Suppression of the Slave-Trade*, Appendix B; Poore, *Federal
and State Constitutions*, I, 395 (art. iv, § 11).

[2] *Statutes at Large of Virginia*, Hening, II, 301.

[3] *Ibid.*, 2d Series, III, 252.

[4] See above, §§ 119-121.   DuBois, *Suppression of the Slave-Trade*,
85-86; Humanitas, *Reflections on Slavery*, 18-31.

[5] DuBois, *Suppression of the Slave-Trade*, 86 f.; *Statutes at Large of
South Carolina*, VII, 449.

[6] *Cf.* §§ 119, 120, above.   American Convention, *Minutes of Proceedings*
1797, pp. 24-25, 7-8, 18-20.

[7] *Annals of Congress*, 6 Cong., 1 sess., 229-230.

[8] *Ibid.*, 230-245.   See also § 126.

[9] *Annals of Congress*, 6 Cong., 1 sess., 199, 200.

regarding the slave-trade was finally referred.[1] The result was an act which considerably strengthened the former act,[2] though the Abolition Societies still found occasion for activity and continued to make exertions for the capture and trial of offenders.[3] Some years later a memorial was presented to Congress by the American Convention (February 7 and 13, 1806), requesting still further amendment. This was referred to a committee,[4] but the time for a possible prohibition of the trade was now so near that the subject was allowed to drop.

After the failure of Mr. Parker's resolution, the impost measure slept for nearly fifteen years; but the challenge sent forth by South Carolina in reopening her ports to the trade in 1803 met with a prompt response. This time (January 6, 1804) it was Mr. Bard of Pennsylvania who offered the resolution,[5] and its chief supporters were not from Virginia but from the Middle States; New England took little part in the debate.[6] Mr. Bard's resolution was adopted after considerable discussion, and a bill was brought in (February 16) and referred to the Committee of the Whole House; but its passage was postponed until March, by a vote of 56 to 50, in order to give South Carolina an opportunity to repeal her recent act, and so the measure quietly dropped out of sight.[7] The subject, however, was revived in the next session (February 8, 1805) by Mr. Southard of New Jersey,[8] and the following session (December 10, 1805) by Mr. Sloan of the same State.[9] Delay was still urged in order that South Carolina might take advantage of the long neglected opportunity for repeal.[10] Mr. Sloan's resolution reached the stage of a bill (January 27, 1806) and even a third reading, but then disappeared by recommitment.[11] Mr. Southard's had not even gone through the form of a debate.

160. Revival of the impost measure.

---

[1] *Annals of Congress*, 6 Cong., 1 sess., 229, 244–245.

[2] *Ibid.*, 668, 676, 686–690, 697, 699, 1512–1513. Approved May 10, 1800.

[3] See above, § 120.

[4] *Annals of Congress*, 9 Cong., 1 sess., 445, 92. Text in 9 Cong., 2 sess., Appendix, 992–993.

[5] *Ibid.*, 8 Cong., 1 sess., 820.

[6] *Ibid.*, 991–1036 (February 14–17).

[7] *Ibid.*, 1020, 1021, 1035–1036

[8] *Ibid.*, 8 Cong., 2 sess., 1189.

[9] *Ibid.*, 9 Cong., 1 sess., 272, 273.

[10] *Ibid.*, 274.

[11] *Ibid.*, 346–352, 358–375, 397, 434–440, 442–444.

The debates on the resolutions of Mr. Bard and Mr. Sloan were similar to those of 1789. The chief objects of the tax were said to be a public expression of disapprobation of the trade and the preservation of the character of the republic.[1] The argument from the political dangers of slavery was emphasized by recent events in St. Domingo ;[2] and the injuries to the industry and the wealth of the country, to arts, science, and manufactures, and to the condition of the laboring classes were dealt with at considerable length.[3] There were one or two attempts to propitiate the sensitive Southern element by explaining that the remarks of the speakers were directed not against slavery, but against the trade ;[4] but from neither North nor South was there any defence of either. Mr. Mitchell of New York spoke of slavery as "a dark spot on some members of the national body, which was spreading wider, turning blacker, and threatening a gangrene all around."[5] Mr. Macon of North Carolina regarded it as an evil which no one regretted more than himself, but to which it was necessary to submit until an adequate cure could be found.[6] All agreed in reprobation of the conduct of South Carolina and in the desire to put a stop to the slave-trade,[7] but opinions differed as to the effects of the measure proposed.

The arguments of the opposition were directed against drawing revenue from an act that rivets the chains of slavery on any of the human race, against staining the national coffers with the price of liberty, and against pointing "the finger of scorn" at a sister State.[8] It was also urged that as South

(margin note: 161. Debates on the resolutions, 1804–1806.)

---

[1] *Annals of Congress*, 8 Cong., 1 sess., 994–995. Speech of Mr. Bard of Pennsylvania.

[2] *Ibid.*, 1003, speech of Mr. Mitchell of New York, and 996, speech of Mr. Bard.

[3] *Ibid.*, 996, 1000–1002, 1009. Speeches of Messrs. Bard and Mitchell and of Mr. Lucas of Pennsylvania.

[4] *Ibid*, 1019. Speech of Mr. Southard of New Jersey. *Ibid.*, 9 Cong. 1 sess., 373. Speech of Mr. Broom of Delaware.

[5] *Ibid.*, 8 Cong., 1 sess., 1003.

[6] *Ibid.*, 9 Cong , 1 sess., 361.

[7] See especially the speeches of Messrs. Moore, Huger, and Marion of South Carolina, *Ibid.*, 8 Cong., 1 sess., 1004, 1006–1007, 9 Cong., 1 sess. 347–348 ; also that of Mr. Macon of North Carolina, *Ibid.*, 361.

[8] *Ibid.*, 8 Cong., 1 sess., 1004, 1005. Speeches by Mr. Moore and Mr Huger ; and 9 Cong., 1 sess., 361, 364, speeches by Mr. Macon and by Mr. Early of Georgia.

Carolina had been unable to execute her previous acts against the slave-trade, the present measure would be worse than useless.[1] Slavery was said to be decreasing in South Carolina, the people of the State were declared to be as desirous as any others of doing away with the institution, and if they were let alone they would of themselves repeal their act.[2] Notwithstanding these flattering promises, however, it is evident that the action of South Carolina in removing her prohibition aroused an anti-slavery sentiment which was becoming somewhat languid ; and the defiance must have done much to promote the passage of the prohibitory act of Congress in 1807.

The same stimulus, no doubt, following so closely upon the annexation of Louisiana, stirred to action the American Convention of Delegates of the Abolition Societies. This assembly addressed a memorial to Congress (presented January 23, 1804) praying for a law prohibiting the importation of slaves into the new Territory.[3] The memorial received little attention. In the Senate it was merely read. In the House it was referred to the committee on the government of Louisiana.[4] A few weeks later Mr. Logan of Pennsylvania gave notice in the Senate (February 18) that he should bring in a bill for a duty on the importation of slaves. A motion to expunge this notice was made two days later, but, though it received only 5 votes against 21, the bill was not brought in.[5] A clause similar to Mr. Harper's amendment for the Mississippi Territory was introduced into the bill for regulating the government of Louisiana, and a motion to strike out the phrase " from any port or place without the limits of the United States " and substitute " for sale," received in the Senate but 6 votes against 22. An attempt to limit to one year the term of servitude of all slaves imported into the Territory from the United States or any American

162. Attempt to prevent importation into the Louisiana Territory.

---

[1] *Annals of Congress*, 8 Cong., 1 sess., 992.

[2] *Ibid.*, 1006–1007, 1013. Speeches of Messrs. Huger of South Carolina and Gregg of Pennsylvania.

[3] See below, § 174.

[4] *Ibid.*, 8 Cong., 1 sess., 238, 940. Text of the memorial, *Ibid.*, 8 Cong., 2 sess., Appendix, pp. 1596–1597.

[5] *Ibid.*, 8 Cong., 1 sess., 256–257. A letter from John Dickinson to Senator Logan, Jan. 30, 1804, was written in support of the memorial. Stillé, *Life of Dickinson*, 324–325.

province or colony was voted down, by a vote of 11 to 17, but a motion prohibiting importation except by citizens of the United States moving into the Territory for actual settlement was passed by a vote of 18 to 11.[1]

A House committee, with John Randolph as chairman, recommended the prohibition of the importation of foreign slaves as "a measure equally dictated by humanity and policy;"[2] but importation from within the United States was finally permitted under a provision granting to Louisiana the same privileges as were enjoyed by the Mississippi Territory (March 2, 1805).[3] The slave-trade of South Carolina was now flourishing. A representative of that State, however, moved (February 7, 1806) a resolution for an inquiry as to what measures might be necessary to prevent the importation of slaves into the Territories.[4] If, as is probable, he meant only the importation directly from foreign ports in evasion of existing laws, his weapon returned upon his own State, for the committee of inquiry reported in favor of a resolution against importing into any of the Territories any slaves thereafter imported into the United States. This resolution was adopted and a bill was brought in and committed to the Whole House (March 27, 1806), but went no farther.[5]

The importation of slaves into the Territories was regarded with a surprising amount of indifference; but the events connected with it were among the influences which brought about the Act prohibiting the Slave-Trade in 1807, and it was probably the anticipation of this act that caused much of the lethargy and apparent indifference of the preceding years. It was believed that the time for action had not yet come and that the prohibitory law soon to be enacted would be all-sufficient.

163. Anticipation of a prohibitory act.

There were symptoms of uneasiness, however, from the time of the South Carolina repeal, and pressure was brought to bear upon Congress some time before that body could fairly be expected to take action. Early in 1805 the legislature of

[1] *Annals of Congress*, 8 Cong., 1 sess., 240–244.

[2] *Ibid.*, 8 Cong., 2 sess., 1016.

[3] *Ibid.*, Appendix, 1674–1675.

[4] *Ibid.*, 9 Cong. 1 sess., 445.   Speech of Mr. Williams.

[5] *Ibid.*, 473, 522, 878.

Massachusetts passed a resolution instructing their senators and requesting their representatives in the national legislature to take measures for a constitutional amendment which should empower Congress to prohibit the importation of slaves from Africa, the West Indies, and other places to the United States or any part thereof, whenever they should consider it expedient.[1] It is claimed by a representative from North Carolina that such a measure was suggested by his State to the legislatures of the other States immediately after the South Carolina repeal.[2] Massachusetts was followed in 1806 by the legislatures of Vermont and New Hampshire, which proposed a constitutional amendment prohibiting importation or empowering Congress to do so.[3] Similar resolutions were soon after adopted by the legislatures of Maryland and Ohio.[4]

In the Senate Mr. Bradley of Vermont, December 16, 1805, introduced a bill to prohibit the slave-trade after January 1, 1808, but after a second reading further consideration was postponed until the first Monday of the following December.[5] February 4, 1806, while Mr. Sloan's bill in favor of a tax of ten dollars was before the House, Mr. Bidwell of Massachusetts moved to limit the tax to the period before January 1, 1808, and offered another amendment prohibiting the trade after that date.[6] Nothing was really accomplished, however, until the opening of the session of 1806–1807, when President Jefferson introduced the subject in his Message to Congress, December 2, 1806.[7] The part of the Message relating to the slave-trade was referred to a select committee of the House, who brought in a bill.[8] In the Senate Mr. Bradley of Vermont gave notice that he should bring in a bill on the subject and it was this bill with amendments which finally became law.[9] It is a happy coincidence that the State

164. Introduction of the bill.

---

[1] *Annals of Congress*, 8 Cong., 2 sess., 1221–1222. *Acts and Laws of the Commonwealth of Massachusetts*, 1804–1805, pp. 348–349.

[2] *Annals of Congress*, 9 Cong., 1 sess., 360.

[3] *Ibid.*, 343–344, 448 (January 20 and February 10).

[4] *Ibid.*, 229 (April 7, 1806) and 9 Cong., 2 sess., 32 (Jan. 15, 1807).

[5] *Ibid.*, 9 Cong., 1 sess., 20–21.

[6] *Ibid.*, 434, 436–438.

[7] *Ibid.*, 9 Cong., 2 sess., 14.

[8] *Ibid.*, 113–114, 151.

[9] *Ibid.*, 16, 19, 33, 36, 45–46, 47, 68–71, 79, 87, 93–94.

which had been first to emancipate its slaves led also in the prohibition of the slave-trade.

The House Bill was debated at considerable length and with great warmth of feeling.[1] The two chief difficulties were (a) the penalty to the importer and (b) the disposal of the cargo. By the committee who reported the bill, the crime was regarded as felony, to be punished with death. An amendment was offered changing the nature of the crime to a " high misdemeanor " and the penalty to imprisonment for from five to ten years.[2] This amendment was supported by the plea that the nature of the crime was not sufficiently serious to justify the extreme penalty, and that the law would be utterly ineffectual under such severe conditions.[3] It was said that no one would inform against the slave-trader, that " it would cost him more than his life is worth; "[4] it was argued also that the importer, if brought into court, might plead that judge and jury in holding slaves were equally criminal with himself.[5] The South, it was said, did not look upon slavery as a crime but only as a political evil, and a large majority of the people did not even regard it as an evil. How then could they consent to execute such a law? It would be broken every day of their lives.[6]

In opposition to the amendment it was urged that the crime was worse than piracy or forgery, since a crime against liberty is more serious than a crime against property.[7] One member satirically proposed that the importer himself should be enslaved.[8] It was declared that if the South were sincere in her objections to the slave-trade the law could and would be executed, and that the death penalty would put an end to the trade. The importers were assumed to be Northern men, and the South was assured that it need feel no compunctions about

Marginal note: 165. Debate on the bill. (a) The penalty.

[1] Text of the House Bill, *Annals of Congress*, 9 Cong., 2 sess., 167–168. Debate, *Ibid.*, 168–179, 180–190, 200–203, 220–228, 231–244, 254, 264–267, 270–273.

[2] *Ibid.*, 231.

[3] *Ibid.*, 235–239. Speeches of Messrs. Elmer of New Jersey, Lloyd of Maryland, Early of Georgia, and Holland of North Carolina.

[4] *Ibid.*, 238. Speech of Mr. Early.

[5] *Ibid.*, 239. Speech of Mr. Holland.

[6] *Ibid.*, 238–239. Speech of Mr. Early.

[7] *Ibid.*, 228. Speech of Mr. Hastings of Massachusetts.

[8] *Ibid.*, 243. Speech of Mr. Barker of Massachusetts.

informing against them. As for the great body of people at the North, said one member from that region, "so far from charging their Southern brethren with cruelty or severity in hanging them, they would acknowledge the favor with gratitude."[1] It was urged also that the South would inform out of "a regard to their own lives, and the lives of their posterity."[2] But when the question was finally put (December 31), the death penalty was struck out by a vote of 63 to 53, and imprisonment for from five to ten years was substituted. In the bill as finally passed the penalty was increased by a fine.[3]

The disposal of the cargo was a still more difficult question; the committee proposed simply forfeiture; the opponents of this clause regarded it as assuming a right of prop- (*b*) Disposal erty in the imported negroes, and as implying that of the cargo. the negroes would afterwards be sold, thus establishing a monopoly of the slave-trade by the national government and recognizing slavery to an extent never before known in the national laws or constitution.[4] The title to the slave would in this case be given directly by the United States, and it was hoped that the national government would never degrade itself by selling human beings as merchandise.[5] It would be equally effective, it was thought, and more in consonance with the truth, to state that the importer had no property rights in the case.[6]

The supporters of the original proposition declared that forfeiture was the only practicable method, that otherwise slaves would be smuggled in from East Florida or Mobile, and that although the South would gladly put an end to the "nefarious traffic" she would never consent to the introduction of free blacks.[7] It might be cruel to sell them, but would it not be more cruel to place them in a position where it would be neces-

[1] *Annals of Congress*, 9 Cong., 2 sess., 232–234. Speeches of Messrs. Tallmadge and Moseley of Connecticut.

[2] *Ibid.*, 241. Speech of Mr. Dwight of Connecticut.

[3] *Ibid.*, 243–244, 483–484.

[4] *Ibid.*, 170, 200–202. Speeches of Mr. Smilie of Pennsylvania, Mr. Bidwell of Massachusetts, and others.

[5] *Ibid.*, 227–228. Speech of Mr. Hastings.

[6] *Ibid.*, 220–221. Speech of Mr. Bidwell.

[7] *Ibid.*, 169, 174, 185, 203, 225. Speeches of Mr. Early of Georgia and others.

sary to " get rid of them "?   If they were allowed their freedom,
said Mr. Early of Georgia, " not one of them would be left alive
in a year."[1]   An attempt was made to simplify the question by
considering forfeiture as a preliminary stage and the later disposition of the cargo as a distinct matter.   Mr. Quincy of
Massachusetts summed up the situation by declaring that all
were agreed in wishing to stop the importation, and that it was
evidently impracticable to introduce free blacks into the Southern States; it would be possible, however, he thought, to
accept the proposition of forfeiture and to trust to the wisdom
and justice of the national government to make suitable provision for the negroes thus placed in its hands.[2]   Without the
assumption of forfeiture, said another member, how could the
United States claim jurisdiction over the negroes, even to bind
them out as apprentices?[3]   And to leave them to the tender
mercies of the States to which they were imported, urges Mr.
Quincy, is the same as condemning them to slavery outright.[4]
The principles of those opposing the proposition of the committee were denied by none, he says, but forfeiture is the only
practicable method.[5]   Thus, as so often in the history of the
slavery question, principle gave way to what was regarded as
practicable, and with the usual results.   The amendment opposing forfeiture was lost by a vote of 36 to 63 (December 29), and
a similar measure was lost a few days later (January 7, 1807)
by a vote of 39 to 77.[6]

Now came the opportunity for the national government to
fulfil the hopes of those optimists who had trusted in its wisdom and justice to make suitable provision for the helpless
beings placed in its hands; but the Southern members next
insisted that the negroes should be sold by the United States.[7]
Mr. Sloan of New Jersey had wished that they might be declared free as soon as they set foot on American soil, as was
the case in England, but as this seemed out of the question he

[1] *Annals of Congress*, 9 Cong., 2 sess., 174.

[2] *Ibid.*, 221–224.

[3] *Ibid.*, 226. Speech of Mr. Cook.

[4] *Ibid.*, 184. Some Southern members also doubted the expediency of
leaving the fate of the negroes to State regulations. *Ibid.*, 203.

[5] *Ibid.*, 222. Speech of Mr. Quincy of Massachusetts.

[6] *Ibid.*, 228, 264.

[7] *Ibid.*, 266.

proposed that only those brought to the free States should be immediately declared free, and others should be transported back to Africa or bound out as apprentices. A few days later he proposed that those brought to the Southern States should be declared free and suitably cared for until they should be transported back to Africa or removed to the free States, where they should be bound out for a term of years.[1] The Southern members, however, failed to find any satisfaction in these devices; they declared that no information would be given; that the national government, now by the principle of forfeiture becoming a slave-owner itself, would be subject to the State laws which required the immediate sale of the negroes, and that any provision other than sale would affect the rights of property.[2] The amendment against sale was finally lost, on a vote of 60 to 60, by the casting vote of the Speaker, Nathaniel Macon of North Carolina (January 7).[3] The bill was now recommitted to a committee of seventeen, including one member from each State, which reported January 20. It was then referred to the Committee of the Whole House.[4] By this time the Senate Bill was nearly ready for the third reading. It was sent down January 28, and was also referred to the Committee of the Whole.[5] The questions of penalty and disposal of the cargo were still the main points of discussion. The proposal of the Senate against enslavement of the persons imported, somewhat more definitely stated than by Mr. Sloan, was finally lost, and the final arrangement left the imported negroes subject to future regulations of the States and Territories into which they were brought.[6]

At the last moment came the question of the domestic slave-trade, through an amendment to the Senate Bill, introduced in

---

[1] *Annals of Congress*, 9 Cong., 2 sess., 168, 226, 254. The plan for apprenticeship was favored by Mr. Pitkin of Connecticut, p. 186, Mr. Findley of Pennsylvania, p. 220, and Mr. Fisk of Vermont, p. 225. Mr. Smilie of Pennsylvania was willing that the negroes should be sent back to Africa, and Mr. Macon of North Carolina thought this suggestion a good one, but doubted if it were practicable. *Ibid.*, 170, 176–177.

[2] *Ibid.*, 266.

[3] *Ibid.*

[4] *Ibid.*, 270–274, 373.

[5] *Ibid.*, 16–47, 427.

[6] *Ibid.*, 1266–1270 (Appendix); *Laws of the United States*, 9 Cong., 2 sess., ch. lxvii, pp. 262–272. Approved March 2, 1807.

the House by Mr. Early of Georgia, relating to transportation from one part of the United States to another.[1] The Senate

(c) The domestic slave-trade. refused to concur in the amendment, and a committee of conference was appointed which finally forbade transportation of slaves coastwise in vessels of less than forty tons, with a view to sale.[2] This limitation called forth violent opposition from Southern members of the House, especially from Mr. Randolph of Virginia, who declared that the clause might some time be made the pretext for universal emancipation, that it affected the rights of property and "went to blow up the Constitution in ruins." If disunion should ever occur, he said, the line of separation would be between the slave-holding and the non-slave-holding States. He despaired of ever getting any help against the slaves from the Northern States. All that he asked was that they should remain neutral and not erect themselves into an abolition society.[3] His excitement over this feature of the bill is significant of the new attitude which Virginia was taking at this time, indicated also by her own legislation with regard to the slave-trade.[4] After this, an expression of anti-slavery sentiment is seldom found in Virginia, and that usually in comparatively humble quarters.

In the debates whose history has here been traced, no genuine anti-slavery sentiment has been found to the south of Vir-

166. Signifi-cance of the debates, 1789-1807. ginia. There are apologies and regrets and palliations, but the institution is evidently there to stay. Objections to slavery, such as there are, are based not on justice or humanity or the rights of man, not on any feeling for the negro, whatever may have existed in the heart of an individual owner, but solely on the sense of danger. There seems to have been little if any appreciation of the economic disadvantages of slavery. At the same time, slavery is not yet regarded as a positive good: it is only by many not considered an evil; and while reflecting men apprehend that "incalculable evils" may arise from it, " few, very few, consider it as a crime."[5] From the Border States, Delaware and Maryland,

---

[1] *Annals of Congress*, 9 Cong., 2 sess., 484.
[2] *Ibid.*, 501, 527–528, 621, 626.   [3] *Ibid.*, 626–627, 636–637.
[4] See above, § 158.
[5] *Annals of Congress*, 9 Cong., 2 sess., 238. Speech of Mr. Early.

little of a decided character is heard on either side of the question. Of those to the north, Pennsylvania, New Jersey, and Massachusetts are the most conspicuous, and the attitude in these States is distinctly a moral one. Congressmen allude to the sentiments of their constituents as " so repugnant to slavery that no consideration whatever could induce them to give it their sanction." [1] They refuse to consider the prohibition of the slave-trade as a purely commercial question or one merely of political expediency. It is to them a question of the rights of nations and of humanity. Morality, says Theodore Dwight of Connecticut, is concerned in the question, and has long been eager to proscribe the trade.[2]

The direct results of the crusade against the slave-trade were less satisfactory than they appeared at the time. If the Southern members had really expected that the trade would be entirely suppressed by the Act of 1807, they would hardly have been so apprehensive of the disposition to be made of the negroes after forfeiture. The law was in fact continually evaded,[3] and the abandonment of the cargo to State regulations was of course utterly opposed to the principles upon which the prohibition was supposed to be based. Worst of all, the act served to quiet the public conscience and to give room for an impression that slavery would gradually disappear in the wake of the slave-trade. The troubles with England, following so closely on this event, occupied men's minds so fully that the question was probably allowed to drop more easily than it would otherwise have been; and by the time the war was over King Cotton had established himself on the throne of slavery and could not be easily disturbed.

167. Results of the movement.

In regard to the Territories, the prohibition of importation from outside the United States must be considered of less importance than the failure to prohibit importation from within its limits; for the new lands of the Southwest still furnished the much needed outlet for the expansion of slavery, and gave a stimulus to the revival and continuance of the slave-trade.

The movement against the foreign slave-trade, however, though its direct results were of no great importance, accom-

---

[1] *Annals of Congress*, 9 Cong., 2 sess., 265.

[2] *Ibid.*, 241.

[3] DuBois, *Suppression of the Slave Trade*, 108 ff.

plished much more than its immediate object. It aroused the Abolition Societies to something beyond their local interests and gave them greater breadth of purpose; it united them in a common cause, and led to the formation of an association which continued its activity until a new era of State and national anti-slavery societies for which the earlier societies had prepared the way; above all, it furnished a legitimate outlet for anti-slavery energy in connection with a national cause. Cut off from interference with the importation or emancipation of slaves or even with the regulation of their treatment in the several States, the national conscience might have gone to sleep for almost a score of years had it not been for this opportunity. It was in fact the " entering wedge " for the anti-slavery sentiment behind it.

CHAPTER VII

CHECK TO ANTI-SLAVERY ON THE TERRITORIAL QUESTION, 1783–1808

LIMITATION of slavery by national authority was not seriously contemplated during the period now under consideration. There were no such stirring appeals for general emancipation as those of Samuel Hopkins and John Dickinson, which appeared in the years of the Revolutionary War.[1] The confederation was too inadequate to its own problems to attempt to assert power in a question involving such additional difficulties. The Federal Convention, although anti-slavery speeches were not wanting, did nothing to restrict slavery; and it added to the Constitution several distinct acknowledgments that slavery existed. The federal ratio of representation became a motive for the preservation and extension of slavery, because, as Gouverneur Morris said, it gave the slave-holder votes in proportion to his inhumanity.[2] On the other hand the federal ratio compromise led to a political jealousy in the free States, which found utterance in anti-slavery speeches[3] and anti-slavery writings;[4] its existence intensified the feeling against slavery, and it came to be regarded as one of the reasons why slavery should be limited in territorial area, if it could not be altogether extinguished. So, too, the very weakness of the efforts for national emancipation, due to the feeling that the regulation of slavery was a matter concerning the individual States and not a national affair, left to anti-slavery sentiment the regulation of the Territories as the only possible outlet for activity.

Here, however, was a matter of distinctly national interest, and one which fell naturally into the hands of Congress, whose

> 168. Conditions. Difficulty of national limitation of slavery.

[1] See above, §§ 62, 69, 72, 73.

[2] Elliot, *Debates on the Adoption of the Federal Constitution*, V, 392–393.

[3] *E. g.*, Speeches of S. W. Dana of Connecticut, in *Annals of Congress*, 7 Cong., 1 sess., 927, 1073, 1290.

[4] See below, §§ 182, 183.

power in this direction was to be denied only by the ingenious subterfuges of a later generation; and here was a promising field of action for the anti-slavery sentiment of the day. The western land-cessions from New York (1781), Virginia (1784), Massachusetts (1784), and Connecticut (1786) necessitated national regulation of the territory which was now the national domain, and the lands in the Southwest were likely soon to follow. In this vast region, then, the opponents of slavery at once perceived the desirability of establishing free institutions.

169. Rise of the territorial question.

The first proposal, originating with Thomas Jefferson in 1784, was intended to prohibit slavery in the whole region west of the Alleghanies after the year 1800.[1] This provision failed for lack of a single vote;[2] for it was substituted that of the Northwest Ordinance of 1787, which provided for the abolition of slavery but applied only to the territory north of the Ohio River.[3] Even this arrangement was executed with difficulty. After the admission of Ohio to the Union, Indiana Territory was impatient to obtain a population sufficient for the formation of State governments, and clamored for permission to retain slavery for a limited term in order to attract slave-holding emigrants.[4] A committee of Congress, of which John Randolph was chairman, made a report (March 2, 1803) decidedly adverse to the petitions: the committee declared that they deemed it "highly dangerous and

170. The Northwest Ordinance.

---

[1] *Journal of Congress*, April 19, 1784, pp. 138–139; *Notes for Encyclopédie Méthodique*, in Jefferson, *Writings*, Ford's Edition, IV, 181.

[2] Of this failure Jefferson writes: "Thus we see the fate of millions unborn hanging on the tongue of one man, & heaven was silent in that awful moment!" *Ibid.*

[3] Text in Poore, *Federal and State Constitutions*, I, 432, art. vi. March 16, 1785, Rufus King of Massachusetts moved that the following resolution, to be made an article of compact between the thirteen original States and each of the States described in the Resolution of 1784 be committed: "That there shall be neither slavery nor involuntary servitude in any of the states, described in the resolution of Congress of the twenty-third of April, 1784, otherwise than in punishment of crimes, whereof the party shall have been personally guilty." This was committed by a vote of 8 to 4, all the States north of the Potomac voting ay and the Southern States no. *Journal of Congress*, 1785, pp. 481–482. The resolution in nearly the same language was adopted by Mr. King's colleague from Massachusetts, Nathan Dane, in the Ordinance of 1787. Appleton, *Encyclopedia*.

[4] *Annals of Congress*, 7 Cong., 2 sess., 613, 1353.

inexpedient " to suspend the prohibition; that the rapid settlement of Ohio showed that slavery was unnecessary; that slave-
labor, " demonstrably the dearest of any," could only be
employed to advantage in the cultivation of the most valuable
products; and that the prohibition was necessary in order to
give security and strength to the frontier.[1] The agitation, however, continued, and a suspension of the article for ten years
was nearly carried.[2]

South of the Ohio River, slavery was quietly permitted to
continue and increase. For the lands west of Virginia no

[1] *Annals of Congress*, 7 Cong., 2 sess., 1353–1354.

[2] *Ibid.*, 8 Cong., 1 sess., 783, 1023; 9 Cong., 1 sess., 293, 466–468, 848–
849; 9 Cong., 2 sess., 375–376, 482–483. In 1807 the Territorial Legislature
authorized owners of negroes over fifteen years of age to bring them into
the Territory, and taking them before the clerk of the Court of Common
Pleas enter into an agreement with each negro as to the number of years he
should serve. If the slave refused, he could be removed within sixty days
to any slave State or Territory. Slaves under fifteen could be held until
thirty-five in the case of males and twenty-five in the case of females; and
children of indentured parents were to serve until thirty and twenty-eight.
The important question whether the limitation of slavery in the Territories
by Congress should be absolutely conclusive in the States formed from that
Territory arose in the Northwest soon after the admission of Indiana and
Illinois to the Union, and the principle of congressional restriction was
severely tested. In both States there was a large pro-slavery element in
the population, and soon after the establishment of the Missouri Compromise
(March 3, 1820), a vigorous effort was made to repeal the clauses in their
State constitutions which prohibited slavery. The undertaking aroused
an equally vigorous opposition which extended to Ohio, Pennsylvania, and
other States. The inspirer, organizer, and leader of the anti-slavery party
in Illinois was Edward Coles, then governor of the State. As a student at
William and Mary College he had begun to doubt the right of slave-holding,
and some years later, after an unsuccessful appeal to Thomas Jefferson to
use his influence toward emancipation in Virginia, he had emigrated to the
Northwest, taking his slaves with him, pronouncing them free upon the
deck of a steamboat as they sailed down the Ohio River and afterward
formally manumitting them, giving them land and aiding them to become
self-supporting. During the struggle over the State Constitution he corresponded with the Pennsylvania abolitionists, directing their energy into
useful channels and distributing their pamphlets. He secured the publication of newspaper articles, and became the proprietor of *The Illinois Intel-
ligencer* that it might be used for this purpose. Methodist and Baptist
clergymen, many if not most of them from the Southern States, gave energetic and efficient aid, and some recent immigrants from England who had
chosen this region as their home on account of its exclusion of slavery took
an important part in the contest. The question was finally decided against
the revision of the Constitution by a vote of 4,950 to 6,882. Washburne,
Sketch of Edward Coles, 19–212.

special provision was made, and Kentucky entered the Union as a slave State in 1792.[1]   The North Carolina cession, ac-

171. Slavery in the Southwest.
companied by a condition that Congress should not apply the anti-slavery principles of the Northwest Ordinance, was the occasion of some debate; and an amendment was proposed and discussed but not adopted.[2]   On the organization of the Mississippi Territory (1798) a motion was made in Congress, " touching the rights of man," to strike out the clause by which a prohibition of slavery like that of the Northwest Ordinance was to be omitted.   This motion aroused considerable debate and gave an opportunity for the anti-slavery sentiment of Massachusetts and Pennsylvania to declare itself and for Virginia to give evidence of her declining interest in emancipation and her desire for new fields for her laborers.[3]

This debate is a forerunner of that on the Missouri Compromise.   The condition of the slaves would be ameliorated,

172. Debate on the organization of the Mississippi Territory.
thinks Mr. Giles of Virginia, by spreading them over a wider area.   It is not for Congress, says his colleague, Mr. Nicholas, "to attempt to make a particular spot of country more happy than all the rest."   If slavery, he adds, is a misfortune to the Southern States, would it not be doing a service not only to them but to the whole country to spread the negroes over a larger area, so that in time it may be safe to effect their emancipation?   When the territory is ready to form a State government, he argues, then its own legislature can, if it wishes, take measures for emancipation; and perhaps by that time other States will be in a position to join it.[4]

Against the weak optimism or insincere philanthropy of Virginian Congressmen stood Albert Gallatin of Pennsylvania and Messrs. Thatcher and Varnum of Massachusetts.   Slavery, says Mr. Thatcher, is acknowledged even by the slave-holders to be an evil.   It has on former occasions been so described by the gentleman from Virginia himself.   Even if it is impracticable to liberate the slaves of the Southern States on account of their great numbers, it is practicable to prevent the further extension

1 Poore, *Federal and State Constitutions*, I, 646–647, 653, art. ix.
2 *Annals of Congress*, 1 Cong., 2 sess., 1477.
3 *Ibid.*, 5 Cong., 2 sess., 1306–1311.
4 *Ibid.*, 1310.

of this evil in the new territory. This is moreover the duty of the government, a duty arising from the very foundations of the government itself. This government, says Mr. Thatcher, " originated from, and was founded on the rights of man, upon which ground we mean to protect it, and could there be any propriety in emanating a government from ours, in which slavery is not only tolerated, but sanctioned by law? Certainly not." [1]

This is a critical moment in the history of the new country, and the responsibility of the government and the dangers of delay are distinctly pointed out by that clear-headed and far-sighted statesman, Albert Gallatin. " If this amendment is rejected," says Gallatin, " we establish slavery for the country, not only during its temporary Government but for all the time it is a State; for, by the constant admission of slaves, the number will increase to a certain degree, and when the Territory shall become a State, the interest of holders will procure a Constitution which shall admit of slavery, and it will be thereby made permanent." [2] By another speaker the prosperity of the North-west Territory and the high value of the lands there are urged as evidences of the advantage of the prohibition of slavery. " If the Southern States could get clear of their slaves," says Mr. Varnum, " the price of their land would immediately double." As for the moral aspect of the question, "he looked upon the practice of holding blacks in slavery in this country to be equally criminal with that of the Algerines carrying our citizens into slavery," a remark deeply resented by Mr. Rutledge of South Carolina.[3]

The chief arguments against the prohibition of slavery were based on the rights of property and, as already mentioned, the desirability of extending slavery and thereby ameliorating the conditions and making ultimate emancipation possible. To these it was replied that the prohibition in the Mississippi Territory would not affect the peace or property of other States any more than did the prohibition already existing in the Northern States and the Northwest Territory. As for those already holding slaves in the Mississippi Territory, they might, as under the terms of the Northwest Ordinance, continue to hold slaves for a limited period. Even if the property of some individ-

---

[1] *Annals of Congress*, 5 Cong., 2 sess., 1310–1311.
[2] *Ibid.*, 1309.   [3] *Ibid.*, 1307.

uals were injured, declared the uncompromising Mr. Thatcher, the government still had a right to take all due measures to diminish and destroy this greatest of evils; "for he never could be brought to believe that an individual can have a right in anything which goes to the destruction of our Government, viz: that he can have a right in a wrong. A property in slaves is founded in wrong, and never can be right." As for the extension of slavery in order to mitigate its evils, if the Southern States were determined to keep slaves, "he wished only they should be plagued with them." [1]

While the debate gave an opportunity for the opponents of slavery to air their sentiments, it is noticeable that but few took **173. Results in the Southwest.** part in the discussion, and that when the question was put to vote, the amendment in favor of the limitation of slavery had but twelve in its favor.[2] Thus a compromise was practically agreed upon by which the Ohio River became the dividing line between the free and slave States of the West.

While the fate of both the Northwest and the Southwest Territories was by 1808 virtually decided, a new element entered **174. Louisiana Territory.** into the controversy in the annexation of the territory west of the Mississippi River. At first the question of the slave-trade was raised, and here, supported by the votes of Virginia, Congress took a decided stand against the importation of slaves from foreign ports.[3] The question of the prohibition of slavery also received some attention, more than had been bestowed upon its exclusion from the Mississippi Territory. The slavery problem was one of the grounds of the Federalist opposition to the new acquisition, and memorials and other anti-slavery literature indicate that the question was considered a critical one.[4]

A memorial was addressed to Congress by the American Convention for promoting the Abolition of Slavery (presented January 23, 1804), praying that the introduction of slaves into the new territory might be prohibited and suggesting a pro-

---

[1] *Annals of Congress,* 5 Cong., 2 sess., 1310–1311.

[2] *Ibid.,* 1312.

[3] See above, § 162.

[4] Typical of the Federalist anti-slavery opposition is D. Humphreys, *Valedictory to the Cincinnati,* July 4, 1804, pp. 24–27.

vision like that of the Northwest Ordinance. It was urged that slavery had been entailed upon the country by our ancestors, and that many people now recognized the evil but felt the difficulty of getting rid of it; and Congress was implored, for the honor of the country and the welfare of posterity, to preserve the new territory from similar calamities.[1] This memorial was followed a year later by one from the Yearly Meeting of the Society of Friends in Philadelphia (presented January 21, 1805), "praying that effectual measures may be adopted by Congress to prevent the introduction of slavery into any of the Territories of the United States."[2] Both memorials were referred in the House to committees on the government of Louisiana Territory, but the whole region without regard to latitude was finally granted the privileges of the Mississippi Territory instead of those of the Northwest (March 2, 1805).[3]

The District of Columbia was another point of attack which was not left to the later abolitionists to discover. As early as 1804 a movement in this direction was suggested by John Parrish, in his *Remarks on the Slavery of the Black People*. After a protest against the Fugitive Slave Law of 1793, he says: "And as it is manifest that Congress supposed they had a right to make laws to oppress this description of the great family of mankind, which is apparent by the aforesaid law; I apprehend there can be no doubt of their authority, if not in other places, at least in the district of Columbia, to prevent some of those evils this degraded part of our fellow-men are groaning under. And where could it begin better than at the seat of Government?"[4] Early the following year (January 18, 1805) a resolution was introduced in the House of Representatives by James Sloan of New Jersey to the effect that after July 4 of that year all blacks born within the District of Columbia or born of a mother belonging to a resident of the District should be free at a certain age. The resolution was rejected by a vote of 31 to 77,[5] but another "entering wedge" had been introduced.

175. The District of Columbia.

---

[1] *Annals of Congress*, 8 Cong., 1 sess., 238, 940. For text, see 8 Cong., 2 sess., Appendix, 1596–1597.

[2] *Ibid.*, 8 Cong., 2 sess., 39, 996.

[3] *Ibid.*, 8 Cong., 1 sess., 940; 8 Cong., 2 sess., 996, 1674.

[4] Parrish, *Remarks on the Slavery of the Black People*, 15.

[5] *Annals of Congress*, 8 Cong., 2 sess., 995.

With all its incompleteness the political movement of this period marks a distinct advance in the cause of universal liberty, **176. Results of the political movement.** both in the work of voluntary associations and in the attitude of the State.   It is noticeable that the principal elements of the later movement are all present and the foundations for the later work firmly laid.   The organization and work of the Abolition Societies, the orations, addresses, pamphlets, and " pictorial representations," the work in court and legislature, the presentation of petitions and the advocacy of the right of petition, the endeavor to exclude slavery from the Western Territories and from the District of Columbia, and the concern about fugitives, kidnapping, and the foreign and domestic slave-trade are all more or less conspicuous in this movement.   Though the actual work was but half accomplished, at least precedents were set and traditions established which were an inspiration and an example to the later age.

Two other gains for the cause of freedom may also be noted. The first was that the importation of slaves had been prohibited by law, never to be revived except in a clandestine trade; though the Act of 1807 was inefficient and the government lax in its execution,[1] the establishment of the principle is of no slight importance as a check to the trade and a support to the opponents of slavery.   In the second place, provision for emancipation had been made in all the States north of Mason and Dixon's Line and the country north of the Ohio River, and a sectional division had thus been established on the slavery question.   A solid South had been left to slavery, but the solid North was to be free.   The development of national feeling would cause men again and again to lay aside anti-slavery scruples for the sake, as they thought, of preserving the Union, and even in 1861 it was love for the Union, not hatred of slavery, that roused the North to arms; but the energetic protest against the Dred Scott decision in 1857 testifies to another conviction, best voiced by Lincoln in 1858: the system of compromises inaugurated by the Federal Convention could only delay the inevitable. In the South slavery might flourish and extend itself to a degree undreamed of by the Fathers of the Republic.   The

[1] DuBois, *Suppression of the African Slave-Trade*, 109–112.

Northern States might shut their eyes and cry, "Am I my brother's keeper?" Even in the North slavery might die a very lingering death. But the free States, with such a history behind them, could never again allow slavery to gain a foothold upon their soil: if the Union must become "either all slave or all free," it was slavery that was doomed.

CHAPTER VIII

ANTI-SLAVERY LITERATURE AFTER THE REVOLUTION,
1783–1808

THE series of parallel movements which have been described in the preceding chapters was accompanied by an anti-slavery literature, more abundant and more varied than that of any previous time. There is comparatively little which is directly connected with the political movement, since that was accomplished chiefly by petitions and resolutions, and by work in court and council which was of a practical rather than a literary character. A few memorable speeches were made, such as those of William Pinkney, David Rice, and Theodore Dwight, which have already been described.[1] The addresses of the American Convention of Delegates of the Abolition Societies have also been mentioned in connection with the political movement.[2] But the great bulk of the literature of this time has no such definite political purpose, and yet is of considerable importance as an expression of anti-slavery sentiment, and an element in the formation of public opinion.

177. General character.

No one who studies this literature can fail to be struck by the likeness of the arguments and methods to those of the later anti-slavery agitation. In the first place, the abolitionists were quick to make use of a new medium, the literary magazines which now began to spring up in the United States. Like most of the anti-slavery literature of the time, the magazine articles lack the simplicity, directness, and force which characterize the earlier writings; they are filled with weak sentiment and florid rhetoric. But these are faults of the period, and it would be as unfair to consider the feeling insincere because of the attempt to clothe it in the fine language which was considered requisite to the occasion, as it would be on the other hand to consider that the coarse attacks upon

178. Magazine articles.

---

[1] See above, §§ 128, 131, 137.   [2] See above, §§ 117–119.

President Jefferson in Dennie's *Portfolio* were prompted by pure anti-slavery sentiment rather than by party virulence.

The sentimental type of magazine article may be illustrated by *An Address to the heart, on the subject of American slavery*, in which the African is described as "reclining in the arms of balmy rest" on a couch of reeds, and smiling at the innocent gambols of his children. All sorts of festive joys abound, and "innocence and virtue reign." Then come flames and shrieks and clanking chains, the desert march, the rolling sea, and the devouring monsters of the deep, until at last the survivors are brought to the "fathers of oppression" in the West, whose "flinty hearts regard them as beasts of burden."[1] Tales are related, one of them a continued story running through a year's issue of *The American Museum*, illustrating the exemplary virtues of dark-hued heroes and heroines, and describing their tragic fate.[2] The magazine literature also includes anecdotes, such as the clever retort of a negro whose master has been preaching on liberty, and of another arrested for buying stolen goods.[3] Travellers' descriptions of the condition of the slave States as compared with the free are occasionally inserted, and the reviews of books of travel notice and comment on the subject.[4] Anti-slavery "poetry" also appears occasionally. This is usually intended to be either humorous or pathetic, but in general the humorous verses are dreary and the pathetic ones are funny.

Not all of the current literature, however, is of so light a character. In *The American Museum* are several essays on negro slavery, one of them by "A Free Negro,"[5] and two others, of unusual vigor, signed by "Othello."[6] Extracts from addresses and orations are also given,[7] and during Jefferson's

---

[1] *Address to the heart, on the subject of American slavery*, in *The American Museum*, I, 465–468.

[2] *The Negro equalled by few Europeans*. Translated from the French [by Phyllis Wheatley]. In *The American Museum*, Vols. IX, X (January to December, 1791).

[3] *The American Museum*, X, 28, VII, 332.

[4] *The Monthly Anthology*, 1806; *The Portfolio*, 1806–1807.

[5] A Free Negro, *Letter on slavery*, in *The American Museum*, VI, 77–80.

[6] Othello, *Essays on negro slavery*, in *Ibid.*, IV, 414–417, 509–512.

[7] *Speech of an American quaker, on African slavery*, in *Ibid.*, IV, 173; J. P. Martin, *Rights of Black Men*, in *Ibid*, XII, 299–300; *Extract from an oration delivered July 4, 1790, by the rev. William Rogers*, in *Ibid.*, VII, 255; *Extract from an oration delivered by mr. William Whittington*, in *Ibid.*, XII, 191–196.

administration there is considerable literature of a semi-political character, consisting chiefly of attacks on the professions of the Republican party. Jefferson's remarks on the natural inferiority of the negro [1] are severely commented on,[2] but it would be difficult to say how much of the criticism is inspired by anti-slavery sentiment and how much by political rancor. The partisan spirit appears more distinctly in connection with a poetical description of the woes of the slave, which is introduced by a sarcastic editorial commenting on the instruction of the negro in " the beautiful *republican* theory, of *equality*, amid the whole-some exhalations of a rice plantation," and advising the author of the poem to dedicate it to Mr. Jefferson.[3] Another author, with some geographical inaccuracy, alludes to the "rice-swamps" at Monticello as "the favorite haunt of philosophy, liberty, and other French fairies." [4] The development of the political antagonism to slavery at the same time with the development of the sentimental style, although it leads to a suspicion of mixed motives, had after all a certain value ; it gave a more manly and healthful tone to the literature, just when it was most needed. Without this prejudice the maunderings of the sentimental tales and "select poetry" would be vapid indeed, and the magazine literature would be worth little consideration. For this reason *The Portfolio*, though less decidedly anti-slavery in its character than *The American Museum*, is a suitable successor, and serves to carry on the work.

The influence of political conditions, though not so marked as in the Revolutionary period, is still great. Elsewhere than in the magazines both the sentimentalist and the political partisan are less conspicuous, and the anti-slavery spirit usually reigns undisputed whenever it appears at all; but, as in the magazines the sentimentalist of the early constitutional period gives way to the political partisan of Jefferson's administration, so the mild, optimistic essayists and orators, such as Dana and Swift, Rogers and Whittington, are followed by a more vigorous and even violent type, stimulated by political conditions, and especially by the development of party politics on somewhat sectional lines. These facts do not in any way indicate a progressive or systematic anti-slavery movement.

179. Influence of political conditions.

---

[1] See above, § 50.

[2] See below, § 190.

[3] *The Portfolio*, IV, 117, 118–119.

[4] *Ibid.*, 150.

There were isolated instances, all the way along, of uncompromising hostility to slavery; and there is little ground for judging whether the sentiment which they represent was more or less general at the end of the period than at the beginning. The differences to be noticed in the character of the literature are the effects of the political conditions in their relation to slavery, rather than of any change in the sentiment itself; and the less hopeful tone and more vigorous denunciations of the later writers indicate the natural reaction of a spirit which had hoped all things from the rising republic, and had waited in vain for the fulfilment of its hopes.

The careful readers of the anti-slavery argument of this time must admit that, like that of the Garrisonians, it spared neither the prejudices nor the fears of the South. There was, to be sure, a difference of opinion, even among 180. **Radical abolitionists.** the most single-minded, as to the most effective methods of educating public sentiment. One orator speaks of the specious enemies of freedom who profess to acknowledge the wickedness of slavery but use every artifice to continue it under pretence of expediency.[1] Another alludes to the intemperate zeal of the immediate abolitionists, who will counteract their own purposes and make the condition of the slaves worse than before.[2] That these immediate abolitionists were always to be reckoned with is indicated by the attitude of Southern Congressmen with their suspicion of entering wedges and their continual expectation of some further move against their peculiar institution;[3] there was said to be as much anxiety over a question affecting slavery in any degree as if the debate were upon its abolition.[4] The fear of an invasion from St. Domingo accompanied by an insurrection of the slaves in the South, which gave occasion for special congressional legislation in the session of 1797–1798[5]

---

[1] Dwight, *Oration before the Connecticut Society for the Promotion of Freedom*, 21.

[2] Webster, *Effects of Slavery on Morals and Industry*, 34

[3] See the speeches of Mr. Smith of South Carolina, in *Annals of Congress*, 4 Cong , 2 sess., 1731, and elsewhere as noted in previous chapters ; also the speeches of Mr. Williams of South Carolina and Mr. Baldwin of Georgia, in *Ibid.*, 5 Cong., 2 sess., 1963, 1969.

[4] *Ibid.*, 5 Cong., 1 sess., 664. Speech of Mr. Bayard.

[5] *Ibid.*, 5 Cong., 3 sess., 2752. See also 6 Cong., 1 sess., 267–268, 276–277 ; 7 Cong., 2 sess., 156, 194.

as well as for some of the State legislation of this decade,[1] was increased by the feeling that in case of such an insurrection the Northern States would give their aid reluctantly, if indeed they would not fan the flame.[2]

Nor can it be denied that the language of some of the abolitionists furnished ground for these apprehensions.   Slaves, says Theodore Dwight, quite openly, having been brought into our society by force without taking part in the social compact or in legislation, " form no part of the social body; and therefore cannot justly be the object of laws." "No Custom and no Law," he declares, "which a state where slavery is practised, either has made, or can make, ought to affect the enslaved negroes at all, unless designed as a partial compensation for the injuries which they have suffered — injuries, for which all the wealth of man can never atone." As for slave-insurrections, he considers that "if defensive war is susceptible of justification, in any possible instance, this is that instance. . . . The same law, which justifies the enormities, committed by civilized nations, when engaged in war, will justify slaves for every necessary act of defence, against the wicked, and unprovoked outrages, committed against their peace, freedom, and existence."[3]

181. Attitude toward slave-insurrections.

David Rice of Kentucky in a similar spirit speaks of the blacks of St. Domingo as "the brave sons of Africa, engaged in a noble conflict with their inveterate foes, . . . fired with a generous resentment of the greatest injuries, and bravely sacrificing their lives on the altar of liberty."[4] Another sympathizer compares them with the patriots of 1776, asking, "Is not their cause as just as ours?"[5] The fate of their exiled masters is even described by Dwight as "a dispensation of Providence which Humanity must applaud."[6] Another St. Domingo is prophesied for the continent, and in this event, it is thought, the Almighty will be implored in vain to give his aid to the oppressors.[7] As for human assistance, "where

---

[1] DuBois, *Suppression of the Slave-Trade*, 70–73.

[2] *Annals of Congress*, 9 Cong., 2 sess., 626–627.

[3] Dwight, *Oration before the Connecticut Society*, 11–13.

[4] Rice, *Slavery inconsistent with Justice and Good Policy*, 9.

[5] J. P. Martin, *Rights of Black Men*, in *The American Museum*, XII, 299.

[6] Dwight, *Oration before the Connecticut Society*, 19.

[7] Branagan, *The Penitential Tyrant*, Notes, 147–148.

shall they [the inhabitants of the Southern States] look," says Dwight, " for auxiliaries in such an iniquitous warfare? Surely, no friend to freedom and justice will dare to lend them his aid." [1] " The political claims which they will have upon us," says another, " will be opposed by the claims, and the remonstrances of Conscience; " [2] and still another writes: " As slavery is generally reprobated in the northern states the people would go, more reluctantly, to lend their aid in such a contest, than in any other; because it would, in effect, be upholding what they know to be wrong in itself." [3]

The suggestion that slavery might lead to the breaking up of the Union belongs also to this period. Such a separation was probably apprehended by a few far-sighted statesmen at the very foundation of the republic; and the sectionalizing of party politics made such a catastrophe still more imminent. The Federalists were particularly exasperated by the professions of liberty and equality made by the opposite party and by the charges of aristocracy brought against themselves. Those, said James Bayard of Delaware, are the real aristocrats who have been " habituated from infancy to trample on the rights of man . . . when I see these high-priests of liberty so zealously proclaiming freedom on one hand while on the other they are rivetting the chains of slavery, I cannot forbear tearing aside the veil." [4] " We are shocked," writes a correspondent of the *Connecticut Courant*, in more violent language, " to hear reverential ideas of liberty and equality, uttered by mouths, worn smooth with curses against their fellowmen who blacken all the surrounding territory. Who does not abhor the hand professedly raised up to check the progress of aristocracy in the land, when its fingers are stained with blood, drawn by the scourge from the veins of a slave? Who will give any credit to a man for sincerity when in one moment he breathes forth enthusiastic praises of Liberty, and the next, like the Bohon Upaz, sheds poison, and death all around him? " [5] The federal ratio of representation and the

182. Separation of the free and slave States contemplated.

---

[1] Dwight, *Oration before the Connecticut Society*, 19–20.
[2] *Pelham Letters*, *No.* 2, in *The Connecticut Courant*, Dec. 12 1796.
[3] *Letters of Gustavus*, *No.* 3, in *Ibid.*, Aug. 28, 1797.
[4] *Annals of Congress*, 5 Cong., 2 sess., 1229. See also 3 Cong., 2 sess., 1039–1043. *Cf.* Amynto, *Reflections on the Inconsistency of Man*, 9–15.
[5] *Pelham Letters*, *No.* 2, in *The Connecticut Courant*, Dec. 12, 1796.

annexation of Louisiana were also sources of discontent, partly from jealousy of the political power of the South and partly from sincere scruples against slavery; and it was more directly in these connections that the separation of the Union was contemplated.

Of the feeling on the federal ratio, the Letters of Pelham and Gustavus which appeared in *The Connecticut Courant* in 1796 and 1797, though violent and overdrawn, may be taken as an illustration. " Negroes," says one of the writers of these letters, "are in all respects, except in regard to life and death, the CATTLE of the citizens of the southern states. If they were good for food, the probability is, that even the power of destroying their lives would be enjoyed by their owners, as fully as it is over the lives of their cattle. It cannot be that their laws prohibit the owners from killing their slaves, because they are human beings, or because it is regarded as a moral evil to destroy them. If that were the case, how can they justify their being treated in all other respects like brutes? for it is in this point of view alone that negroes in the southern states are considered in fact as different from cattle. . . . On what principle, then, were they noticed among their masters in the scale of representation? " [1]

183. The Federal Ratio.

Of the annexation of Louisiana David Humphreys, in a valedictory to the Cincinnati, July 4, 1804, says, after enumerating various political objections: " And, what is infinitely more pernicious, . . . it cannot be cultivated to advantage without the introduction of great numbers of Africans. An abomination, sooner or later, I fear, to be expiated in blood ! " After remarking on " the species of republicanism which will characterize their fellow-citizens, in the newly-acquired territory," the orator suggests that " every candid person must also be left to judge for himself, whether this event will be likely to contribute to the preservation or destruction of the Union ! " [2]

184. The annexation of Louisiana.

The possibility of separation was not only suggested but elaborately discussed in the series of papers by Pelham and Gustavus, and among the arguments in favor of separation

[1] *Pelham Papers*, *No.* 1, in *The Connecticut Courant*, Nov. 21, 1796.
[2] D. Humphreys, *A Valedictory Discourse delivered before the Cincinnati of Connecticut*, 26.

slavery is conspicuous. " The existence of Slavery," says Pelham, " may be viewed as one forcible cause of a final separation of the United States. . . . The extreme wickedness of holding our fellowmen in chains, merely to serve our own interested plans, is very generally acknowledged in the northern states, and the sentiment is steadily gaining ground. . . . How can the hands of men, accustomed to do to others, as they would that others should do to them, clasp in the fraternal embrace, those who brood over misery and blood, who smile at murder and ridicule despair?" [1] ·Division is inevitable from both political and moral causes, is the argument of Gustavus, and the sooner it takes place the better: for if division is postponed until the opposition becomes more virulent, as it certainly must from the nature of the causes of opposition, the friction, before separation is accomplished, will involve the country in civil war; whereas, if the division is soon brought about, it may be effected without bloodshed.[2]

Independently of party politics, the most radical of the anti-slavery writers of this period are to be found either in connection with the movement for emancipation in the States, as in the case of Theodore Dwight and David Rice, or soon after the annexation of Louisiana and the repeal of the South Carolina prohibition. 185. Notable radicals outside of politics. The two former agitators have been frequently mentioned. Of those stimulated to action by the South Carolina repeal the most conspicuous are Thomas Branagan and John Parrish, men of very different types but both remarkable for their earnestness of purpose and their appreciation of the vital importance of the slavery question.

Thomas Branagan, the " Penitential Tyrant or Slave-Trader Reformed," represents to some degree the type of reformed slave-holder, later to be so manfully represented by John G. Birney and Cassius M. Clay. At the 186. Thomas Branagan. same time he is the man of one idea represented in the earlier time by Ralph Sandiford and Benjamin Lay. He was born in Dublin, Ireland, in 1774. At the age of thirteen he went to sea, but as he approached manhood he became convinced that privateering was no better than

---

[1] *Pelham Letters, No.* 2, in *The Connecticut Courant*, Dec. 12, 1796.
[2] *Letters of Gustavus*, in *Ibid.*, Aug. 14, 21, 28, and Sept. 11, 1797.

piracy and left the service. He then became overseer on a plantation at Antigua, but gave up this position also from conscientious scruples and went to Philadelphia. The cruises of his youthful years had made him acquainted with the slave-trade, and his experience on the coast of Africa and on the West India plantation led to a conviction of sin which forced him to write a confession of his deeds. He also felt bound to make what compensation he could by trying to convince others of the iniquity of slavery and warning them of the fate which awaited the slave-holder and the nation unless the evil were abolished.[1] Although when he began his career as an author, according to his own account, he " did not know what a note of admiration, a note of interrogation, or quotation marks meant,"[2] he did not allow his ignorance of punctuation to set limits to the ambition of his style. Two epic poems of several cantos each are written " in the style of Homer" and of Pope.[3] But his frank avowal of illiteracy, tautology, and servile imitation disarms the critic, and the honesty of his purpose makes up in some degree for the tediousness of his lines.

Avenia, the earlier of these poems, is preceded by *A Preliminary Essay* announcing its preparation and calling for subscribers to defray expenses. The call was responded to by a considerable number of subscribers, chiefly if not all of them citizens of New York and Philadelphia.[4] *Avenia* is a tragic tale beginning with the innocent joys of Africa, which are soon disturbed by the arrival of the slave-trader, and ending with the suicide of the heroine on account of the brutal treat-

---

[1] Branagan, *Compendious Memoirs*, in *The Penitential Tyrant*, 1–38 ; Ibid., *A Preliminary Essay on the Oppression of the Exiled Sons of Africa*, 9–28.

[2] Ibid., *The Penitential Tyrant*, Notes, 144.

[3] The motive of *The Penitential Tyrant* is thus expressed in the opening lines : —

> " Awake, my muse, tho' sorrowful to name,
> The crimes of baptiz'd infidels proclaim,
> Their complicated villainies explore
> From Afric's golden coast to India's shore;
>
> . . . .
>
> Sing Adam's exil'd sons, by them oppress'd,
> With grief, despair, and mighty woe depress'd."

[4] Ibid., *A Preliminary Essay*, Advertisement, 5–8, and *The Penitential Tyrant*, Appendix, 291 ff. The list of subscribers is mutilated in the copy found in the Boston Public Library.

ment of her master. *The Penitential Tyrant*, although written in response to a midnight vision of a somewhat thrilling nature,[1] is much less interesting than its title would lead one to expect. It has no definiteness of purpose, and but little distinct anti-slavery sentiment in its lines, which are mainly of a religious character. It is on Branagan's prose that his claim to be ranked among anti-slavery writers must rest. Here he deals with the subject in its moral, political, and economic aspects with some incoherence but plenty of vigor. He addresses the legislature of South Carolina on the subject of the slave-trade;[2] he urges on the Northern States an amendment of the federal constitution abolishing the three-fifths ratio of representation, which, as long as it exists, he says, will prevent the South from giving up slavery or the slave-trade;[3] he suggests that Congress undertake the immediate amelioration of the condition of the slaves;[4] and he follows the policy of Anthony Benezet in suggesting the colonization of the negroes in the Western territory.[5]

When, in 1849, Joshua R. Giddings set forth his vigorous doctrine that the Constitution was an anti-slavery document and urged Congress to exercise its powers against slavery, he probably did not know that more than forty years earlier another had trodden the same path. John Parrish, writing at about the same time as Thomas Branagan and under the influence of the same political conditions, was a man of very different character and antecedents. He was a native of Baltimore County, Maryland, and a member of the Society of Friends.[6] Though advanced in years when he published his *Remarks on the Slavery of the Black People* (1806), he has all the vigor and uncompromising morality of youth. In his charity of heart and keenness of vision he reminds one of John Woolman; he is no man's enemy and would do a kindness even to a slave-holder; he does not wish to call down fire from heaven to destroy the wicked. Yet he feels, as was felt during the

187. John Parrish.

---

[1] Branagan, *The Penitential Tyrant*, canto ii, pp. 71–81.

[2] Ibid., *A Preliminary Essay*, 211–220.

[3] Ibid., *Serious Remonstrances*, xiii, xiv, 27–31; *Political Disquisition*, 54–56, 59-63.

[4] Ibid., *A Preliminary Essay*, 220–223.

[5] Ibid., *Serious Remonstrances*, 17–22, 35–64.

[6] Appleton, *Encyclopedia*.

French and Indian War and the Revolution,[1] that the judgment of the Lord is at hand. Judgments, indeed, are already following South Carolina's apostasy in regard to the slave-trade. Since the rights of man have been investigated, people can no longer plead ignorance, and the continuance of slavery in spite of the Declaration of Independence and the State bills of rights must lead to further visitations of the Almighty.[2]

Like the Pennsylvania Abolition Society in its memorial of 1790, he regards slavery as contrary not only to the principles of the Declaration of Independence but to those of the Constitution as stated in the preamble. For, he argues, to deprive the colored people of the rights which have been proclaimed would not " form a more perfect union" or "ensure domestic tranquillity." "And nothing," he adds, " can be more contrary to the blessing of liberty than to make them liable to unconditional bondage, without the consoling prospect of ever being redeemed therefrom." The Constitution, he declares further, affirms the validity of all engagements entered into before its adoption, and the declaration of the universal right to liberty he regards as such a pledge. Since these are the principles of the Constitution, he argues, any expression in such a document calculated to admit of partial construction or a different meaning in order to enslave a particular race of men would be ignoble; and any act of legislation by which slavery is countenanced would be a perversion of the fundamental principles of government.[3]

With equal vigor he declares that the only sure basis of good government is the principle of the Golden Rule,[4] and that no government is secure in which one half of the citizens trample upon the rights of the other half. In one splendid sentence he anticipates by half a century the prophecy of Abraham Lincoln. " A house divided against itself," says Parrish, "cannot stand; neither can a government or constitution." [5] Lincoln's use of the scriptural figure is more effective than the earlier author's, for he not only hits the nail on the head but drives it home. Lincoln, moreover, is referring to a sectional division with the expectation not that the house will fall, not that the Union will be dissolved, but that it will become either all slave or all free;

---

[1] Parrish, *Remarks on the Slavery of the Black People*, 1–7.
[2] *Ibid.*, 39–40.
[3] *Ibid.*, 8–9.
[4] *Ibid.*, 14.
[5] *Ibid.*, 9.

Parrish is referring to the race problem, and his idea of the issue is based on a religious conviction that the cry of the oppressed will be heard. " There is a God that judgeth in the earth ! " is the continual cry of this Jeremiah. There is a curse upon the house that is builded by unrighteousness.[1] God's justice cannot sleep forever, and we cannot " hope for the long continuance of his blessing upon a government which neglects or refuses its duty in respect to these people."[2] " All the combinations of human policy," he believes, " shall not be able to prevent the deliverance of these people from their wretched state of thraldom."[3] " The day is hastening when these people will become free; and it is desirable it should be with the consent of those who have authority over them."[4]

Parrish not only realizes the seriousness of the situation, but has a keen eye for specific abuses and suggests definite remedies. He protests against the Fugitive Slave Law of 1793. He declares that the domestic as well as the foreign slave-trade must cease, and suggests that the State legislatures might prohibit transportation through their respective territories.[5] Not only must further importation be prohibited at the earliest possible moment, but something must be done to relieve those already under the lash, and that can be begun at once.[6] He suggests that Congress, which had power to make laws for the oppression of the slave, as in 1793, is surely competent also to ameliorate his condition, and that the District of Columbia would be a suitable place to begin.[7] He argues in favor of emancipation on economic as well as moral and political grounds, and like Branagan advocates a scheme of colonization in the West, where he fondly imagines that " there are millions of acres likely to continue many ages unoccupied."[8] After the sentimental platitudes of the magazines, the weak optimism of most of the occasional orators, the political acrimony of the federalist writers, and the incoherent extravagances of *The Penitential Tyrant*, it is refreshing to find a man so fair-minded and reasonable, so sure-sighted and so far-seeing, so prompt and practical in his

[1] Parrish, *Remarks on the Slavery of the Black People*, 29.
[2] *Ibid.*, 24.
[3] *Ibid.*, 7.
[4] *Ibid.*, 41.
[5] *Ibid.*, 31.
[6] *Ibid.*, 39.
[7] *Ibid.*, 15. *Cf.* § 175, above.
[8] *Ibid.*, 23–25, 43.

action. No other writer of his time has grasped the whole situation so thoroughly or dealt with it so effectively.

An examination of the anti-slavery arguments of this period shows little that is new, since the fundamental principles had already been established. The inconsistency of slavery with the teachings of Scripture is still urged,[1] though much less conspicuously than its inconsistency with the principles and professions of the American Revolution. The moral argument of the degrading effects of slavery on both master and slave is often repeated on the same lines as in the earlier period. Slavery, it is said, "destroys all sense of moral rectitude and natural justice."[2] "It debases and contaminates the immortal soul, as well as torments and lacerates the mortal body."[3] It necessitates inhumanity.[4] It deprives the negro of the social and domestic relations favorable to the practice of virtue.[5] Idleness is a result of slavery, and idleness is the nurse of vice.[6] "On the whole," says Theodore Dwight, "every species of wickedness results from slavery, wherever it exists."[7]

188. Anti-slavery arguments, scriptural and moral.

Although in this period the "Rights of Man" began to suffer some eclipse on account of the excesses of the French Revolution, it is still the principles of 1776 that stimulate the anti-slavery writers to greatest enthusiasm.[8] Slavery is regarded by them as a "monu-

189. The Rights of Man.

---

[1] Crawford, *Observations upon Negro Slavery*, 3–14, 13 ; Dana, *The African Slave-Trade*, 5–12, 26–30; Edwards, *The Injustice and Impolicy of the Slave-Trade and Slavery*, 13–18 ; Hopkins, *Discourse upon the Slave-Trade and Slavery of the Africans*, in Hopkins, *Works*, II, 600–604 ; Buchanan, *Oration upon the Moral and Political Evil of Slavery*, 9, 15.

[2] Branagan, *Serious Remonstrances*, 58.

[3] *Ibid.*, 32.

[4] Tucker, *Dissertation on Slavery*, 48–65.

[5] A Free Negro, *Letter on Slavery*, in *The American Museum*, VI, 79.

[6] Rice, *Slavery inconsistent with Justice and Good Policy*, 10.

[7] Dwight, *Oration before the Connecticut Society*, 16. For comments on the effects of slavery on the character see also Morse, *American Geography*, 65–66, 352–353, 388–391, 432–433; Webster, *Effects of Slavery on Morals and Industry*, 6–14, 18–22; Sutcliffe, *Travels in some Parts of North America*, 71-72; Edwards, *The Injustice and Impolicy of the Slave-Trade and Slavery*, 10–12 ; *The American Museum*, VII, 72–73; Imlay, *A Topographical Description of the Western Territory of North America*, 58 ; Miller, *Discourse before the New York Society*, 24–25.

[8] Dwight, *Oration before the Connecticut Society*, 8–13, 23–24 ; Pinkney, *Speech in the House of Delegates of Maryland*, 6–8; Buchanan, *Oration*

ment of the tyranny and inconsistency of human governments."[1] "It will not do," says William Pinkney, in his oration before the Maryland House of Delegates, in 1789, "thus to talk like philosophers, and act like unrelenting tyrants; to be perpetually sermonizing it with liberty for our text, and actual oppression for our commentary."[2] Can Americans so soon forget their principles, asks "Othello," and "after the noble contempt they expressed for tyrants, meanly descend to take up the scourge?"[3] The same sentiment appears in pictorial form in the frontispiece of Branagan's *Avenia*. Here the goddess of liberty is represented as seated in her temple, which is supported by columns inscribed with the names of appropriate virtues, and as gazing mournfully on a band of African slaves, who, as the author explains, "are brought to view, in order to demonstrate the hypocrisy and villainy of professing to be votaries of liberty, while, at the same time, we encourage or countenance, the most ignoble slavery."[4]

This argument is forcibly presented in the remarkable oration of Dr. George Buchanan, July 4, 1791 : —

"Deceitful men! who could have suggested, that American patriotism would at this day countenance a conduct so inconsistent; that while America boasts of being a land of freedom, and an asylum for the oppressed of Europe, she should at the same time foster an abominable nursery for slaves, to check the shoots of her glorious liberty? . . . Cruel and oppressive she wantonly abuses the *Rights of Man*, and willingly sacrifices her liberty at the altar of slavery: What an opportunity is here given for triumph among her enemies? Will they not exclaim, that upon this very day, while the Americans celebrate the anniversary of Freedom and Independence, abject slavery exists in all her States but one."[5]

In Dennie's *Portfolio* (1803), Fraternal, a Virginia planter, is represented as abandoning the rehearsal of a speech on liberty

---

upon the Moral and Political Evil of Slavery, 7–14; Tucker, *Dissertation on Slavery*, 9–11, 27–30, 50 ; Imlay, *A Topographical Description of the Western Territory*, 222.

[1] Rice, *Slavery inconsistent with Justice and Good Policy*, 8–9.

[2] Pinkney, *Speech in the House of Delegates of Maryland*, 8.

[3] Othello, *Essay on Negro Slavery, No.* 1, in *The American Museum*, IV, 415.

[4] The picture is described in Branagan, *The Penitential Tyrant*, iii.

[5] Buchanan, *Oration upon the Moral and Political Evil of Slavery*, 13.

and equality in order to beat a slave.[1] By this time the doctrines of Jefferson had become unpopular among the Federalists, and it was said even at the North that the negroes had become less industrious and less prosperous " since their heads had been turned by the modern jargon of liberty, and the rights of man;"[2] but except among violent partisans these principles remained the favorite argument against slavery. The light, as John Parrish said, had been set upon the candlestick where all men could see it.[3] The phrases of the Declaration of Independence were the handwriting on the wall, and woe to those who failed to regard it![4]

Besides the general argument from the inalienable rights of man there are often special arguments on the natural equality

190. Natural equality. of the negroes, using this term in a less restricted sense than when it was defined by the philosopher of the English Revolution.[5] The common humanity of blacks and whites is argued in language that recalls Franklin's adaptation of Shylock.[6] Differences of color and other physical distinctions, if they proved anything, argues Branagan, would prove too much.[7] The somewhat equivocal position of Thomas Jefferson on this question arouses a native of the Virginia back country, Gilbert Imlay, to champion the cause of the negro. " Mr. Jefferson . . . asks," says Imlay, "' if the difference [of color] is of no real importance?' I answer, that it is of no real importance, when compared with the object of rescuing some millions of miserable human beings from the odious prejudices which have degraded a whole race of men to the rank of beasts of burden, because they had the misfortune not to have the tinge of *red and white*."[8]

---

[1] *The Portfolio*, III, 245–246.

[2] *Ibid.*, I, 163–164.

[3] Parrish, *Remarks on the Slavery of the Black People*, 2–3.

[4] Luther Richardson, *Address before the Roxbury Charitable Society*, Sept. 17, 1804, in *The Monthly Anthology*, I, 609.

[5] Natural equality as defined by John Locke is a state " wherein all the power and jurisdiction is reciprocal, no one having more than another." Locke, *Essay concerning the true Original, Extent and End of Civil Government*, ch. ii.

[6] [Franklin], *Essay on the Slave-Trade*, 5. See also Crawford, *Observations upon Negro Slavery*, 4; A Free Negro, *Letter on Slavery*, in *The American Museum*, VI, 78.

[7] Branagan, *A Preliminary Essay*, 96–100.

[8] Imlay, *A Topographical Description of the Western Territory*, 225–

As for equality of mental powers, the general inferiority which exists is regarded, as in the Revolutionary period, as the effect of slavery. Jefferson's discriminations against the negro call forth another indignant response. "One would have thought," says a reviewer of the *Notes on Virginia*, in 1804, "that modern philosophy himself could not have the face to declare that the wretch who is driven out to labour at the dawn of day, and who toils until evening with the whip flourishing over his head, ought to be a poet." [1] The negro poetess, Phyllis Wheatley, is still quoted as an instance of the natural ability of the race,[2] and other cases of exceptional talent, such as Benjamin Banneker and Thomas Fuller, the phenomenal calculators, are occasionally brought forward.[3]

The political arguments on the destructiveness of slavery to republican institutions and perhaps to the very existence of the republic are much the same as in the Revolutionary period, though with new illustrations drawn from the events of the passing years. That reverence for liberty which is the vital principle of a republic, says William Pinkney, will be destroyed.[4]   Liberty and peace, says Theodore Dwight, "can never flourish, on the bleak and barren soil of Slavery." [5]   Our free institutions, writes Othello, are only "'painted sepulchres,' containing within them nought but rottenness and corruption." [6]   Slavery, says Branagan, "is to the body politic what a yellow fever or a gallopping consumption is

191. Danger to republican institutions.

---

226. See also Pinkney, *Speech in the House of Delegates of Maryland*, 15–17 ; Dana, *The African Slave-Trade*, 28–29; Rice, *Slavery inconsistent with Justice and Good Policy*, 4–6; Buchanan, *Oration upon the Moral and Political Evil of Slavery*, 7 ; Swift, *Oration on Domestic Slavery*, 11.

[1] *Observations upon certain passages in Mr. Jefferson's Notes on Virginia*, in *The Portfolio*, IV, 251–252, 268. On this subject, see also Imlay, *A Topographical Description of the Western Territory*, 227–228 ; Branagan, *A Preliminary Essay*, 100–110.

[2] Imlay, *A Topographical Description*, 228; Crawford, *Observations upon Negro Slavery*, 5–7, note. See above, p. 56, note.

[3] *Accounts communicated by Dr. Rush*, published by the Pennsylvania Abolition Society in *The American Museum*, V, 61–63; An Account of Benjamin Banneker by James M'Henry, *Ibid.*, XII, 185–187; Branagan, *A Preliminary Essay*, 102–108; Brissot, *New Travels in the United States*, I, 241–243.

[4] Pinkney, *Speech in the Maryland House of Delegates*, 9.

[5] Dwight, *Oration before the Connecticut Society*, 24.

[6] Othello, *Essay on Negro Slavery*, in *The American Museum*, IV, 511.

to an individual body," [1] and "every slave ship that arrives at Charleston, is to our nation what the Grecians' wooden horse was to Troy." [2]   The insurrection in St. Domingo furnished a fruitful text for the anti-slavery Jeremiads, [3] at the same time that it intensified the reluctance of the Southern States to increase the number of free blacks; and the possibilities of domestic insurrection and even of a dissolution of the Union were, as has already been seen, touched upon with an unsparing hand. [4]

Listen to the warnings of the Maryland orator, Dr. George Buchanan, on this point: —

" Hark !   Methinks I hear the work begun, the Blacks have already sought for Allies and found them in the wilderness ; they have called the rusty savages to their assistance, and are preparing to take revenge of their haughty masters.

" A revenge, which they consider as justly merited ; for being no longer able to endure their unnatural and unlawful bondage, they are determined to seek Liberty or Death." [5]

Another aspect of the subject is treated by Dr. Buchanan with equal earnestness:

" Slavery, the most implacable enemy of your country . . . threatens you with destruction.   Already has it disturbed the limpid stream of liberty, it has polluted the minds of your youth, sown the seeds of despotism, and without a speedy check to her ravages, will sink you into a pit of infamy where you shall be robbed of all the honours you have before acquired." [6]

To the argument of vested rights the anti-slavery writers address themselves resolutely, and rights of property in the slave **192. Rights of property.** are as vehemently denied as by the old-time Quakers. The old Puritan idea of slavery as a permissible result of captivity in war is now entirely exploded.   Slavery as a punishment for crime is the only possibility admitted at all,

---

[1] Branagan, *Avenia*, 311.

[2] Ibid., *The Penitential Tyrant*, 51.

[3] Thomas Branagan frequently refers to this subject. *Political Disquisition*, 23–26, 65–68, 82; *The Penitential Tyrant*, 51, 149–161 ; *A Preliminary Essay*, 218 *et passim*, 133–163.

[4] See above, §§ 181–184.

[5] Buchanan, *Oration upon the Moral and Political Evil of Slavery*, 17.

[6] *Ibid.*, 14–15.

and this but seldom. "No man can have a property in stolen goods," says Charles Crawford, in his *Observations upon Negro Slavery*, in 1784, " and it is immaterial whether a man, or his ancestors, or the persons of whom they were bought, stole the goods." [1] "One man can never become the property of another," says Thomas Branagan, following a different line of thought, " till the latter become more, and the former less, than a man." [2] Theodore Dwight, too, declares such property " impossible, in any situation, or under the authority of any laws." [3] If that right existed, says Jonathan Edwards, there would be no reason why the skins and teeth of negroes should not be taken for sale as well as those of elephants, if only they were equally valuable.[4] By David Rice the slave-owners are regarded as licensed robbers, not as just proprietors, and their claims as entitled to no respect.[5] The claim to compensation, even if it were valid, reasons Theodore Dwight, would still be a distinct question from that of giving the slave his liberty, the latter of which admits of no doubt whatever.[6] The owner may not even plead the dangers of emancipation, says Dr. Edwards, any more than a robber may murder the man he has robbed in order that he may have a better chance for his own life.[7] The master's suffering in any case, Rice reminds his hearers, is the result not of the emancipation of the slave, but of the conditions produced by the existence of slavery, and even though there should be undeserved loss, he asks, " is nobody intitled to justice, but slave-holders?" [8]

The necessities of climate received comparatively little attention. " A thing radically wrong," said John Parrish, " will not admit of such fig-leaf coverings." [9] The impossibility of carrying

[1] Crawford, *Observations upon Negro Slavery*, 12–13. See also Edwards, *Injustice and Impolicy of the Slave-Trade and Slavery*, 24–28; Rice, *Slavery inconsistent with Justice and Good Policy*, 3–4.

[2] Branagan, *A Preliminary Essay*, 127.

[3] Dwight, *Oration before the Connecticut Society*, 9.

[4] Edwards, *Injustice and Impolicy of the Slave-Trade and Slavery*, 21–22.

[5] Rice, *Slavery inconsistent with Justice and Good Policy*, 13.

[6] Dwight, *Oration before the Connecticut Society*, 8–9. See also Miller, *Discourse before the New York Society*, 15.

[7] Edwards, *Injustice and Impolicy of the Slave-Trade and Slavery*, 33–34.

[8] Rice, *Slavery inconsistent with Justice and Good Policy*, 13.

[9] Parrish, *Remarks on the Slavery of the Black People*, 25.

on a plantation without negro labor was doubted,[1] and in any case the importance of the work was regarded as subordinate to the interests of humanity, justice, and religion.[2]

193. Economic necessity. Thomas Branagan believed that the free negroes, if kindly treated, would work, as they did at the North, and that their masters would gain rather than lose by the change; [3] but in general the possibility that free negroes might do the work as well as slaves seems to have received little consideration. In fact, even some zealous emancipationists were appalled at the prospect of idleness, famine, and vice which would follow the sudden abolition of slavery. St. George Tucker pictured the freed blacks as " the caterpillars of the earth, and the tigers of the human race,"[4] and the general opinion evidently was that the dreaded disasters attendant upon a free black population must be avoided by some safe and gradual means of emancipation still to be discovered.

In this period appeared a more prominent and elaborate statement of the economic effects of slavery than ever before. The great lexicographer, Noah Webster, writing in a scientific spirit and believing that the most effective appeal is to self-interest, devoted his attention especially to this aspect of the question. Other authors, too, urged the economic arguments with more appreciation of their real importance than had been shown in earlier times except by Benjamin Franklin and Dr. Rush. The unprofitableness of slave-labor to both the slave-holder and the community was perhaps more fully realized at this time than either earlier or later. Before this, economic principles were not so carefully considered, and economic differences between the free and slave States were not sufficiently developed to point the moral ; while afterwards the realms of King Cotton were colored by a glow of apparent prosperity which disguised the real disadvantages of the system.

194. Economic effects of slavery.

---

[1] Webster, *Effects of Slavery on Morals and Industry*, 35–36.

[2] Crawford, *Observations upon Negro Slavery*, 12. *Cf.* Dr. Rush, in § 66, above.

[3] Branagan, *Suggestions to Congress*, in *A Preliminary Essay*, 233. See also Miller, *Discourse before the New York Society*, 24–26; Amynto, *Reflections on the Inconsistency of Man*, 18–19.

[4] Tucker, *Dissertation on Slavery*, 79–80. See also Webster, *Effects of Slavery on Morals and Industry*, 34–35.

Nevertheless at the time under consideration slavery was not yet regarded as "a positive good." In Maryland and Virginia it was admitted to be unprofitable.[1] It was argued that land in the free States was worth more than that of the same quality in the South,[2] and the labor of a freeman was said to be worth twice that of a slave.[3] Experiments in the use of free labor were tried in the Shenandoah Valley and on the Eastern Shore of Virginia with apparent success,[4] although ultimately only to prove that free and slave labor cannot exist on the same soil. The greater cost of slave labor in proportion to the product was so well understood by John Randolph that he confessed that but few productions would bear the expense.[5] Noah Webster, from an elaborate comparison of the advantages of free and slave labor in their effects on the cost of production, the relative value of land, and the amount of exports, draws similar conclusions, noting that the annual product of the South is much less than that of the North in proportion to the population; and he goes still further in asserting that "the most luxuriant soil and most salubrious climate are advantages which in no country, counterbalance the tendency of slavery . . . to weaken and impoverish a country."[6]

These conclusions were supplemented by the observations of travellers, who did not fail to comment on the differences between the free and slave States.[7] John Parrish, too, speaks of the worn-out soil, the destruction of timber, the broken

[1] Pinkney, *Speech in the Maryland House of Delegates*, 10–11; Buchanan, *Oration upon the Moral and Political Evil of Slavery*, 16; Tucker, *Dissertation on Slavery*, 80–81, note; La Rochefoucauld-Liancourt, *Travels through the United States*, II, 118, 233; Chastellux, *Travels in North America*, II, 168, 197. But compare Brissot de Warville, *New Travels in the United States*, I, 237, 244.

[2] *Annals of Congress*, 4 Cong., 2 sess., 1939. Speech of Mr. Page of Virginia.

[3] Morse, *American Geography*, 65.

[4] Brissot, *New Travels in the United States*, I, 244; Webster, *Effects of Slavery on Morals and Industry*, 49.

[5] Report of the committee on Indiana Territory, *Annals of Congress*, 7 Cong., Appendix, 1353. See also, § 170, above.

[6] Webster, *Effects of Slavery on Morals and Industry*, 22–23, 40–54.

[7] Sutcliffe, *Travels in some Parts of North America*, 108–109; T. M. Harris, *Journal*, 58–59; T. Ashe, *Travels in America*, 182–183; Brissot, *New Travels in the United States*, I, 237–244.

fences, saying, " The land is made barren, by the wickedness of those that dwell therein." [1] The effects on density
of population are noticed in some detail by Noah Webster
and Jonathan Edwards.[2] The dishonoring of labor, the conse-
quent lack of industry and the waste arising from a large
number of unemployed are also subjects of comment. " When
slavery becomes common," says Rev. David Rice, " industry
sinks into disgrace. To labour, is to *slave;* to work, is to work
like a Negroe." [3] And as labor becomes dishonored, he adds,
poverty and crime take its place.

The effects of slavery upon the development of commerce
and manufactures received some attention from Webster,[4] but
elsewhere were hardly touched upon, and that aspect of the
subject was probably little understood. Manufactures were
still in their infancy, and the differences which were to arise in
respect to the density of population, the character and variety
of industries, and the accumulation of wealth could hardly be
dreamed of.

Although it is impossible to make a chronological division
on this basis, it may be said in general that the earlier writers
of the period were radiant with hope and courage,
and that as years passed without any progress in those
regions where it might naturally be looked for next,
the note of warning was more frequently sounded and suggestions were offered for the sake of relieving the conscience of the
writer rather than with any hope of their adoption. Among the
more sanguine it was believed that the American Revolution
was the beginning of political liberty for the whole world[5] and
that, the march of Freedom once begun, " nothing but the arm

195. Antici-
pations and
warnings.

---

[1] Parrish, *Remarks on the Slavery of the Black People*, 29.

[2] Webster, *Effects of Slavery on Morals and Industry*, 47; Edwards,
Injustice and Impolicy of the Slave-Trade and Slavery, 12. See also
Imlay, *A Topographical Description of the Western Territory*, 58.

[3] Rice, *Slavery inconsistent with Justice and Good Policy*, 11. See also
Edwards, *Injustice and Impolicy of the Slave-Trade and Slavery*, 10–11;
Webster, *Effects of Slavery on Morals and Industry*, 22–33, 40–54.

[4] *Ibid.*, 22, 41 f. For manufactures see also Sutcliffe, *Travels in some
Parts of North America*, 156. Cf. " *Lee's Add.*" in *Views of American
Slavery*, 109.

[5] Swift, *Oration on Domestic Slavery*, 19–23; Dana, *The African Slave-
Trade*, 30; Campbell, *Oration*, July 4, 1787, in *The American Museum*,
III, 21; Rogers, *Oration*. July 4, 1790, in *Ibid*, VII, 255.

of Omnipotence can prevent it from reaching the miserable Africans."[1] To some it seemed hardly necessary to make any further effort, as so much had already been accomplished. Rev. James Dana in 1790 notes the progress made during the previous twenty years, and asks, "Could wisdom and philanthropy have advanced further for the time?"[2] Even to Jonathan Edwards, who was not a man to shrink from vigorous exertion, it seemed in 1791 that at the present rate of progress it would within fifty years "be as shameful for a man to hold a Negro slave, as to be guilty of common robbery or theft."[3] Noah Webster, after his historical and statistical researches, is less hopeful. Judging by the history of villeinage in Europe, he thinks, it will be about two centuries before slavery is naturally extinguished.[4] James Sullivan in writing to Dr. Belknap takes a similar view. The time required for emancipation, he thinks, "must be as extensive, at least, as that in which slavery has been endured here."[5]

Others no less energetic take a still more gloomy view, and dwell less on the prospect of emancipation than on the retribution which is awaiting the nation and particularly the slave-holders unless emancipation is speedily accomplished. Thomas Branagan, for instance, warns his readers that "the scourge of God is now shaking over the American commonwealth."[6] "Many are the abominations," says John Parrish, "which draw down Divine displeasure, and bring judgments on lands and on individuals, but nothing appears to me equal, nor fraught with so many evils, as enslaving our fellow-men."[7] Rev. Samuel Hopkins, who felt in 1776 that the war had been sent by Providence to show the nation its sin, and that a happy issue could not be expected without previous repentance and reform, feels again in 1787 that the hand of God is upon the country. The suppression of the slave-trade, he says, has car-

---

[1] Dwight, *Oration before the Connecticut Society*, 24.

[2] Dana, *The African Slave-Trade*, 30.

[3] Edwards, *The Injustice and Impolicy of the Slave-Trade and Slavery*, 30. The oration was delivered in 1791.

[4] Webster, *Effects of Slavery on Morals and Industry*, 37.

[5] Letter of J. Sullivan in Deane, *Letters and Documents relating to Slavery*, 5 *Mass. Hist. Soc. Coll.*, III, 414.

[6] Branagan, *The Penitential Tyrant*, 146.

[7] Parrish, *Remarks on the Slavery of the Black People*, 38.

ried the colonies through the Revolution; but by continuing to hold the negroes in bondage and by the renewal of the slave-trade the country has forfeited the favor of the Almighty and another visitation of Providence has been necessary. The nation, he affirms, is not prospering; it is despised by European powers; there is discontent and anarchy and insurrection at home. Especially-marked are the disasters of Rhode Island, the headquarters of the reviving slave-trade. The hand of God is again upon the country, urging to repentance and reform.[1]

The dangers of insurrection, as has already been noted, furnish a particularly fruitful field for the prophets of impending destruction.[2] As for the slave-holders themselves, nothing less than eternal sufferings, thinks Othello, can make adequate retribution for their offences, and at the day of judgment the oppressor will be forced to " dart deeper into the flames" in order to avoid the just reproaches of his former slaves.[3] The same consoling thought inspires the verses of " The Penitential Tyrant": —

> " Soon, soon that God his justice will display,
> And chase oppressors from the face of day;
> Hurl'd down to hell by Heaven's Almighty Sire,
> Transfix'd with vengeance and involv'd in fire." [4]

Of the possible remedies for slavery none was neglected in the writings of this period. The members of the Society of Friends had done little beyond accomplishing emancipation throughout their own sect and urging individual manumission outside. The Revolutionists had begun to apply to the State, and their work was accomplished through that agency. Now that the efforts for political action had spent their strength, nearly every anti-slavery writer seems to have some pet scheme for encountering or avoiding the prejudice, timidity, or avarice which left the work of emancipation still incomplete. The individual projects of this period are therefore more definite and more elaborate than those of the previous one, as well as of greater variety.

196. Remedies for slavery.

---

[1] Hopkins ("Crito"), *The Slave-Trade and Slavery, Works,* II, 613-624.

[2] See above, §§ 181, 191.

[3] Othello, *Essays on Negro Slavery, No.* 2, in *The American Museum,* IV, 511.

[4] Branagan, *The Penitential Tyrant,* canto i, p. 66.

Various half-way measures were urged, either as palliatives to the lot of the slave or as appeals to the self-interest of the master. It was hoped that the abolition of the slave-trade together with a mitigation of the lot of the slave and a gradual improvement in the relation between him and his master would by and by make emancipation a safe and natural process.[1] Proposals were therefore made for legislation in regard to the treatment of the slave, granting him some time to himself and providing for his instruction.[2] Several enthusiastic accounts appeared of an arrangement said to be in operation in the Spanish West Indies, where the slave was allowed to work one day in the week for wages, with the privilege of buying his other days and so gradually working out his freedom.[3] Another idea, according to Abbé Bonnet, was to sell all the slaves to the planters of the West Indies![4]

A favorite scheme was to make slavery unprofitable by the refusal to buy or use the produce of slave labor. The consumption of sugar in Philadelphia was perceptibly diminished at one time by "the qualmishness of some of the Quakers."[5] At about the same time the sugar-maple came into great favor as the probable means of destroying slavery. "I cannot help contemplating a sugar maple-tree with a species of affection and even veneration," writes Dr. Rush; "for I have persuaded myself to behold in it the happy means of rendering the commerce and slavery of our african brethren in the sugar islands as unnecessary, as it has always been inhuman and unjust."[6] Brissot de Warville, then travelling in America, and later, as a leader in the French Revolution, to be identified with the emancipation of slaves in

197. Beginning of the free produce movement.

---

[1] Letter of John Adams in Deane, *Letters and Documents relating to Slavery*, 5 *Mass. Hist. Soc. Coll.*, III, 416; Letter of J. Sullivan, in *Ibid.*, 413-415.

[2] Branagan, *A Preliminary Essay*, 117-125.

[3] Crawford, *Observations upon Negro Slavery*, 14-15 and note; Parrish, *Remarks on the Slavery of the Black People*, 41-42; *The American Museum*, VI, 317 and VIII, Appendix IV, pp. 14-15.

[4] Abbé Bonnet, *A summary of proposed means of abolishing negro slavery*, in *Réponse aux principales Questions*, II, 39-40.

[5] *Annals of Congress*, 3 Cong., 2 sess., 1089.

[6] Rush, Letter to Thomas Jefferson, vice-president of the American Philosophical Society. In Imlay, *A Topographical Description of the Western Territory*, 23, note, 157-158.

the French colonies, writes with equal confidence and enthusiasm.[1] A society was organized for the special purpose of encouraging this movement. Estimates were made of the capacity of the trees of New York and Pennsylvania to supply the demands of the United States, and it was calculated that 263,000 acres of trees would serve the purpose.[2] Thomas Jefferson, at this hopeful period, is said to have planted an orchard of sugar-maples and to have used no other sugar in his family.[3] Good Abbé Bonnet, in America at about this time, indulges in pleasing anticipations of the effects of this sugar culture upon the future deliberations of Congress. Although humanity itself prescribe delays, he says, the triumph of liberty is none the less decreed by nature; " for in fifteen years Congress will have to declare itself in regard to the liberty of the negroes, and what can it reply to them, when, each bearing in his hand a branch of the sugar-maple, they shall come to say to it; Look, and read upon this leaf the decree of nature; we were enslaved in order to cultivate the sugar cane ! What can it reply, I say, but you *are free*." [4] The slaves unfortunately did not appear in the halls of Congress with their branches of sugar-maple, and the beautiful tree which was to destroy slavery was soon overshadowed by the gigantic proportions of the cotton plant.

The free produce movement was taken up by the Abolition Societies and never wholly died out. In 1807 Thomas Branagan calls on all Christians, particularly Methodists and Quakers, to unite against buying and using " the price and produce of human blood." [5] The American Convention of Delegates of the Abolition Societies makes an appeal to the same effect.[6] It is said that the number of those who have joined in the movement " is large and is increasing daily," and that " no bounds can be assigned to its future progress; " [7] and although the movement

---

[1] Brissot, *New Travels in the United States*, I, 255–260.

[2] Imlay, *Topographical Description*, 163.

[3] *Ibid.*, 158, note; Brissot, *New Travels*, I, 257.

[4] Bonnet, *Réponse aux principales Questions*, 46–47.

[5] Branagan, *Buying Stolen Goods synonymous with Stealing*, in *The Penitential Tyrant*, Appendix, pp. 219–250.

[6] American Convention, *Minutes of Proceedings*, 1796, pp. 18, 27–29. See also *Ibid.*, 1828, pp. 7, 25–27.

[7] Branagan, *The Penitential Tyrant*, Appendix, 250. See also *The Mirror of Misery*, 3.

disappointed the hopes of its originators in the achievement of definite results, it must, as in the later anti-slavery movement, have had considerable moral influence.

Suggestions for measures of emancipation in the South were very much along the lines that had already proved practicable in the North, though it was impossible to overlook the difference of conditions in States having large numbers of slaves. The remedy of colonization was now distinctly brought forward. Individual manumission was insisted on by Jonathan Edwards as absolutely and immediately obligatory.[1] Legislative action, however, was regarded as altogether the most promising resource, and the chief problem was to overcome the opposition of those who would suffer immediate loss by the measure. The most important efforts in this direction have already been described.[2] Among minor suggestions were that of Dr. Buchanan for the emancipation of one or two generations at a certain age,[3] and the bolder one of " Othello," for immediate abolition with a provision for colonizing the freed negroes in some place west of the Alleghanies.[4]

198. Suggestions for emancipation.

The greatest difficulties which the abolitionists had to contend with were connected with the free negroes, and no scheme of emancipation which left them out of account could hope for success in the States where there was a large negro population. Even the abolitionists generally admitted the unfitness of the blacks for freedom, though contending that this was no argument for continuing to hold them in slavery, but rather the reverse.[5] Emancipation, it was thought, was no less a duty because it was not the whole duty, but it must be supplemented by other measures;[6] the negroes must at least be taught to take care of themselves and to obey the laws of the country. There were, however, social and political distinctions even in Massachusetts, and it was sup-

199. Problem of the free blacks.

---

[1] Edwards, *Injustice and Impolicy of the Slave-Trade and Slavery*, 24–28.
[2] See especially § 141, above.
[3] Buchanan, *Oration upon the Moral and Political Evil of Slavery*, 17–18.
[4] Othello, *Essay on Slavery, No.* 1, in *The American Museum*, IV, 417.
[5] Rice, *Slavery inconsistent with Justice and Good Policy*, 20–22; Branagan, *Serious Remonstrances*, 32–39, 58–59, 68.
[6] Webster, *Effects of Slavery on Morals and Industry*, 13. See also Miller, *Discourse before the New York Society*, 30–32; Amynto, *Reflections on the Inconsistency of Man*, 18–22.

posed that the full enjoyment of equal rights and liberties was practically impossible, and that there could never be any real harmony of interests.[1]   The degradation of the blacks, as well as custom and prejudice among the whites, would prevent such a united community.   The generous loyalty of the Afro-American had not yet been tested, and the free negro was expected to resent his own past injuries and those of his race to such an extent as to be a source of danger to the commonwealth, even more serious than when he was a slave.[2]

All these difficulties it was hoped might be met by colonization.   This had been a favorite idea of Dr. Hopkins ever since **200. Coloni-** 1773, when he and President Stiles undertook the **zation.** education of some promising young colored men who were to act as leaders in establishing a colony in Africa.[3] The enterprise received some financial aid from churches in Massachusetts, Connecticut, and New York, and from London and Edinburgh, but the establishment of the colony was prevented by the Revolutionary War.[4]   Meanwhile Jefferson and other leading Virginians had taken up the idea, and a plan was proposed by Jefferson providing for the previous instruction of the negroes in agriculture and various handicrafts, the equipment of the colonists, and arrangements for their support and defence until they should be able to take care of themselves.[5] After the close of the Revolutionary War, Dr. Hopkins renewed his efforts for the execution of his scheme, and Dr. William Thornton volunteered to act as a leader in the enterprise.[6]   The colony of Sierra Leone, derived partly from Hopkins's ideas, was founded in 1787 by Granville Sharp and other English philanthropists; and as Dr. Thornton failed to secure sufficient funds for his own undertaking, efforts were made for a combination with the English colony.   In regard to this project Dr. Hopkins corresponded with Granville Sharp and Zachary

[1] Brissot, *New Travels in the United States*, I, 138, 261–263; Hopkins, *Works*, II, 610–611.

[2] Branagan, *Serious Remonstrances*, 38–39, 43–46, 67; Jefferson, *Writings*, VIII, 380.

[3] Park, *Memoir of Samuel Hopkins*, in Hopkins, *Works*, I, 129–138.

[4] *Ibid.*

[5] See above, § 85; Jefferson, *Writings*, VIII, 380.

[6] Park, *Memoir of Hopkins*, 139; Brissot, *New Travels in the United States*, I, 138–139, 261–263.

Macaulay.[1]   He also tried to obtain aid from the State legislatures and the Abolition Societies; [2] although he was never
able to carry out his scheme, he never abandoned it, and the
Liberia of a later day may justly look upon him as first among
its founders.

In 1790 a " Plan for liberating the negroes within the
united states" was published in *The American Museum* " by
mr. Ferdinando Fairfax." It was here proposed that Congress
should make a plan for African colonization on a national
scale along the lines already proposed by Jefferson for Virginia.[3]   The insurrection in Virginia in 1800 revived the project again in that State, and for several years efforts toward
colonization were made, President Jefferson taking a prominent
part.[4] Plans for colonization in the West, however, were often
regarded as more feasible than the African scheme.   It was
proposed that a tract of the unoccupied land should be allotted
to the free negroes by Congress, with conditions similar to
those suggested by Jefferson.[5]   In the earlier proposals this
land was vaguely located west of the Alleghanies; after the
purchase of Louisiana the location was transferred to that
region.   The land, according to one plan, was to be sold at
moderate terms, on credit, to Africans only, who had been
brought up as farmers.[6]   Funds were to be raised in the various
States for the accommodation of emigrants and their equipment
with the necessary outfit.[7]   The blacks already free were to
go first, and it was expected that voluntary manumission would
go on rapidly when the problem became simplified in this way.
One sanguine writer even thought that emancipation might be
almost instantly realized.[8]

Objections to the colonization schemes were raised, then as

---

[1] Park, *Memoir of Hopkins*, 140–153.

[2] Hopkins, *Works*, II, 610–612; Park, *Memoir*, 145–149.

[3] *Plan for liberating the negroes within the united states. By mr.
Ferdinando Fairfax.* In *The American Museum*, VIII, 285–287.

[4] See above, § 141; McPherson, *History of Liberia*, 17–18.

[5] Othello, *Essay on Slavery, No.* 1, in *The American Museum*, IV, 417;
Parrish, *Remarks on the Slavery of the Black People*, 41–42; Branagan,
Serious Remonstrances, 35 ff., 92–93.

[6] Rush, Letter to Nicholson, April 12, 1793, in *Pa. Mag. Hist. and
Biog.*, VI, 113.

[7] Branagan, *Serious Remonstrances*, 35–37.

[8] *Ibid.*, 64.

later, on account of the expense, the length of time required, the mischievousness of a plan which would involve such delay, and the injustice to the negroes deported, especially if they should be sent to Africa. It was considered unwise, too, to banish the whole laboring class from the Southern States.[1] It had been thought that the free blacks would not work, but it was evident that somebody must. This policy was compared to the expulsion of the Moors from Spain, and dire famine was predicted if such a measure should be carried out.[2] Jefferson had proposed that the place of the negro should be filled by soliciting emigration from Europe,[3] but here, too, there were practical difficulties.[4] Even the plan of St. George Tucker for inducing the voluntary emigration of the freedmen by restricting their rights and privileges at home[5] would share in these disadvantages.

201. Objections to colonization.

For these reasons it seemed to some writers more practicable as well as more just to arrange for some system of overseers or of tenant farming by which the negroes could be kept under supervision at least during the transition period. One plan was for the appointment of overseers from among the negroes themselves to look after the conduct of the rest and report to the proper authorities; incapable or vicious negroes were to be placed out for a year or other term as was done in the case of whites.[6] Another plan was to raise the negroes gradually to the condition of free tenants; the most promising should be taken first and equipped with tools and other necessaries, and assistance and guidance should be given them until they learned to manage their own farms.[7] According to still another suggestion the slave might receive a portion of the waste lands which were so plentiful among the plantations, and bring it under cultivation for himself, although he should still for a term of years or even for life be attached to the soil and held responsible by his master. The next genera-

202. Tenant farming.

---

[1] Webster, *Effects of Slavery on Morals and Industry*, 35–36; Imlay, *Topographical Description*, 223.

[2] Webster, *Effects of Slavery on Morals and Industry*, 36, note.

[3] Jefferson, *Writings*, VIII, 380.

[4] Imlay, *Topographical Description*, 223.

[5] See above, § 141.

[6] Edwards, *Injustice and Impolicy of the Slave-Trade and Slavery*, 34.

[7] Webster, *Effects of Slavery on Morals and Industry*, 37–38.

tion, in this case, might be free at the age of twenty-five. This arrangement was intended to give time for the reclaiming of the waste land and the training of the negroes to self-dependence, and was expected to leave the proprietors better off than before through the greater productiveness of the system. At the same time there would be opportunity, in case the negroes proved unequal to the occasion, for the importation of European emigrants.[1]

All these schemes, well as they looked on paper, had very little chance of showing how they would actually work. To the South, however much the existence of slavery might be regretted, emancipation seemed impossible, though ever so gradual, if the blacks were to remain in the country. 203. Causes of failure. Even the slightest allusion to the subject was beginning to arouse suspicion or fear, and measures or even phrases which had the remotest connection with the negro were regarded as offensive because they were likely to affect that species of property. Mr. Randolph's excitement because slaves might not be carried from one port to another in vessels of less than forty tons, and Mr. Early's declaration that if the negroes illegally imported were allowed to go free not one of them would be left alive within a year, sufficiently illustrate the situation.

Looking back over the period it may seem at first one of promise unfulfilled. In the light of later events the good that was done is overshadowed by what was left undone. It is necessary to realize the conditions of the time, in order to estimate fairly the progress made since James Otis asserted the rights of the British colonies. When the Declaration of Independence was adopted there was not a foot of free soil in the country. The blacks in the South had been regarded as a source of danger for nearly a century, yet their numbers had been continually increasing. The history of St. Domingo in the years immediately following the adoption of the Constitution was not an incentive to the citizens of a still unstable and very experimental government to attempt an additional experiment in the way of emancipation. That the blacks would work in a state of freedom, that they could be peaceful, useful, and law-abiding citizens, and that the productiveness of a free South would be greater than was ever possible under a system of slavery could be known only by

[1] Imlay, *Topographical Description*, 223–224.

actual experience.   With visions of famine, fire, and massacre, of all the possible horrors of an insurrection by a barbarous people situated at their very hearth-sides and burning for revenge, with the daily spectacle of the difficulties of obtaining a reasonable amount of labor from the negro even by constant oversight and severe discipline, it is not to be wondered at that the slave-holders of the South could arrive at emancipation only at the point of the sword.   Yet whatever the difficulties of emancipation, there never was a time when it could not have been accomplished with more ease and less disaster than was the case in the final crisis of the Civil War.   It was only because avarice and timidity, selfishness and sloth, at the North as well as at the South, had combined to tie the knot tighter and tighter, that only the sword could finally loose it.   Gradual abolition became more and more impossible, and a voice must cry, " Emancipation total, universal, and immediate" before the end could come.

Abolitionists of the earlier day had seen the truth as clearly and spoken it as boldly as any of the later generation.   If their language was usually more temperate it was **204. Work of the early abolitionists.** not from timidity or indifference, but because they believed that persuasion was more effective than provocation.   They did what they could to save their country from the doom which they foresaw, and it was not the insufficiency of their zeal nor the defects of their organization that made it impossible to avert that doom.   A democracy must move slowly.   The masses cannot keep the pace of the leaders. An intelligent autocrat or an enlightened and patriotic aristocracy might have put an end to slavery much more easily than was done by the great mass of the American people through their representatives in 1865 ; but the toilsome paths by which a great people have been led upward have been through fields of promise that would not have been open to the citizens of an oligarchy or an autocracy.   The abolition of slavery in America has been accomplished through the political, economic, and moral education of the whole nation, and its history will be a lesson, a warning, and an inspiration as long as the nation endures.   Honor to those who led in the movement and pointed out the way! Their schemes for universal emancipation were looked upon as impracticable, their exhortations and warnings fell for the most part on unlistening ears. Nevertheless, they accomplished the prohibition of the slave-trade, the establishment of universal liberty in the Northern States, the regulation of territorial slavery by Congress, and the custom of petitioning for further legislation. They formed the Abolition Societies and propagated anti-slavery ideas through their agency. They produced a constant outpour of anti-slavery pamphlets, orations, and newspaper and magazine articles. In these ways they laid the foundations of the work of Lundy and Garrison and the Anti-Slavery Societies, and made possible the petitions presented by John Quincy Adams and the development of the Liberty, Free Soil, and Republican parties.

BIBLIOGRAPHY

Libraries consulted: Boston Athenæum (B. A.); Boston Public Library (B.); Harvard College Library (H.); Massachusetts State Library (M. S. L.); Massachusetts Historical Society (M. H. S.); New York Historical Society (N. Y. H. S.); New York Public Library, Astor (A.) and Lenox (L.); Pennsylvania Historical Society (P. H. S.); Philadelphia Library Company (P. L. C.); Yale University Library (Y.).

Adams, Henry. The Life of Albert Gallatin. Philadelphia and London, J. B. Lippincott and Co., 1880.

Adams, John. The Works of John Adams, the Second President of the United States. With a Life of the Author, Notes and Illustrations, by his Grandson, Charles Francis Adams. 10 vols. Boston: Little, Brown, and Company. 1856.

Address, An, to the People of North Carolina, on the Evils of Slavery. By the Friends of Liberty and Equality. [The North Carolina Manumission Society. — General Association.] William Swaim, Printer, Greensborough, N. C., 1830. [Reprinted about 1860.] [H.]

Allen, William. American Biographical Dictionary. . . Boston: John P. Jewett and Company. 1851.

American Anti-Slavery Almanac, The, for 1844. . . . Compiled by D. L. Child. . . . New York: American Anti-Slavery Society, 143 Nassau Street. [H.]

[American Colonization Society.] The eighth annual Report of the American Society for colonizing the Free People of Colour of the United States. With an Appendix. Washington City, 1825. [H.]

[American Convention of Abolition Societies.] Minutes of the Proceedings of a Convention of Delegates from the Abolition Societies established in different Parts of the United States, assembled at Philadelphia on the first Day of January, one thousand seven hundred and ninety-four, and continued, by Adjournments, until the seventh Day of the same Month, inclusive. Philadelphia: Printed by Zachariah Poulson, Junr., Number Eighty Chesnut-Street, eight doors below Third-Street. 1794. pp. 30. [B.]

—— Minutes of the Proceedings of the Second Convention of Delegates from the Abolition Societies established in different Parts of the United States, assembled at Philadelphia on the seventh Day of January, one thousand seven hundred and ninety-five, and continued by Adjournments until the fourteenth Day of the same Month, inclusive. Philadelphia: Printed by Zachariah Poulson, Junr. . . . 1795. pp. 32. [B.]

American Convention, *continued.* Minutes of the Proceedings of the Third Convention of Delegates from the Abolition Societies established in different Parts of the United States, assembled at Philadelphia on the first Day of January, one thousand, seven hundred and ninety-six, and continued, by Adjournments, until the seventh Day of the same Month, inclusive. Philadelphia: Printed by Zachariah Poulson, Junior, . . . 1796. pp. 32.   [B.]

—— Address to Free Africans and other free People of Colour in the United States [1796]. *In* Cuffe, Paul, A Brief Account of the Settlement . . . of Sierra Leone. *See* Cuffe.   [H.]

—— Minutes of the Proceedings of the Fourth Convention of Delegates from the Abolition Societies established in different Parts of the United States, assembled at Philadelphia on the third Day of May, one thousand seven hundred and ninety-seven, and continued by Adjournments, until the ninth Day of the same Month, inclusive. Philadelphia, Printed by Zachariah Poulson, Junior, . . . 1797. pp. 59, including Appendix. [B.]

—— Minutes of the Proceedings of the Fifth Convention of Delegates from the Abolition Societies established in different Parts of the United States, assembled at Philadelphia, on the first Day of June, one thousand seven hundred and ninety-eight, and continued, by Adjournments, until the sixth Day of the same Month, inclusive. Philadelphia: Printed by Zachariah Poulson, Junior, . . . 1798. pp. 20.   [N. Y. H. S.]

[No Minutes published for 1799.]

—— Minutes of the Proceedings of the Sixth Convention of Delegates from the Abolition Societies established in different Parts of the United States, assembled at Philadelphia, on the fourth Day of June, one thousand eight hundred, and continued by Adjournments, until the sixth Day of the same Month, inclusive. Philadelphia: Printed by Zachariah Poulson, Junior, . . . 1800. pp. 35.   [N. Y. H. S.]

—— Minutes of the Proceedings of the Seventh Convention of Delegates from the Abolition Societies established in different parts of the United States, assembled at Philadelphia, on the third Day of June, one thousand eight hundred and one, and continued by Adjournments until the sixth Day of the same Month, inclusive. Philadelphia: Printed by Zachariah Poulson, Junior, . . . 1801. pp. 55.   [N. Y. H. S.]

[No Minutes published for 1802.]

—— Minutes of the Proceedings of the Eighth Convention of Delegates from the Abolition Societies established in different Parts of the United States, assembled at Philadelphia, on the tenth Day of January, one thousand eight hundred and three, and continued by Adjournment until the fourteenth Day of the same Month, inclusive. Philadelphia: Printed by Zachariah Poulson, Junior, . . . 1803. pp. 34.   [N. Y. H. S.]

—— Minutes of the Proceedings of the Ninth American Convention for promoting the Abolition of Slavery and improving the Condition of the African Race; assembled at Philadelphia, on the ninth Day of January, one thousand eight hundred and four, and continued by Adjournments until the thirteenth Day of the same Month, inclusive. Philadelphia: Printed by Solomon W. Conrad. 1804.   [Y.]

American Convention, *continued.* Address of the American Convention for promoting the Abolition of Slavery and improving the Condition of the African Race, assembled at Philadelphia, in January, 1804, to the People of the United States. Philadelphia : Printed by Solomon W. Conrad. 1804. pp. 8. [B. A.]

—— Minutes of the Proceedings of the Tenth American Convention for promoting the Abolition of Slavery and improving the Condition of the African Race : assembled at Philadelphia, on the fourteenth Day of January, one thousand eight hundred and five, and continued by Adjournments until the seventeenth Day of the same Month, inclusive. Philadelphia : Printed by Kimber, Conrad, & Co. 1805. pp. 44, 3.
[N. Y. H. S.]

—— Minutes of the Proceedings of the Eleventh American Convention for promoting the Abolition of Slavery and improving the Condition of the African Race : assembled at Philadelphia, on the thirteenth Day of January, one thousand eight hundred and six, and continued by Adjournments until the fifteenth Day of the same Month, inclusive. Philadelphia : Printed by Kimber, Conrad, and Co. 1806. pp. 42.   [N. Y. H. S.]

—— Minutes of the Proceedings of a Special Meeting of the Fifteenth American Convention for promoting the Abolition of Slavery and improving the Condition of the African Race, assembled at Philadelphia on the tenth Day of December, 1818, and continued by Adjournments until the fifteenth Day of the same Month, inclusive. Philadelphia : Printed for the Convention by Hall and Atkinson. 1818. pp. 68, iv. [B.]

—— Constitution of the American Convention for promoting the Abolition of Slavery, and improving the Condition of the African Race. Adopted on the eleventh Day of December, 1818, to take effect on the fifth Day of October, 1819. Philadelphia : Printed for the Convention by Hall and Atkinson. 1819. [B.]

—— Minutes of the Eighteenth Session of the American Convention for promoting the Abolition of Slavery, and improving the Condition of the African Race. Convened at Philadelphia, on the seventh Day of October, 1823. Philadephia : Printed by order of the Convention, by Daniel Neall, upon the Vertical Press. 1823. pp. 43 ; Appendix, pp. 44–65.
[B.]

—— To the Clergy and Pastors throughout the United States. N. t.-p. [Dated Philadelphia, September 18, 1826.] pp. 3. [B.]

—— Minutes of the Adjourned Session of the Twentieth Biennial American Convention for promoting the Abolition of Slavery. Held at Baltimore, November 28. Philadelphia : Published by order of the Convention. Samuel Parker, Printer, 1828. pp. 68. [B.]

American Convention for Promoting the Abolition of Slavery, &c. Address to the Citizens of the United States. [Dated Baltimore, November, 1828.] [1] N. t.-p., pp. 4. [B.]

----

[1] A more complete bibliography of the Abolition Societies from 1808 to 1830 is now being prepared by Miss Alice D. Adams in her monograph on Anti-Slavery from 1808 to 1830.

American Museum, The: or, Annual Register of fugitive Pieces, ancient and modern. For the Year 1798. [Edited by Matthew Carey.] Printed for Matthew Carey, Philadelphia, June 20, 1799.   [H.]

American Museum, The, or, Repository of ancient and modern fugitive Pieces, &c. prose and poetical. Vols. I–IV. First and second Editions, Philadelphia: Printed by Matthew Carey, 1788. Third Edition, Philadelphia: Carey, Stewart and Co., 1790.   [H.]

American Museum, The, or Universal Magazine, containing, Essays on Agriculture — Commerce — Manufactures — Politics — Morals — and Manners. Sketches of National Characters — Natural and Civil History — and Biography. . . . Vols. V–XII. Philadelphia: Carey, Stewart and Co., Vols. V–X; Vols. XI, XII, from the Press of M. Carey. 1789–1792.   [H.]

[Amynto.] Reflections on the Inconsistency of Man, particularly exemplified in the practice of Slavery in the United States. New-York: Printed and sold by John Buel. 1796. [According to Act of Congress.] pp. 27.   [N. Y. H. S.]

[Annals of Congress.] The Debates and Proceedings in the Congress of the United States. . . . Washington: Gales and Seaton. 1834.

Anti-Slavery Record, The. New York: Published by the American Anti-Slavery Society. 1835–1837.   [H.]

Appleton, Nathaniel. Considerations on Slavery. In a Letter to a Friend. Boston: Edes and Gill. 1767. pp. 16.   [B.]

Δppletons' Cyclopædia of American Biography. Edited by James Grant Wilson and John Fiske. New York, D. Appleton and Company, 1887–1889.

Appleton, The New American Encyclopædia. . . . New York: D. Appleton and Company. 1859–1863.

Ashe, Thomas. Travels in America, performed in 1806, for the Purpose of exploring the Rivers Alleghany, Monongahela, Ohio, and Mississippi, and ascertaining the Produce and Condition of their Banks and Vicinity. London: Printed. Newburyport — Reprinted for William Sawyer and Co. 1808.

Athenian Oracle, The. The second Edition, printed at London, 1704. [Boston of the Massachusetts; December 5, 1705. Printed by Bartholomew Green, and are to be sold by Samuel Phillips at the Brick Shop above the Town-House.]   [M. H. S.]
Same, *in* Hepburn, American Defence of the Christian Golden Rule, 37–40, *and in* Moore, Notes on Slavery in Massachusetts, 91–94.

Atherton, J. Speech [in the New Hampshire Convention for the Investigation, Discussion and Decision of the Federal Constitution]. *In* Walker, Joseph B., History of the New Hampshire Convention [etc.], Appendix, pp. 112–114.   [B.]

Baird, Samuel J. A Collection of the Acts, Deliverances, and Testimonies of the Supreme Judicatory of the Presbyterian Church, from its Origin in America to the present Time: with Notes and Documents explanatory and historical: constituting a complete Illustration of her

Polity, Faith and History. Philadelphia: Presbyterian Board of Publications. N. d. [B.]

Baldwin, Simeon. An Oration pronounced before the Citizens of New-
Haven, July 4th, 1788; in commemoration of the Declaration of Independence and Establishment of the Constitution of the United States
of America. New-Haven, J. Meigs, 1788. [H.]

Bangs, Nathan. The Life of the Rev. Freeborn Garrettson: compiled
from his printed and manuscript Journals, and other authentic documents. Fifth Edition. New York: Carlton & Porter. 200 Mulberry-
Street. N. d.

Barry, John Stetson. The History of Massachusetts. The Commonwealth Period. (The History of Massachusetts, Third Period.) Boston: Published for the Author. 1857.

Bassett, John Spencer. Anti-Slavery Leaders of North Carolina (Johns
Hopkins University Studies in historical and political Science, Series
XVI, No. 6.) The Johns Hopkins Press, Baltimore, June, 1898.

—— Slavery and Servitude in the Colony of North Carolina. (Johns
Hopkins University Studies in historical and political Science. Four-
teenth Series, IV–V.) Baltimore, The Johns Hopkins Press, April and
May, 1896.

—— Slavery in the State of North Carolina. (Johns Hopkins University Studies in historical and political Science. Series XVII, No. 7–8.)
The Johns Hopkins Press, Baltimore, July–August, 1899.

Baxter, Richard. The Christian Directory: The Practical Works of the
Late Reverend and Pious M^r. Richard Baxter, in four Volumes. Lon-
don: Printed for Thomas Parkhurst at the Bible and Three Crowns in
Cheapside: Jonathan Robinson at the Golden Lyon in St. Paul's Church-
Yard, and John Lawrence at the Angel in the Poultrey. 1707.

[H. and B.]

Bayard, Ferdinand M. Voyage dans l Intérieur des Etats-Unis, à Bath,
Winchester, dans la Vallée de Shenandoah, etc., etc., pendant l'Été de
1791. Seconde Edition, augmentée de descriptions et d'anecdotes sur
la vie militaire et politique de Georges Washington. Paris, Batilliot
frères, An VI? [H.]

Benedict, David. An Abridgement of the General History of the Baptist
Denomination in America, and other Parts of the World. 2 vols. in 1.
Boston: Lincoln & Edmands. 1820. [B.]

—— A General History of the Baptist Denomination in America, and
other Parts of the World. 2 vols. Boston: Printed by Manning and
Loring, for the Author. 1813. [B.]

Benezet, Anthony. The Case of our Fellow-Creatures, the Oppressed
Africans, respectfully recommended to the serious Consideration of
the Legislature of Great-Britain, by the People called Quakers. London: James Phillips. 1783. [B.]

—— A Caution to Great Britain and her Colonies, in a short Representation of the calamitous State of the enslaved Negroes in the British
Dominions. A new Edition. Philadelphia, printed: London, reprinted
by James Phillips. 1784. [H.]

Benezet, Anthony, *continued.* Observations on the inslaving, importing and purchasing of Negroes; with some Advice thereon, extracted from the Epistle of the Yearly-Meeting of the People called Quakers, held at London in the Year 1748. Second Edition. [*Anon.*] Germantown: Printed by Christopher Sower. 1760. pp. 11. [B.]

—— The potent Enemies of America laid open: being some Account of the baneful Effects attending the use of distilled spirituous Liquors, and the Slavery of the Negroes. . . . Philadelphia: Joseph Crukshank. N. d. pp. 48, 83, 16. [H.]

—— A Short Account of that Part of Africa, inhabited by the Negroes. With respect to the *Fertility* of the Country; the *good Disposition* of many of the *Natives,* and the *Manner* by which the SLAVE TRADE is carried on. The second Edition, with large additions and Amendments. [*Anon.*] Philadelphia: W. Dunlap. 1792. pp. 80. [H.]

—— Short Observations on Slavery, introductory to some Extracts from the Writing of the Abbé Raynal, on that important Subject. [*Anon.*] N. t.-p., n. d. pp. 12. [H.]

—— Some Historical Account of Guinea, its Situation, Produce, and the general Disposition of its Inhabitants. With an Inquiry into the Rise and Progress of the Slave Trade, its Nature and lamentable Effects. London: J. Phillips. 1788. pp. 132. [H.]

Bernard, John. Retrospections of America, 1797-1811. Edited from the Manuscript by Mrs. Bayle Bernard with an Introduction, Notes, and Index by Laurence Hutton and Brander Matthews. New York, Harper and Brothers, 1887. [H.]

Bettle, Edward. Notices of Negro Slavery as connected with Pennsylvania. Read before the Historical Society of Pennsylvania, 8th mo., 7th, 1826. *In* Pa. Hist. Soc. Mem., I, 365-416. Philadelphia, J. B. Lippincott and Co., 1864.

Birkbeck, Morris. Extracts from a supplementary Letter from the Illinois; an Address to British Emigrants; and a Reply to the Remarks of William Cobbett, Esq. London: Printed for James Ridgway. 1819. [H.]

—— Letters from Illinois. London: Printed for Taylor and Hessey. 1818. [H.]

—— Notes on a Journey in America, from the Coast of Virginia to the Territory of Illinois. London: Printed for Ridgway and Sons. 1818. [H.]

Birney, William. James G. Birney and his Times. The Genesis of the Republican Party with some Account of the Abolition Movements in the South before 1828. New York, D. Appleton and Company, 1890.

[Blane, William Newnham.] An English Gentleman. An Excursion through the United States and Canada during the Years 1822-23. Printed for Baldwin, Cradock, and Joy, London, 1824.

[Bonnet, Abbé J. E.] Réponse aux principales Questions qui peuvent être faites sur les Etats-Unis de l'Amérique, par un citoyen adoptif de la Pensylvanie. 2 vols. Lausanne, Henri Vincent, 1795. [H.]

Bonnet, M. [J.] E. Tableau des États-Unis de l'Amérique, au Commencement du XIX? Siècle. Paris, Testu et C?, 1816. [H.]

[Boston Town Records.] A Report of the Record Commissioners of the City of Boston containing the Records of the Boston Selectmen. Boston: Rockwell and Churchill. 1874– .

Bourne, George. Man-Stealing and Slavery denounced by the Presbyterian and Methodist Churches. Together with an Address to all the Churches. Boston: Garrison and Knapp. 1834 [B.]

Brackett, Jeffrey R. The Negro in Maryland A Study of the Institution of Slavery. Baltimore, Johns Hopkins University, 1889.

—— The Status of the Slave. 1775–1789. *In* Essays in the Constitutional History of the United States in the formative Period, 1775–1789, by Graduates and former Members of the Johns Hopkins University. Edited by J. Franklin Jameson. pp. 263–311. Boston and New York, Houghton, Mifflin and Company, 1899.

Bradford, Alden. History of Massachusetts from 1764 to 1820. 3 vols. Boston: Richardson and Lord [etc.]. 1822–1829.

Branagan, Thomas. Avenia: or, a Tragical Poem, on the Oppression of the human Species, and Infringement of the Rights of Man. In six Books, with Notes explanatory and miscellaneous. Written in imitation of Homer's Iliad. Philadelphia: Printed for Silas Engles and Samuel Wood. 1805. pp. 358. [B.]

—— Buying Stolen Goods synonymous with Stealing; or, The Immorality of using the Products of Slavery demonstrated. Addressed to Christians of all Denominations. *In* The Penitential Tyrant, Appendix, pp. 219–239.

—— The Penitential Tyrant or Slave-Trader Reformed. A Pathetic Poem in four cantos [and other pieces]. [New York: 1807.] N. t.–p. pp. 302. [B.]

—— Political & theological Disquisitions on the Signs of the Times, relative to the present Conquests of France etc. Trenton: Printed for the Author. 1807. pp. 216. [B]

—— A Preliminary Essay on the Oppression of the exiled Sons of Africa, consisting of Animadversions on the Impolicy and Barbarity of the deleterious Commerce and subsequent Slavery of the human Species. . . . Philadelphia: Printed for the Author by John W. Scott. 1804. pp. 282. [B]

—— Serious Remonstrances, addressed to the Citizens of the Northern States and their Representatives, being an Appeal to their Natural Feelings and Common Sense; consisting of Speculations and Animadversions, on the recent Revival of the Slave Trade in the American Republic. Philadelphia: Thomas T. Stiles. 1805. pp. 133. [B.]

Brief Statement, A, of the Rise and Progress of the Testimony of the Religious Society of Friends, against Slavery and the Slave Trade. Published by direction of the Yearly Meeting, held in Philadelphia, in the Fourth month, 1843. Philadelphia: Joseph and William Kite. 1843. pp. 59. [H.]

Brissot de Warville, J. P. New Travels in the United States of America, performed in 1788. . . 2 vols. Second Edition, corrected. London: Printed for J. S. Jordan. 1794. [H.]

—— An Oration upon the Necessity of establishing at Paris, a Society to promote the Abolition of the Trade and Slavery of the Negroes. *In* Clarkson, Essay on the Slave Trade, Appendix. [B. A.]

Bristed, John. The Resources of the United States of America; or a View of the agricultural, commercial, manufacturing, financial, political, literary, moral and religious Capacity and Character of the American People. New-York: James Eastburn and Co. 1818. [H.]

British Bostonian, A. An Oration, on the Beauties of Liberty, or the essential Rights of the Americans. Delivered at the Second Baptist-Church in Boston, upon the last annual Thanksgiving, Dec. 3ᵈ, 1772. . . . The third Edition, carefully corrected by the Author, in which are many Additions . . . and Remarks on the Rights and Liberties of the Africans, inserted by particular Desire. Boston: N. E. Printed and sold by E. Russell, next the Cornfield. 1773. pp. 78. [H.]

Brown, David Paul. The Forum; or Forty Years Full Practice at the Philadelphia Bar. 2 vols. Philadelphia: Robert H. Small, Law Bookseller. 1856. [H.]

Brown, John Mason. The Political Beginnings of Kentucky. A Narrative of public Events bearing on the History of that State up to the Time of its Admission into the American Union. Louisville: John P· Morton and Company, Printers to the Filson Club. 1889.

Bruce, Henry. Life of General Oglethorpe. (Makers of America Series.) New York, Dodd, Mead and Company, 1890.

Buchanan, George. An Oration upon the Moral and Political Evil of Slavery. Delivered at a Public Meeting of the Maryland Society, for promoting the Abolition of Slavery, and the Relief of Free Negroes, and others unlawfully held in Bondage. Baltimore, July 4th, 1791. Baltimore: Philip Edwards. 1793. pp. 20. [B. A.]

Buckingham, Joseph T. Specimens of Newpaper Literature : with personal Memoirs, Anecdotes and Reminiscences. Boston: Redding and Company. 1852. [H.]

Burling, William. An Address to the Elders of the Church upon the Occasion of some Friends compelling certain Persons, and their Posterity, to serve them continually and arbitraryly, without Regard to Equity or Right, not heeding whether they give them any thing near so much as their Labour deserveth. [1718.] *In* Lay, All Slave-Keepers Apostates, pp. 6–10. [P. L. C.]

[Candler, Isaac] An Englishman. A Summary View of America : comprising a Description of the Face of the Country, and of several of the principal Cities ; and Remarks on the social, moral and political Character of the People : being the Result of Observations and Enquiries during a Journey in the United States. London: Printed for T. Cadell. 1824. [H.]

Channing, Edward. The Narragansett Planters. A Study of Causes. (Johns Hopkins University Studies in historical and political Science. Fourth Series, III.) Baltimore, Johns Hopkins University, March, 1886.

Chastellux, François Jean, Marquis de. Travels in North-America, in the Years 1780, 1781, and 1782. Translated from the French by an English Gentleman [J. Kent], who resided in America at that Period. With Notes by the Translator. 2 vols. London : Printed for G. G. J. and J. Robinson. 1787. [H.]

Chateaubriand, [François Auguste] Vicomte de. Voyages en Amérique, en France, et en Italie. 2 vols. Paris, Ambroise Dupont et Cⁱᵉ, 1828. [H.]

Child, Lydia Maria. Isaac T. Hopper: A True Life. Boston: John P. Jewett and Co. 1853.

Clarkson, T. An Essay on the Impolicy of the African Slave Trade. In two Parts. To which is added An Oration upon the Necessity of establishing at Paris, a Society to promote the Abolition of the Trade and Slavery of the Negroes, by J. P. Brissot de Warville. Philadelphia : Printed by Francis Bailey, at Yorick's Head, in Market-street. 1788.
[B. A.]

[Clarkson, Thomas.] An Essay on the Slavery and Commerce of the Human Species, particularly the African, translated from a Latin Dissertation, which was honoured with the first Prize in the University of Cambridge, for the year 1785, with Additions. London, printed : Philadelphia : Re-printed by Joseph Crukshank. 1786. pp. 155. [B.]

Coffin, Joshua. A Sketch of the History of Newbury, Newburyport, and West Newbury, from 1635 to 1845. Boston : Samuel G. Drake. 1845. [H.]

Coleman, Elihu. A Testimony against that Anti-Christian Practice of making Slaves of Men, wherein it is shewed to be contrary to the Dispensation of the Law and Time of the Gospel, and very opposite both to Grace and Nature. Printed in the year 1733. New Bedford : Reprinted for Abraham Shearman, Jun. 1825. pp. 24. [H.]

Colman, Benjamin. [Extracts from Essay in The Essex Journal, Newburyport, July 20, 1774, and from Letter in ibid., Sept. 16, 1775], *in* Coffin, Sketch of the History of Newbury, 339–345. [B.]

Computation that the Importation of Negroes is not so profitable as that of White Servants. *In* Moore, Notes on Slavery in Massachusetts, pp. 107–108.
Reprinted from the Boston News-Letter, No. 112, June 10, 1706.

Connecticut. Acts and Laws of the State of Connecticut, in America. New-London: Timothy Green. 1784–1792. [M. S. L.]
—— —— Hartford : Hudson and Goodwin. 1796. [H.]
—— The Public Records of the Colony of Connecticut. [1636–1776.] With notes etc. by J. Hammond Trumbull [etc.]. 15 vols. Hartford, 1850–1890. [H.]

Conscience. [An article without title, refused by the newspapers.] *In* A British Bostonian, Oration on the Beauties of Liberty, Appendix, pp. 76–78. [H.]

Cooley, Henry Scofield. A Study of Slavery in New Jersey. (Johns Hopkins University Studies in historical and political Science. Fourteenth Series, IX–X.) Baltimore, The Johns Hopkins Press, September and October, 1896.

[Cooper, James Fenimore.] Notions of the Americans: picked up by a Travelling Bachelor. 2 vols. London: Henry Colburn. 1828. [H.]

Crawford, Charles. Observations upon Negro-Slavery. Philadelphia: Joseph Crukshank. 1784. pp. 24. [H.]

[Crèvecœur,] J. Hector St. John [de]. Letters from an American Farmer ; describing certain provincial Situations, Manners, and Customs, not generally known ; and conveying some Idea of the late and present interior Circumstances of the British Colonies in North America. Written for the Information of a Friend in England. London, printed for Thomas Davies and Lockyer Davis, 1782. [H.]

Cuffe, Paul. A Brief Account of the Settlement and present Situation of the Colony of Sierra Leone in Africa . . . to which is subjoined, an address to the people of colour, from the Convention of Delegates from the Abolition Societies in the U States [1796], pp. 10–12. New York: Samuel Wood. 1812.

Cursory Remarks on the Character of Anthony Benezet. Read in the Franklinian Society, March, 1791. *In* The American Museum, Vol. IX, pp. 192–194.

Dana, James. The African Slave Trade. A Discourse delivered in the City of New-Haven, September 9, 1790, before the Connecticut Society for the Promotion of Freedom. New-Haven: Thomas and Samuel Green. 1791. pp. 33.

Dane, Nathan. A General Abridgment and Digest of American Law, with occasional Notes and Comments. 8 vols. Boston: Cummings, Hilliard and Co. 1824.

Danish Laws, The: or, The Code of Christian the Fifth. Faithfully translated for the Use of the English Inhabitants of the Danish Settlements in America. London: Printed for N. Gibson. 1756. [H.]

Darby, William. A Geographical Description of the State of Louisiana: presenting a View of the Soil, Climate, Animal, Vegetable and Mineral Productions ; . . . with an Account of the Character and Manners of the Inhabitants. . . . Printed for the Author, and published by John Melish, Philadelphia. 1816. [H.]

Davis, Daniel. An Oration, delivered at Portland, July 4th, 1796, in commemoration of the Anniversary of American Independence. Portland. Thomas Baker Wait. N. d. [H.]

Dawson, Henry B. The Assault on Stony Point, by General Anthony Wayne, July 16, 1779. Prepared for the New York Historical Society, and read at its regular monthly meeting, April 1, 1862. . . . Morrisania, N. Y., 1863. [H.]

Deane, Charles. The Connection of Massachusettts with Slavery and the Slave-Trade. Read at the annual Meeting of the American Antiquarian Society at Worcester, Mass., Oct. 21, 1886. Worcester, Charles Hamilton, 1886. [H.]

Deane, Charles, Editor. Letters and Documents relating to Slavery in Massachusetts. Edited with a Preface and Notes by Charles Deane. Reprinted from the Collections of the Massachusetts Historical Society [5th Series, Vol. III. pp. 373–442]. Cambridge : John Wilson and Son. 1877. [H.]

Delaware. Laws of the State of Delaware, from the fourteenth Day of October, one thousand seven hundred, to the eighteenth Day of August, one thousand seven hundred and ninety-seven. 2 vols. New-Castle : Samuel and John Adams. 1797. [H.]

Dickinson, John. Draft of an Act for the gradual Abolition of Slavery in Delaware. (From the original in the hand-writing of John Dickinson in the Historical Society of Pennsylvania.) *In* Stillé, Life and Times of John Dickinson, Appendix VIII, pp. 424–431. [H.]

—— *See* A Farmer.

Dixon, William Hepworth. William Penn : An Historical Biography, from new Sources . . . Philadelphia : Blanchard and Lea. 1851. [H.]

Drake, Francis S. Dictionary of American Biography, including Men of the Time. . . . Boston : James R. Osgood and Company. 1872.

DuBois, W. E. B. The Suppression of the African Slave-Trade to the United States of America, 1638–1870. (Harvard Historical Studies, Vol. I.) New York, London, and Bombay : Longmans, Green and Co. 1896.

Duncan, John M. Travels through Part of the United States and Canada in 1818 and 1819. 2 vols. Glasgow : Printed for Hurst, Robinson, and Company, London. 1823. [H.]

Dunlevy, A. H. History of the Miami Baptist Association ; from its organization in 1797 to a division . . . in 1836. Cincinnati, Geo. S. Blanchard and Co., 1869. [B.]

Dwight, Theodore. An Oration, spoken before the Society of the Cincinnati, of the State of Connecticut, met in Hartford, on the 4th of July, 1792. Hartford, Hudson and Goodwin, 1792. [H.]

—— An Oration, spoken before " the Connecticut Society, for the Promotion of Freedom and the Relief of Persons unlawfully holden in Bondage." Convened in Hartford, on the 8th Day of May, A.D. 1794. Hartford, Hudson and Goodwin, 1794. pp. 24. [H.]

Dwight, Timothy. Travels ; in New-England and New-York. 4 vols. New-Haven : Timothy Dwight. 1822. [H.]

Edwards, Jonathan. The Injustice and Impolicy of the Slave-Trade, and of the Slavery of the Africans : illustrated in a Sermon preached before the Connecticut Society for the Promotion of Freedom, and for the Relief of Persons unlawfully holden in Bondage, at their annual Meeting in New-Haven, September 15, 1791 . . . Providence : John Carter. 1792. pp. 38 ; Appendix, pp. 38–60. [H.]

Elliot, Jonathan, *Editor.* Debates on the Adoption of the Federal Constitution, in the Convention held at Philadelphia, in 1787 ; with a Diary of the Debates of the Congress of the Confederation ; as reported by James Madison. Complete in one volume, supplementary to Elliot's Debates. (The Madison Papers.) Washington : Printed for the Editor. 1845.

Elliot, Jonathan, *Editor, continued.* The Debates in the several State Conventions, on the Adoption of the Federal Constitution, as recommended by the General Convention at Philadelphia in 1787. 4 vols. Washington, printed for the Editor, 1836.

Evans, Estwick. A Pedestrious Tour, of four thousand Miles, through the Western States and Territories, during the Winter and Spring of 1818. Interspersed with brief Reflections upon a great Variety of Topics: religious, moral, political, sentimental, &c., &c. Concord, N. H., Joseph C. Spear, 1819. [H.]

Farmer, A [John Dickinson]. A Serious Address to the Rulers of America on the Inconsistency of their Conduct respecting Slavery : forming a Contrast between the Encroachments of England on American Liberty, and, American Injustice in tolerating Slavery. Trenton printed : London, reprinted by J. Phillips, 1783. pp. 24. [H.]

Faux, W. Memorable Days in America : being a Journal of a Tour to the United States, principally undertaken to ascertain, by positive Evidence, the Condition and probable Prospects of British Emigrants. . . . London : Printed for W. Simpkin and R. Marshall. 1823. [H.]

Fearon, Henry Bradshaw. Sketches of America. A Narrative of a Journey of five thousand Miles through the eastern and western States of America; contained in eight Reports addressed to the thirty-nine English Families by whom the Author was deputed, in June 1817, to ascertain whether any, and what Part of the United States would be suitable for their Residence. . . . London : Printed for Longman, Hurst, Rees, Orme, and Brown. 1816. [H.]

Felt, Joseph B. Annals of Salem. Second Edition. 2 vols. Salem : W. & S. B. Ives. Boston : James Munroe & Co. 1845, 1849. [H.]

Flint, James. Letters from America, containing Observations on the Climate and Agriculture of the Western States, the Manners of the People, the Prospects of Emigrants, &c., &c. Edinburgh : Printed for W. & C. Tait [etc.]. 1822. [H.]

Flint, Timothy. Recollections of the Last Ten Years, passed in occasional Residences and Journeyings in the Valley of the Mississippi . . . In a Series of Letters to the Rev. James Flint, of Salem, Massachusetts. Boston : Cummings, Hilliard, and Company. 1826. [H.]

Flower, Richard. Letters from Lexington and the Illinois, containing a brief Account of the English Settlement in the latter Territory, and a Refutation of the Misrepresentations of Mr. Cobbett. London : Printed for J. Ridgway. 1819. [H.]

Force, Peter, *Editor.* American Archives : consisting of a Collection of authentick Records, State Papers, Debates and Letters and other Notices of publick Affairs. . . . In six series. Fourth Series, containing a Documentary History of the English Colonies in North America, from the King's Message to Parliament, of March 7, 1774, to the Declaration of Independence by the United States. 6 vols. Washington, 1837–1846. [H.]

A Forensic Dispute on the Legality of enslaving the Africans, held at the public Commencement in Cambridge, New-England, July 21st, 1773;

by two Candidates for the Bachelor's Degree [Theodore Parsons and Eliphalet Pearson]. Boston : Printed for Thomas Leverett. 1773. pp. 48. [H.]

Fowler, William C. The Historical Status of the Negro, in Connecticut. A Paper read before the New Haven Colony Historical Society. Reprinted from the Historical Magazine. New Haven : Tuttle, Morehouse & Taylor. 1875.

Framery, M. Recherches Statistiques sur la Pennsylvanie &c. Accompagnées de quelques Remarques, sur le Sol, le Commerce, sur les Manufactures et sur le Gouvernement des Etats-Unis, et sur les Mœurs des Américains. MS. [About 1816.] [B.]

Franklin, Benjamin. The Complete Works, including his private as well as his official and scientific Correspondence, and numerous Letters and Documents now for the first Time printed, with many others not included in any former Collection. . . . 10 vols. Compiled and edited by John Bigelow. New York and London, G. P. Putnam's Sons, 1887.

—— An Essay on the African Slave Trade. [*Anon.*] Philadelphia : Printed by Daniel Humphreys, in Front-Street, near the Drawbridge. 1790. pp. 15. [H.]

Freeman, F. Yaradee ; A Plea for Africa, in familiar Conversations on the Subject of Slavery and Colonization, Appendix. Philadelphia : J. Whetham. 1836. [H.]

Freeman, Frederick. The History of Cape Cod : the Annals of Barnstable County and of its several Towns, including the District of Mashpee. 2 vols. Boston : Printed for the Author, by Geo. C. Rand & Avery. 1860. [H.]

Garretson, Freeborn. A Dialogue between Do-Justice and Professing Christian. Dedicated to the Respective and Collective Abolition Societies, and to all other Benevolent, Humane Philanthropists, in America. Wilmington : Printed by Peter Brynberg for the Author. N. d. [Between 1803 and 1827.] pp. 58.

Genius, The, of Universal Emancipation, a monthly periodical work, containing original essays, documents, and facts, relative to the subject of African Slavery. Edited by Benjamin Lundy. Greeneville, Tenn., Washington and Baltimore, 1821–1836. [B.]

Georgia Historical Society. Collections. 4 vols. Savannah : Printed for the Society. 1840–1878.

Germantown Friends' Protest against Slavery, 1688. To yᵉ Monthly Meeting held at Richard Worrell's. [With Artotype Facsimile by J. Carbutt, Philadelphia, 1880.] [H.]

Giddings, Joshua R. Relation of the Federal Government to Slavery. [Speech on the bill making appropriations to carry into effect our Treaty with Mexico. Delivered in Committee of the Whole House, February 17, 1849.] *In* Giddings, Speeches in Congress. Boston : John P. Jewett and Company. 1853.

Godwyn, Morgan. The Negro's & Indians Advocate, suing for their Admission into the Church : . . shewing, that as the Compliance therewith can prejudice no Mans just Interest; So the wilful Neglecting and Opposing of it, is no less than a manifest Apostacy from the Christian Faith. London, Printed for the Author, by F. D. and are to be Sold by most Booksellers. 1680. pp. 174. [H.]

Gordon, William. Letter to the Freemen of the Massachusetts-Bay (I). *In* The Independent Chronicle and the Universal Advertiser, April 2, 1778. Massachusetts-State. Boston: Powars and Willis. [B. A.]

Gordon, William. Letter to the Freemen of the Massachusetts-Bay (II). *In* The Continental Journal, and Weekly Advertiser, April 9, 1778. Boston: John Gill. [B.A.]

Gustavus, Letters of. *In* The Connecticut Courant, April to September, 1797. [Summary of contents given September 11. Letters on Slavery, August 14, 21, and 28, September 4 and 11.] Hartford: Hudson and Goodwin. [B.]

Hall, Basil. Travels in North America, in the Years 1827 and 1828. 3 vols. Edinburgh: Printed for Cadell and Co. . . . 1829. [H.]

Hall, Francis. Travels in Canada, and the United States, in 1816 and 1817. Second Edition. London: Printed for Longman, Hurst, Rees, Orme, and Brown. 1819. [H.]

Hamilton, John C. History of the Republic of the United States of America, as traced in the Writings of Alexander Hamilton and of his Cotemporaries. 6 vols. New York: D. Appleton and Company. 1857.

Hammond, Isaac W. Slavery in New Hampshire. *In* The Granite Monthly, Vol. IV, pp. 108–110. Concord, N. H., 1883.

Harris, Thaddeus Mason. The Journal of a Tour into the Territory northwest of the Alleghany Mountains; made in the Spring of the Year 1803. With a geographical and historical Account of the State of Ohio. Illustrated with original Maps and Views. Boston: Manning and Loring. 1805. [H.]

Harris, William Tell. Remarks made during a Tour through the United States of America, in the Years 1817, 1818, and 1819. In a Series of Letters to Friends in England. London: Printed for Sherwood, Neely, & Jones. 1821 [H.]

Hart, Albert Bushnell, *Editor.* American History told by Contemporaries. Vol. II. New York, The Macmillan Company, 1898.

Haynes, Fred Emory. The Struggle for a Constitution in Massachusetts, 1775–1780. MS. [H.]

Hazard, Samuel. Annals of Pennsylvania, from the Discovery of the Delaware, 1609–1682. Philadelphia: Hazard and Mitchell. 1850. [H.]

—— *Editor.* The Register of Pennsylvania. Devoted to the preservation of Facts and Documents and every other kind of useful Information respecting the State of Pennsylvania. 16 vols. Philadelphia: W. F. Geddes. 1828–1835. [H.]

Hening, William Waller. *See* Virginia, Statutes at Large.

Henry, William Wirt. Patrick Henry. Life, Correspondence and Speeches. 3 vols. New York, Charles Scribner's Sons, 1891.

Hepburn, John. The American Defence of the Christian Golden Rule. N. t.-p. [1714.] pp. 40. [B.]

Hodgson, Adam. Letters from North America, written during a Tour in the United States and Canada. 2 vols. London: Printed for Hurst, Robinson, & Co. [etc.]. 1824. [H.]

Holditch, Robert. The Emigrant's Guide to the United States of America; containing the best Advice and Directions . . . also the latest Information concerning the Climate, Productions, Population, Manners, Prices of Land, Labour, and Provisions, and other Subjects, economical and political. . . . London: Printed for William Hone. 1818. [H.]

Holmes, Abiel. Life of Ezra Stiles, DD., LL.D. . . . Published according to Act of Congress. Boston: Printed by Thomas and Andrews, Faust's Statue, No. 45 Newbury St. May, 1798. [H.]

Holmes, Isaac. An Account of the United States of America, derived from actual Observation, during a Residence of four Years in that Republic: including original Communications. London: Printed at the Caxton Press, by Henry Fisher. [1823.] [H.]

Hopkins, Samuel. A Dialogue concerning the Slavery of the Africans, showing it to be the Duty and Interest of the American Colonies to emancipate all the African Slaves. With an Address to the Owners of such Slaves. Dedicated to the Honorable Continental Congress. *In* Hopkins, Works, Vol. II, pp. 547–594. Boston: Doctrinal Tract and Book Society. 1854.

—— A Discourse upon the Slave Trade and the Slavery of the Africans. Delivered before the Providence Society for abolishing the Slave-Trade, etc. at their annual Meeting, May 17, 1793. *In* Hopkins, Works, Vol. II, pp. 595–612.

—— ("Crito"). The Slave Trade and Slavery. Originally published in The Providence Gazette and Country Journal [Oct. 13, 1787]. *In* Hopkins, Works, Vol. II, pp. 613–624.

Howitt, E. Selections from Letters written during a Tour through the United States, in the Summer and Autumn of 1819 . . . Nottingham: J. Dunn. [1820.] [H.]

Humanitas. Reflections on Slavery; with recent Evidence of its Inhumanity. Occasioned by the melancholy Death of Romain, a French Negro. Philadelphia: Printed for the Author, by R. Cochran. 1803. pp. 40. [B.]

Humes, Thomas William. The Loyal Mountaineers of Tennessee. Knoxville, Tenn., Ogden Brothers and Company, 1888.

Humphreys, D. A Valedictory Discourse, delivered before the Cincinnati of Connecticut, in Hartford, July 4th, 1804, at the Dissolution of the Society. Published at the Request of the Society. Boston, Gilbert and Dean, 1804. [H.]

Hurd, John Codman. The Law of Freedom and Bondage in the United States. 2 vols. Boston: Little, Brown and Co. New York: D. Van Nostrand. 1858.

Illinois.] The Slave-Code of the State of Illinois. *In* The Genius of Liberty. Extra. [Lowell, La Salle Co., Ill.] [B.]

Imlay, Gilbert. A Topographical Description of the Western Territory of North America: containing a succinct Account of its Soil, Climate, Natural History, Population, Agriculture, Manners, and Customs. . . . The third Edition, with great Additions. London: Printed for J. Debrett. 1797. [H.]

Inquiry, An, into the Causes of the Insurrection of the Negroes in the Island of St. Domingo. To which are added, Observations of M Garran-Coulon on the same subject, read in his absence by M. Gaudet, before the National Assembly, 29th Feb. 1792. London: Printed: Philadelphia: Re-printed and sold by Joseph Crukshank. 1792. [N. Y. H. S.]

Jameson, John Franklin. William Usselinx, Founder of the Dutch and Swedish West India Companies. (Papers of the American Historical Association, Vol. II, No. 3.) New York and London, G. P. Putnam's Sons, 1887.

Janney, Samuel M. History of the Religious Society of Friends, from its Rise to the Year 1828. 4 vols. Philadelphia: T. Ellwood Zell. 1861.

Jay, John. Correspondence and Public Papers. Edited by Henry P. Johnston. 4 vols. G. P. Putnam's Sons, New York and London [1890].

Jay, William. An Inquiry into the Character and Tendency of the American Colonization, and American Anti-Slavery Societies. New York: Leavitt, Lord & Co. Boston: Crocker & Brewster. 1835. [B.]

—— The Life of John Jay: with Selections from his Correspondence and miscellaneous Papers. 2 vols. New-York: J. & J. Harper. 1833.

Jefferson, Thomas, The Writings of. Collected and edited by Paul Leicester Ford. G. P. Putnam's Sons, New York and London, 1894.

—— —— Being his Autobiography, Correspondence, Reports, Messages, Addresses, and other Writings, official and private. Published by the order of the Joint Committee of Congress on the Library, from the original Manuscripts, deposited in the Department of State. With explanatory notes etc. by H. A. Washington. 9 vols. Published by Taylor & Maury, Washington, D. C., 1853.

Jones, Absalom. A Thanksgiving Sermon preached January 1, 1808, in St. Thomas's, or the African Episcopal, Church, Philadelphia, on account of the Abolition of the African Slave Trade, on that Day, by the Congress of the United States. Philadelphia: Fry and Kammerer. 1808. [B.]

Jones, Charles C., Jr. The History of Georgia. 2 vols. Houghton, Mifflin and Co., 1883.

Jones, Electa F. Stockbridge, Past and Present; or, Records of an old Mission Station Springfield: Samuel Bowles & Company. 1854. [H.]

Journals of Congress and of the United States in Congress assembled, containing the Proceedings from Sept. 5, 1774 to 1788. Published by order of Congress. 13 vols. Philadelphia: 1777-1788. [H.]

Kalm, Peter. Travels into North America; containing its Natural History, and a circumstantial Account of its Plantations and Agriculture in general, with the civil, ecclesiastical and commercial state of the Country, the Manners of the Inhabitants etc. Translated into English by John Reinhold Forster. The second Edition. 2 vols. London: Printed for T. Lowndes. 1772. [H.]

Keith, George. An Exhortation and Caution to Friends concerning buying or keeping of Negroes. Given forth by our Monthly Meeting in Philadelphia, the 13th Day of the 8th Moneth, 1693, and recommended to all our Friends and Brethren . . . *In* The Pa. Mag. Hist. and Biog., Vol. XIII, pp. 265-270.

Kentucky. A Digest of the Statute Laws of Kentucky of a public and permanent Nature, from the Commencement of the Government to the Session of the Legislature, ending February 24, 1834. With references to judicial decisions. 2 vols. C. S. Morehead and Mason Brown. Frankfort, Kentucky, Albert G. Hodges, 1834. [B.]

Kingsley, James L. Life of Ezra Stiles, President of Yale College. (Sparks, Library of American Biography, second Series, Vol. VI.) Boston: Charles C. Little and James Brown. 1845.

Lalor, John J., *Editor*. Cyclopædia of Political Science, Political Economy, and of the History of the United States, by the best American and European Writers. 3 vols. Chicago: Rand, McNally & Company. 1881.

Lambert, John. Travels through Lower Canada, and the United States of North America, in the Years 1806, 1807, and 1808. . . . 3 vols. With Engravings. London: Printed for Richard Phillips. 1810. [H.]

Laurens, Henry. A South Carolina Protest against Slavery: being a Letter from Henry Laurens, second President of the Continental Congress, to his Son, Colonel John Laurens; dated Charleston, S. C., August 14th, 1776. Now first published from the Original. New York: G. P. Putnam. 1861. [H.]

Lay, Benjamin. ALL SLAVE-KEEPERS, that keep the Innocent in Bondage, APOSTATES Pretending to lay Claim to the Pure & Holy Christian Religion; of what Congregation so ever; but especially in their Ministers, by whose Example the filthy Leprosy and Apostacy is spread far and near; it is a notorious Sin, which many of the true Friends of Christ, and his pure Truth, called *Quakers*, has been for many years, and still are concerned to write and bear Testimony against; as a Practice so gross & hurtful to Religion, and destructive to Government, beyond what Words can set forth, or can be declared of by Men or Angels, and yet lived in by Ministers and Magistrates in *America. The Leaders of the People cause them to Err.* Written for a General Service, by him that truly and sincerely desires the present and eternal Happiness of all Mankind, all the World over, of all Colours, and Nations, as his own Soul. PHILADELPHIA: Printed for the AUTHOR. 1737. pp. 271, 6. [P. L. C.]

Lee. "Add." *In* Views of American Slavery taken a Century ago, Appendix, pp. 109-112. [H.]

Lincoln, Levi. Brief in the Slave Case tried 1781. *In* Mass. Hist. Soc. Coll., 5th Series, III, 438-442, *and in* Mass. Hist. Soc. Proc., 1857, pp. 197-201.

Lincoln, William. History of Worcester, Massachusetts, from its earliest Settlement to September, 1836. Worcester: Moses D. Phillips and Co. 1837. [H.]

Livermore, George. An Historical Research respecting the Opinions of the Founders of the Republic on Negroes as Slaves, as Citizens, and as Soldiers. Read before the Mass. Hist. Soc., Aug. 14, 1862. Boston: John Wilson and Son. 1862.

Lyman, Theodore, Jr. Free Negroes and Mulattoes. [Report of a Committee to the Massachusetts] House of Representatives, January 16, 1822. True & Green, Boston. N. t.–p., n. d. [H.]

McCall, Hugh. The History of Georgia, containing brief Sketches of the most remarkable Events, up to the present Day. 2 vols. Savannah: Seymour and Williams. 1811. [H.]

McDougall, Marion Gleason. Fugitive Slaves (1619–1865). (Publications of the Society for the Collegiate Instruction of Women, Fay House Monographs, No. 3.) Boston, Ginn and Company, 1891.

Maclay, William. Journal. 1789–1791. Edited by Edgar S. Maclay. New York, D. Appleton and Company, 1890.

McLeod, Alexander. Negro Slavery Unjustifiable. A Discourse by the late Alexander McLeod. 1802. Eleventh Edition. With an Appendix. New York: Alexander McLeod. 1863. pp. 49. [B.]

McPherson, J. H. T. History of Liberia. (Johns Hopkins University Studies in historical and political Science. Ninth Series, X.) Baltimore, The Johns Hopkins University Press, October, 1891.

McTyeire, Holland N. A History of Methodism: comprising a View of the Rise of this Revival of spiritual Religion in the first half of the eighteenth Century. Nashville, Tenn., Southern Methodist Publishing House, 1887. [B.]

Macy, Obed. The History of Nantucket; being a compendious Account of the first Settlement of the Island by the English, together with the Rise and Progress of the Whale Fishery. . . . Boston: Hilliard, Gray, and Co. 1835. [H.]

Madison, James. Letters and other Writings. 4 vols. Published by order of Congress. Philadelphia: J. B. Lippincott and Co. 1865.

—— The Papers of James Madison, purchased by order of Congress; being his Correspondence and Reports of Debates during the Congress of the Confederation and his Reports of Debates in the Federal Convention; Now published from the original Manuscripts . . . under the Superintendence of Henry D. Gilpin. 3 vols. Washington: Langtree & O'Sullivan. 1840.

Maryland. Abridgment and Collection of the Acts of Assembly of the Province of Maryland at present in force. . . . By James Bisset. Philadelphia: printed by William Bradford, for the Author. 1759. [H.]

—— The Laws of Maryland, to which are prefixed the original Charter, with an English Translation, the Bill of Rights and Constitution of the State. . . . Revised and collected under Authority of the Legislature by William Kilty, Attorney at Law. 2 vols. Annapolis: 1799, 1800. [H.]

—— The Laws of Maryland, with the Charter, the Bill of Rights, the Constitution of the State, and its Alterations, etc. 3 vols. Revised by Virgil Maxcy. Baltimore: Philip H. Nicklin & Co. 1811. [H.]

[**Maryland Abolition Society.**] Constitution of the Maryland Society, for promoting the Abolition of Slavery, and the relief of free Negroes, and others, unlawfully held in Bondage. Baltimore: William Goddard and James Angell. 1789. pp. 8. [N. Y. H. S.]

Mason, Jonathan. Extract from a Diary kept by the Hon Jonathan Mason of a Journey from Boston to Savannah in the Year 1804. [Reprinted from the Proceedings of the Massachusetts Historical Society, 1885.] Cambridge: John Wilson and Son. 1885. [H.]

Massachusetts. The Colonial Laws of Massachusetts. Reprinted from the Edition of 1660, with the Supplements to 1672. Containing also, The Body of Liberties of 1641. Published by order of the City Council of Boston, under the supervision of William H. Whitmore, Record Commissioner. Boston: 1889. [H.]

—— The Acts and Resolves of the Province of the Massachusetts Bay, to which are prefixed the Charters of the Province. Boston: 1869. [H.]

—— Acts and Laws of the Commonwealth of Massachusetts. Boston: Benjamin Edes and Sons [etc.], 1781. Reprinted by Wright and Potter. 1890. [H.]

—— Journal of the Convention for framing a Constitution of Government for the State of Massachusetts Bay, from the Commencement of their first Session, September 1, 1779, to the close of their last Session, June 16, 1780 . . . Boston: 1832. [H.]

—— [1766-1767.] Journal of the Honourable House of Representatives of His Majesty's Province of Massachusetts-Bay in New-England, begun and held at BOSTON, in the County of *Suffolk*, on Wednesday the Twenty-eighth Day of *May*, Annoque Domini, 1766. Boston: N. E. Green and Russell. 1766. [Title-page mutilated.] [M. S. L.]

—— [1770–1771.] Journal of the Honorable House of Representatives of His Majesty's Province of the Massachusetts-Bay in New-England, begun and held at Harvard-College in Cambridge, in the County of Middlesex, on Wednesday the Thirtieth Day of May, Annoque Domini, 1770. Boston, New-England: Edes and Gill. 1770. [M. S. L.]

—— [1772–1773.] Journal of the Honorable House of Representatives of His Majesty's Province of the Massachusetts-Bay in New-England, begun and held at Harvard-College in Cambridge, in the County of Middlesex, on Wednesday the Twenty-seventh Day of May, Annoque Domini, 1772. Boston, New-England: Edes and Gill. 1772.

—— [1773–1774.] Journal of the Honorable House of Representatives of His Majesty's Province of the Massachusetts-Bay in New-England, begun and held at Boston, in the County of Suffolk, on Wednesday the Twenty-sixth Day of May, Annoque Domini, 1773. Boston, New-England: Edes and Gill. 1773. [M. S. L.]

—— A Journal of the Honorable House of Representatives of the State of Massachusetts-Bay in New-England, begun and held at Boston, in the County of Suffolk, on Wednesday the Twenty-Eighth Day of May, Anno Domini, 1777. Boston, New England: Thomas and John Fleet. 1777. [M. S. L.]

Massachusetts, *continued.* MS. Journal of the House of Representatives, 1782–1783. [M. S. L.]

—— MS. Journal of the Senate, 1782–1783. [M. S. L.]

—— Records of the Governor and Company of the Massachusetts Bay in New England. [1628–1686.] Printed by order of the Legislature. Edited by Nathaniel B. Shurtleff. 5 vols. Boston : 1853–1854.

—— The Report of a Constitution or Form of Government for the Commonwealth of Massachusetts. Agreed upon by the Committee, — to be laid before the Convention of Delegates, assembled at Cambridge September 1, 1779 . . . Oct. 28, 1780. Boston : Benjamin Edes & Sons. 1779. [H.]

—— Reports of Cases argued and determined in the Supreme Judicial Court of the Commonwealth of Massachusetts. Vol. IV. By Dudley Atkins Tyng. Boston : Charles C. Little and James Brown. 1851.

—— [Manuscript Archives.] Revolutionary Letters, vol. 199. [M. S. L.]

—— Same, Revolutionary Resolves, vol. 212. [M. S. L.]

Mather, Cotton. The Life and Death of the Reverend Mr. John Eliot, who was the first Preacher of the Gospel to the Indians in America. . . . The third Edition carefully corrected. London : Printed for John Dunton, at the *Raven* in the *Poultrey.* 1694. [H.]

Matlack, Lucius C. The History of American Slavery and Methodism from 1789 to 1849 . . . In two Parts. No. 5 Spruce Street, New York, 1849. [B.]

Matlack, T. The Abolition of Slavery in Pennsylvania. A Letter to William Findley, January 11, 1817. *In* Mass. Hist. Soc. Coll., 2d Series, VIII, 184–192.

May, Samuel J. Liberty or Slavery the only Question. Oration : delivered on the Fourth of July, 1856, at Jamestown, Chautauqua Co., New York. Syracuse : J. G. K. Truair, Printer, Daily Journal Office. 1856. [H.]

[**May, Samuel, Jr.**] Catalogue of Anti-Slavery Publications in America [1750–1863]. pp. 157–175, pph. [No place or date.] [H.]

Memorial, A, to the Congress of the United States, on the subject of restraining the Increase of Slavery in new States to be admitted into the Union, prepared in pursuance of a vote of the Inhabitants of Boston and its vicinity, assembled at the State House on the 3d of December, A. D. 1819. [Signed December 15. Published by Sewall Phelps, No. 5 Court st., Boston. 1819.] *In* The Nebraska Question, comprising Speeches in the United States Senate etc., pp. 9–12. Redfield, New York, 1854. [H.]

Memorial of Inhabitants of the District of Columbia, praying for the gradual Abolition of Slavery in the District of Columbia. March 24, 1828. H. Doc. No. 140, 23d Cong., 2d sess. *Reprinted in* Address of the Free Soil Association of the District of Columbia. Washington : Buell and Blanchard. 1849. [H.]

Memorials presented to the Congress of the United States of America, by the different Societies instituted for promoting the Abolition of Slavery, &c. &c. in the States of Rhode-Island, Connecticut, New-York, Pennsylvania, Maryland, and Virginia. Published by order of "the Pennsylvania Society " . . . Philadelphia: Francis Bailey. 1792. pp. 31. [H.]

Mickley, Joseph J. Some Account of William Usselinx and Peter Minuit, two Individuals who were instrumental in establishing the first permanent Colony in Delaware. (Papers of the Delaware Historical Society. III.) The Historical Society of Delaware. Wilmington : 1881.

Mifflin, Warner. The Defence of Warner Mifflin against Aspersions cast on him on account of his Endeavours to promote Righteousness, Mercy and Peace, among Mankind. Philadelphia: Samuel Sansom, jun. 1796. pp. 30. [P. L. C.]

—— A Serious Expostulation with the Members of the House of Representatives of the United States. [*Anon.*] Philadelphia: Daniel Lawrence. 1793. pp. 16. [N. Y. H. S.]

—— Same. [Reprinted in part in 1837, in a pamphlet called Liberty, pp. 31–33. Julius R. Ames, Compiler.]

—— The Memorial alluded to in the foregoing Pamphlet [A Serious Expostulation] with the Introduction thereto ; Taken from The Providence Gazette of December 22, 1792. pp. 8. [*Anon.*] [N. Y. H. S.]

Miller, Samuel. A Discourse, delivered April 12, 1797, at the request of and before the New-York Society for promoting the Manumission of Slaves, and protecting such of them as have been or may be liberated. New-York : T. and J. Swords. 1797. pp. 36. [N. Y. H. S.]

Mirror, The, of Misery : or, Tyranny exposed. Extracted from authentic Documents, and exemplified by Engravings. New-York : Samuel Wood. 1807. [N. Y. H. S.]

Montesquieu. Œuvres complètes. Avec les variantes des premières éditions un choix des meilleurs commentaires et des notes nouvelles par Édouard Laboulaye. Paris, Garnier Frères, 1875. [H.]

Monthly Anthology, The, and Boston Review, containing Sketches and Reports of Philosophy, Religion, History, Arts and Manners. 10 vols. Boston : Munroe & Francis [etc.]. 1804–1811. [H.]

Moore, Frank, *Editor.* American Eloquence : A Collection of Speeches and Addresses, by the most eminent Orators of America ; with biographical Sketches and illustrative Notes. 2 vols. New York and London : D. Appleton and Company. 1857.

Moore, George H. Historical Notes on the Employment of Negroes in the American Army of the Revolution. New York : Charles T. Evans. 1862.

—— Notes on the History of Slavery in Massachusetts. New-York, D. Appleton & Co., 1866.

—— Additional Notes on the History of Slavery in Massachusetts. [A Reply to his Boston Critics.] *From* The Historical Magazine, 186–198, December, 1866.

Morse, Jedidiah. The American Geography ; or, A View of the present Situation of the United States of America. . . . Elizabethtown : Printed by Shepard Kollock, for the Author. 1789. [H.]

Morse, John T., Jr. Thomas Jefferson. (American Statesmen Series.) Houghton, Mifflin and Company, 1883.

Native, A, of America. Arguments against making Slaves of Men. [Dated September 14, 1713.] *In* J. Hepburn, American Defence of the Christian Golden Rule, Appendix, pp. 23–26.   [B.]

Needles, Edward. An Historical Memoir of the Pennsylvania Society, for promoting the Abolition of Slavery; the Relief of free Negroes unlawfully held in Bondage, and for improving the Condition of the African Race. Compiled from the Minutes of the Society and other official Documents and published by Authority of the Society. Philadelphia: Merihew and Thompson. 1848.   [H.]

New Hampshire. Constitutional Conventions in New Hampshire, 1778–1783; with the Constitution established in 1784. *In* Documents and Records relating to Towns in New Hampshire, Appendix, pp. 837–918. (New Hampshire State Papers, Vol. IX.) Concord, N. H., 1875.   [H.]

—— Documents and Records relating to Towns in New Hampshire; with an Appendix embracing the Constitutional Conventions of 1778–1779; and of 1781–1783; and the State Constitution of 1784. (New Hampshire State Papers, Vol. IX.) Concord, N. H., 1875.   [H.]

New-Jersey. Acts of the General Assembly of the Province of New-Jersey, from the Surrender of the Government to Queen Anne, on the 17th Day of April, in the Year of our Lord 1702, to the 14th Day of January, 1776 . . . Compiled and published under the appointment of the General Assembly by Samuel Allinson. Burlington: Printed by Isaac Collins, Printer to the King, for the Province of New-Jersey. 1776.   [B.]

—— Cases adjudged in the Supreme Court of New-Jersey; relative to the Manumission of Negroes and others holden in Bondage. Burlington. Printed for " The New-Jersey Society for promoting the Abolition of Slavery," by Isaac Neale, — 1794. pp. 32.   [H.]

—— Documents relating to the colonial History of the State of New Jersey. (New Jersey Archives.) Edited by William A. Whitehead [etc.], 1631–1776. 19 vols. Newark and Paterson, N. J., 1880–1897.   [H.]

—— The Grants, Concessions, and original Constitutions of the Province of New Jersey, the Acts passed during the proprietary Governments [etc.]. By Aaron Leaming and Jacob Spicer. Philadelphia. W. Bradford [1752?]. [Reprinted, Somerville, N. J., 1881.]   [H.]

—— Laws of the State of New-Jersey. Revised and published, under the Authority of the Legislature by William Paterson. Newark: Matthias Day. 1800.   [B.]

—— Same. New Brunswick: Printed by Abraham Blauvelt. 1800. [H.]

—— Laws of the State of New-Jersey. [From Nov. 11, 1800, to Feb. 23, 1811.] Compiled and published under the Authority of the Legislature. By Joseph Bloomfield. Trenton: James J. Wilson. 1811.   [H.]

[New Jersey Abolition Society.] The Constitution of the New-Jersey Society, for promoting the Abolition of Slavery: to which is annexed, Extracts from a Law of New-Jersey, passed the 2d *March*, 1786, and Supplement to the same, passed the 26th *November*, 1788. Burlington: Printed for the Society, by Isaac Neale. 1793. pp. 14. [N. Y. H. S.]

New Plymouth. Records of the Colony of New Plymouth in New England. Printed by order of the Legislature of the Commonwealth of Massachusetts. . . . 12 vols. Boston: 1855–1861. [H.]

New York. The Colonial Laws of New York, from the Year 1664 to the Revolution, including the Charters to the Duke of York [etc.]. 5 vols. Albany: 1896. [H.]

—— Documents relative to the colonial History of the State of New York; procured in Holland, England and France, by John Romeyn Brodhead, Esq., Agent. . . . 11 vols. Edited by E. B. O'Callaghan. . . . Albany: Weed, Parsons and Company. 1856–1861. [H.]

—— Laws of the State of New York, 1777–1801. 5 vols. Republished by the Secretary of State, pursuant to Chapter three hundred and forty, one of the Laws of eighteeen hundred and eighty-five. Albany, 1886. [H.]

—— Laws of the State of New York, comprising the Constitution, and the Acts of Legislature since the Revolution, from the first to the twelfth Session inclusive. 2 vols. New York: Printed by Hugh Gaines, at his Printing-Office and Book-Store, at the Bible, in Hanover-Square. 1789. [B.]

—— Selections from the revised Statutes of New York: containing all the Laws of the State relative to Slaves, and the Law relative to the Offence of Kidnapping; which several Laws commenced and took Effect January 1, 1830. Together with Extracts from the Laws of the United States. Published on behalf of the New York Manumission Society by Direction of the Standing Committee. New York: Vanderpool and Cole. 1830. [B.]

Niles, Nathaniel. Two Discourses on Liberty; delivered at the North Church, in Newbury-Port, on Lord's-Day, June 5th, 1774, and published at the general Desire of the Hearers. Newbury-Port: J. Thomas and H. W. Tinges. 1774. pp. 60. [B. A.]

[Nisbet, Richard.] A West-Indian. Slavery not forbidden by Scripture. Or a Defence of the West-India Planters, from the Aspersions thrown out against them, by the Author of a Pamphlet, entitled, An Address to the Inhabitants of the British Settlements in America, upon Slave-Keeping. [*See* B. Rush.] Philadelphia: 1773. [H.]

North Carolina. Laws of the State of North-Carolina [1715–1790]. Published, according to Act of Assembly, by James Iredell. Edenton: 1791. [H.]

Public Acts, The, of the General Assembly of North Carolina [1715 to 1803]. Revised and published, under the Authority of the Legislature, by the Honorable James Iredell, Esquire . . . and now revised by François-Xavier-Martin. 2 vols. in 1. Newbern: 1804. [H.]

Ogden, George W. Letters from the West, comprising a Tour through the Western Country, and a residence of two Summers in the States of Ohio and Kentucky: originally written in Letters to a Brother. New-Bedford: Melcher & Rogers. 1823. [H.]

Opinions of the early Presidents, and of the Fathers of the Republic, upon Slavery, and upon Negroes as Men and Soldiers. (Loyal Publication Society, 863 Broadway. No. 18.) New York: Wm. C. Bryant & Co. 1863. [H.]

Othello. Essays on Negro Slavery. [Dated Baltimore, May 10, 1788, and Maryland, May 23, 1788.] *In* The American Museum, Vol. IV, pp. 414-417, 509-512. [H.]

Otis, James. The Rights of the British Colonies asserted and proved. Boston, New-England, printed: London reprinted, for J. Almon. N. d. [H.]

Palmer, John. Journal of Travels in the United States of North America, and in Lower Canada, performed in the Year 1817; containing Particulars relating to the Prices of Land and Provisions, Remarks on the Country and People, interesting Anecdotes, and an Account of the Commerce, Trade, and present State of Washington, New York, Philadelphia . . . &c. . . . London: Printed for Sherwood, Neely, and Jones. 1818. [H.]

[Park, Edwards A.] Memoir of the Life and Character of Samuel Hopkins. *In* Hopkins, Works, Vol. I, pp. 1-266. Boston: Doctrinal Tract and Book Society. 1854.

—— Same, published separately.

Parrish, John. Remarks on the Slavery of the Black People; addressed to the Citizens of the United States, particularly to those who are in legislative or executive Stations in the general or state Governments; and also to such Individuals as hold them in Bondage. Philadelphia: Printed for the Author, by Kimber, Conrad & Co. . . . 1806. pp. 66. [H.]

[Parsons, Theophilus.] Result of the Convention of Delegates holden at Ipswich in the County of Essex, who were deputed to take into Consideration the Constitution and Form of Government, proposed by the Convention of the State of Massachusetts-Bay. Newbury-Port: John Mycall. 1778. [H.]

Patten, William. On the Inhumanity of the Slave-Trade, and the Importance of correcting it. A Sermon, delivered in the Second Congregational Church, Newport, Rhode-Island, August 12, 1792. Providence, J. Carter, 1793. pp. 14. [B.]

[Paulding, James Kirke.] Letters from the South, written during an Excursion in the Summer of 1816. By the Author of John Bull and Brother Jonathan, &c. &c. 2 vols. New-York: James Eastburn & Co. 1817. [H.]

[Pelham Papers, The.] *In* The Connecticut Courant, Nov. 21 and Dec. 12, 1796. Hartford: Hudson & Goodwin. [B.]

Pennsylvania. A Digest of the Laws of Pennsylvania, from the Year 1700 to May 1, 1861. Ninth Edition. John Purdon, Compiler. Philadelphia, Kay and Brother, 1862. [B.]

—— Laws of the Commonwealth of Pennsylvania, from the fourteenth Day of October, one thousand seven hundred, to the sixth Day of April, one thousand eight hundred and two. Republished, under the Authority of the Legislature, by M. Carey and J. Bioren. 6 vols. Philadelphia: Printed by J. Bioren for Matthew Carey and self. 1803. [H.]

Pennsylvania, *continued.* Laws of the Commonwealth of Pennsylvania, from the second Day of October, one thousand seven hundred and eighty-one, to the second Day of October, one thousand seven hundred and ninety. Vol. II. Republished, under the Authority of the Legislature, by Alexander James Dallas. Philadelphia: Hall and Sellers. 1793 [B.]

—— Minutes of the Provincial Council, from the Organization to the Termination of the Proprietary Government. Published by the State. (Pa. Col. Rec., Vols. I–X.) Vols. I–III, Philadelphia, 1852. Vols. IV–X, Harrisburg, 1851–1852. [H.]

—— Minutes of the Supreme Executive Council, from its Organization to the Termination of the Revolution. Published by the State. (Pa. Col. Rec., Vols. XI–XVI.) Harrisburg, 1852–1853. [H.]

—— The Statutes at Large from 1682 to 1801. Compiled by James T. Mitchell and Henry Flanders, Commissioners. 5 vols. [to 1759]. 1896. [H.]

—— Votes and Proceedings of the House of Representatives of the Province of Pennsylvania. Beginning the fourth Day of December, 1682. Philadelphia: Printed and sold by B. Franklin, and D. Hall, at the New-Printing-Office, near the Market. 1752. [B.]

[Pennsylvania Abolition Society.] The Constitution of the Pennsylvania Society for promoting the Abolition of Slavery, and the Relief of free Negroes, unlawfully held in Bondage. Begun in the year 1774 and enlarged on the twenty-third of April, 1787. To which are added, the Acts of the General Assembly of Pennsylvania, for the gradual Abolition of Slavery. Philadelphia: Printed by Francis Bailey, for "the Pennsylvania Society" etc. 1788. [N. Y. H. S.]

—— Constitution and Act of Incorporation of the Pennsylvania Society for promoting the Abolition of Slavery [etc.]. To which are added Abstracts of the Laws of the States of Pennsylvania, New York, New Jersey, Delaware and Maryland, and of the Acts of Congress, respecting Slavery and the Slave Trade. Philadelphia: Printed for the Society, by Hall & Atkinson. 1820. pp. 31. [B.]

[Pennsylvania Anti-Slavery Society.] Proceedings of the Pennsylvania Convention, assembled to organize a State Anti-Slavery Society, at Harrisburg, on the 31st of January and 1st, 2d and 3d of February, 1837. Philadelphia: Merrihew and Gunn. 1837. [H.]

—— Pennsylvania Archives. Selected and arranged from original Documents in the Office of the Secretary of the Commonwealth, conformably to Acts of the General Assembly, February 15, 1851, and March 1, 1852. By Samuel Hazard. 11 vols. Philadelphia: 1853. [H.]

Pennsylvania Magazine, The, of History and Biography. 23 vols. [to 1900]. Philadelphia: Publication Fund of the Historical Society of Pennsylvania. 1877.

Pinkney, William. Speech in the House of Delegates of Maryland, at their Session in November, 1789. Philadelphia: Joseph Crukshank. 1790. pp. 22. [H.]

Poole, William Frederick. Anti-Slavery Opinions before the Year 1800. Read before the Cincinnati Literary Club, November 16, 1872. To which is appended a fac simile Reprint of Dr. George Buchanan's Oration on the moral and political Evil of Slavery. Cincinnati : Robert Clarke & Co. 1873.

Poore, Ben : Perley. The Federal and State Constitutions, colonial Charters, and other organic Laws of the United States. 2 vols. Washington, 1877.

Portfolio, The. By Oliver Oldschool, Esq. [Joseph Dennie]. Philadelphia, 1801–1805. New Series, 1806–1808. [H.]

Priest, William. Travels in the United States of America ; commencing in the Year 1793, and ending in 1797. . . . London : Printed for J. Johnson. 1802. [H.]

[Providence Abolition Society.] Constitution of a Society for abolishing the Slave-Trade. With several Acts of the Legislatures of the States of Massachusetts, Connecticut and Rhode-Island, for that Purpose. Providence : John Carter. 1789. pp. 19. [B.]

Queries respecting the Slavery and Emancipation of Negroes in Massachusetts, proposed by the Hon. Judge Tucker of Virginia, and answered by the Rev. Dr. Belknap. *In* Mass. Hist. Soc. Coll., 1st Series, IV, 191–211.

Randall, Henry S. The Life of Thomas Jefferson. 3 vols. New York : Derby and Jackson. 1858.

Reed, Henry. Life of Joseph Reed. (Sparks, Library of American Biography, second Series, Vol. VIII.) Boston : Charles C. Little and James Brown. 1846.

Rhode Island. [Laws of Rhode Island.] October, 1779. At the General Assembly of the Governor and Company of the State of *Rhode-Island*, and *Providence-Plantations*, begun and holden at *South-Kingstown*, within and for the State aforesaid, on the last *Monday* in *October*, in the Year of our Lord One Thousand Seven Hundred and Seventy-nine and in the Fourth Year of Independence. N. t.-p. [Providence : Bennett Wheeler.] [M. S. L.]

—— —— February, 1784. At the General Assembly of the Governor and Company of the State of *Rhode-Island* and *Providence-Plantations*, begun and holden (by Adjournment) at *Providence*, within and for the State aforesaid, on the last *Monday* in *February*, in the Year of our Lord One Thousand Seven Hundred and Eighty-four, and in the Eighth Year of Independence. N. t.-p. [Providence : Bennett Wheeler.] [M. S. L.]

—— —— February, 1785. At the General Assembly of the Governor and Company of the State of *Rhode-Island* and *Providence Plantations*, begun and holden by Adjournment at *East-Greenwich*, on the last *Monday* of *February*, in the Year of our Lord One Thousand Seven Hundred and Eighty-five, and in the Ninth Year of Independence. N. t.-p. [Providence : John Carter.] [M. S. L.]

—— —— October, 1785. At the General Assembly of the Governor and Company of the State of *Rhode-Island*, and *Providence-Plantations*, begun and holden at *South-Kingstown*, within and for the State aforesaid, on the last *Monday* in *October*, in the Year of our Lord One thousand

Seven Hundred and Eighty-five, and in the Tenth Year of Independence. N. t.-p. [Providence: John Carter.] [M. S. L.]

Rhode Island. [Laws of Rhode Island] *continued.* June, 1787. At the General Assembly of the Governor and Company of the State of *Rhode-Island* and *Providence Plantations*, begun and held by Adjournment at *Newport*, within and for the State aforesaid, on the Second Monday in *June*, in the Year of our Lord One Thousand Seven Hundred and Eighty-seven, and in the Eleventh Year of Independence. N. t.-p. [M. S. L.]

—— —— October, 1787. At the General Assembly of the Governor and Company of the State of *Rhode-Island* and *Providence Plantations*, begun and holden at *South-Kingstown*, within and for the State aforesaid, on the last Monday in *October*, in the Year of our Lord One Thousand Seven Hundred and Eighty-seven, and in the Twelfth Year of Independence. N. t.-p. [M. S. L.]

—— The Public Laws of the State of Rhode-Island and Providence Plantations, as revised by a Committee and finally enacted by the Honourable General Assembly, at their Session in January, 1798 . . . Providence, Carter and Wilkinson, 1798. [H.]

—— Records of the Colony of Rhode Island and Providence Plantations in New England. Printed by order of the Legislature. Transcribed and edited by John Russell Bartlett, Secretary of State. 7 vols. Providence, R. I., 1856–1862. [H.]

Rice, David. Slavery inconsistent with Justice and Good Policy; proved by a Speech delivered in the Convention, held at Danville, Kentucky. Philadelphia printed, 1792. London reprinted, M. Gurney, 1793. pp. 24. [H.]

Rider, Sidney S. An Historical Inquiry concerning the Attempt to raise a Regiment of Slaves by Rhode Island during the War of the Revolution. (Rhode Island Historical Tracts, No. 10.) Providence, Sidney S. Rider, 1880.

Rochefoucauld-Liancourt, Duke de La. Travels through the United States of North America, the Country of the Iroquois, and Upper Canada, in the Years 1795, 1796, and 1797; with an authentic Account of Lower Canada. 2 vols. London: Printed for R. Phillips. 1799. [H.]

Rogers, William. An Oration, delivered July 4, 1789, at the Presbyterian Church, in Arch Street, Philadelphia. . . . Published at the request of the Pennsylvania Society of the Cincinnati. Philadelphia: Printed for T. Dobson. 1789. [H.]

Roosevelt, Theodore. Gouverneur Morris. (American Statesmen Series.) Boston and New York, Houghton, Mifflin and Company, 1888.

Rowland, Kate Mason. The Life of George Mason, 1725–1792. Including his Speeches, public Papers, and Correspondence. With an Introduction by General Fitzhugh Lee. 2 vols. G. P. Putnam's Sons, New York and London, 1892.

[**Royall, Anne.**] **A Traveller.** Sketches of History, Life, and Manners, in the United States. New-Haven: Printed for the Author. 1826. [H.]

[**Rush, Benjamin**]. An Address to the Inhabitants of the British Settlements in America, upon Slave-Keeping. Philadelphia: John Dunlap. 1773. pp. 30. [H.]

—— A Pennsylvanian. An Address to the Inhabitants of the British Settlements, on the Slavery of the Negroes in America. The second Edition. To which is added A Vindication of the Address, in Answer to a Pamphlet entitled, "Slavery not forbidden in Scripture; or, a Defence of the West India Planters" [by Richard Nesbit]. Philadelphia: John Dunlap. 1773. pp. 54. [H.]

Rushton, Edward. Expostulatory Letter to George Washington, of Mount Vernon, in Virginia, on his continuing to be a Proprietor of Slaves. Liverpool, 1797. [H.]

Saffin, John. A Brief and Candid Answer to a late printed Sheet entitled The Selling of Joseph. *In* Moore, Geo. H., Notes on Slavery in Massachusetts, pp. 251–256.

Sandiford, Ralph. A Brief Examination of the Practice of the Times, by the Foregoing and the Present Dispensation: Whereby is manifested, how the Devil works in the Mystery, which none can understand and get the Victory over but those that are armed with the Light, that discovers the Temptation and the Author thereof, and gives Victory over him and his Instruments, who are now gone forth, as in the Beginning, from the true Friends of Jesus, having the Form of Godliness in Words, but in Deeds deny the Power thereof; from such we are commanded to turn away. [Philadelphia:] Printed for the Author [by Franklin and Meredith]. Anno 1729. [P. H. S.]

Semple, Robert R. A History of the Rise and Progress of the Baptists in Virginia. Richmond: Published by the Author. 1810. [B.]

Sewall, Samuel. Diary. 1674–1729. *In* Mass. Hist. Soc. Coll., 5th Series, Vols. V–VII. Boston: Published by the Society. 1878–1882.

—— Letter-Book. *In* Mass. Hist. Soc. Coll., 6th Series, Vols. I, II. Boston: Published by the Society. 1886–1888.

—— The Selling of Joseph. "Boston of the Massachusets; Printed by Bartholomew Green, and John Allen. [3 pp. folio.] June, 24th, 1700." *In* Mass. Hist. Soc. Coll., 5th Series, VI, 16–20, *and in* Mass. Hist. Soc. Proc., 1863–1864, pp. 161–165.

Shaler, N. S. Kentucky. A Pioneer Commonwealth. (American Commonwealth Series.) Houghton, Mifflin and Company, 1885.

[**Sharp, Granville**.] Extract of a Letter to a Gentleman in Maryland; wherein is demonstrated the extreme wickedness of tolerating the *Slave Trade*, etc. Originally printed in America. First printed in London in 1793. The fourth Edition. London: Phillips and Fardon. 1806. pp. 14. [N. Y. H. S.]

Sharp, Granville. Letter to the Maryland Society for promoting the Abolition of Slavery, and the Relief of free Negroes and Others, unlawfully held in Bondage. Published by order of the Society, Baltimore, 1793. pp. 11. [H.]

Singleton, Arthur. [Knight, Henry C.] Letters from the South and West. Boston: Richardson and Lord. 1824. [H.]

Smith, E. H. [Elihu Hubbard.] A ·Discourse, delivered April 11, 1798, at the request of and before the New-York Society for promoting the Manumission of Slaves, and protecting such of them as have been or may be liberated. New York: T. and J. Swords. 1798. pp. 30. [B.]

Smith, George. History of Wesleyan Methodism, Vol. I, Appendix G. Third Edition. London: Longman, Green, Longman, and Roberts. 1862. [B.]

Smith, J. E. A. The History of Pittsfield, (Berkshire County,) Massachusetts, from the year 1734 to the year 1800. Boston: Lee and Shepard. 1869. [H.]

Sons of Africa, The: an Essay on Freedom. With Observations on the Origin of Slavery. By a member of the African Society in Boston. Boston: Printed for the Members of the Society. 1808. pp. 21. [H.]

South Carolina. The Statutes at Large of South Carolina. Edited, under Authority of the Legislature, by Thomas Cooper (Vols. I–V) and David J. McCord (Vols. VI, VII). Columbia, S. C., 1836–1841. [H.]

Sparks, Jared, *Editor.* The Diplomatic Correspondence of the American Revolution. . . . Vol. X. Boston: Nathan Hale and Gray and Bowen: G. & C. & H. Carvill, New York: P. Thompson, Washington. 1830. [H.]

Spencer, David. The Early Baptists of Philadelphia. Philadelphia, William Syckelmoore, 1877. [B.]

Sprague, William B. Annals of the American Pulpit; or Commemorative Notices of distinguished American Clergymen of various Denominations. . . . New York: Robert Carter and Brothers. 1858. [H.]

Staples, William R. Annals of the Town of Providence, from its first Settlement, to the Organization of the City Government, in June, 1832. Providence: Knowles and Vose. 1843. [H.]

Statistical View of the Population of the United States from 1790 to 1830, inclusive. Furnished by the Department of State, in accordance with resolutions of the Senate of the United States of the 26th February, 1833, and 31st March, 1834. Washington: Duff Green. 1835. [H.]

Steiner, Bernard C. History of Slavery in Connecticut. (Johns Hopkins University Studies in historical and political Science. Eleventh Series, IX–X.) Baltimore, The Johns Hopkins Press, September–October, 1893.

Stillé, Charles J. The Life and Times of John Dickinson. Prepared at the request of the Historical Society of Pennsylvania. Philadelphia: J. B. Lippincott Co. 1891.

Stroud, George M. A Sketch of the Laws relating to Slavery in the several States of the United States of America. Philadelphia: Kimber and Sharpless. N. d. pp. 180. [B.]

—— Same, second Edition, revised and enlarged. 1856. pp. 300. [B.]

Stuart, Charles. A Memoir of Granville Sharp, to which is added Sharp's "Law of passive Obedience," and an extract from his "Law of Retribution." New-York: American Anti-Slavery Society. 1836. [B.]

Sumner, Charles. Freedom National; Slavery Sectional. Speech on his Motion to repeal the Fugitive Slave Bill, in the Senate of the United States, August 26, 1852. Boston, Ticknor and Fields, 1852.

—— Same, *in* Sumner, Works, Vol. III.

Sutcliff, Robert. Travels in some Parts of North America, in the Years 1804, 1805, & 1806. Second Edition, improved. York: Printed for W. Alexander. 1813. [H.]

Swan, James. A Dissuasion to Great-Britain and the Colonies, from the Slave Trade to Africa. Shewing, the Contradiction this Trade bears, both to Laws divine and provincial; the Disadvantages arising from it, and Advantages from abolishing it, both to Europe and Africa, particularly to Britain and the Plantations. Also shewing, how to put this Trade to Africa on a just and lawful Footing. Boston: N. E. Printed by E. Russell, near the new Intelligence-Office and Auction-room, and next the Cornfield, Union-street. pp. xvi, 70. [1771 or 1772.] [H.]

Dedicated "to all Friends to Liberty."

—— A Dissuasion to Great Britain and the Colonies, from the Slave-Trade to Africa. Shewing the Injustice thereof, &c. Revised and abridged. Boston: Printed for J. Greenleaf. 1773. pp. x, 41. [H.]

Dedicated to his Excellency the Governor, the Honorable His Majesty Council, and the House of Representatives of the Province of the Massachusetts Bay, in New-England. "This edition appears in the world, at the earnest desire of the Negroes in Boston, in order to answer the purpose of sending a copy to each town." Preface, p. ix.

Swift, Zephaniah. An Oration on Domestic Slavery. Delivered at the North Meeting-House in Hartford, on the 12th Day of May, A.D. 1791. At the Meeting of the Connecticut Society for the Promotion of Freedom, and the Relief of Persons unlawfully holden in Bondage. Hartford: Hudson and Goodwin. 1791. [H.]

Tennessee. A Compilation of the Statutes of Tennessee of a general and permanent Nature, from the Commencement of the Government to the present Time. By R. L. Caruthers & A. O. P. Nicholson. Nashville, Tennessee, 1836. [B.]

—— Laws of the State of Tennessee, including those of North Carolina now in force in this State. From the year 1715 to the year 1820, inclusive. By Edward Scott. 2 vols. Knoxville, Tennessee, 1821. [M. S. L.]

Thomas, David. Travels through the Western Country in the Summer of 1816. Including Notices of the Natural History, Antiquities, Topography, Agriculture, Commerce, and Manufactures. . . . Auburn, (N. Y.), David Rumsey, 1819. [H.]

Thompson, Charles. Letter to Richard Peters, New York, March 21, 1785. [H.]

Published in The Daily Evening Traveller, June 25, 1850, under the title of A Voice from the Revolution for the Prohibition of Slavery.

Tremain, Mary. Slavery in the District of Columbia. The Policy of Congress and the Struggle for Abolition. (University of Nebraska. Seminary Papers, Number 2. April, 1892.) G. P. Putnam's Sons, 1892.

[**Tryon, Thomas.**] Philotheos Phystologus. Friendly Advice to the Gentelmen-Planters of the East and West Indies. In three Parts . . . II. The Complaints of the Negro-Slaves against the hard Usages and barbarous Cruelties inflicted upon them, pp. 75–145. III. A Discourse in way of Dialogue, between the *Ethiopean* or *Negro-Slave* and a *Christian* that was his Master in *America*, pp. 146–222. London, Printed by Andrew Sowle at the Crooked Riket in Halloway Lane near Shoreditch. [1684.] [H.]

Tucker, St. George. A Dissertation on Slavery: with a Proposal for the gradual Abolition of it, in the State of Virginia. Philadelphia: Printed for Mathew Carey. 1796. [H.]

United States, The. Laws of the United States of America, Vols. I–VIII. Published by Authority. Philadelphia: Richard Folwell, 1796–1799 (Vols. I–IV); Washington, 1799– (Vols. V–VIII). [H.]

Vaux, Roberts. Memoirs of the Life of Anthony Benezet. Philadelphia printed. York, reprinted with additións, &c. for W. Alexander, 1817. [H.]

—— Memoirs of the Lives of Benjamin Lay and Ralph Sandiford; two of the earliest public advocates for the emancipation of the Enslaved Africans. Philadelphia: Solomon W. Conrad. 1815. [B.]

Vermont. Statutes of the State of Vermont, passed by the Legislature in February and March, 1787. [Earlier laws included.] Windsor: Hough and Spooner. 1787. [M. S. L.]

Views of American Slavery, taken a Century ago. Anthony Benezet, John Wesley. [Lee, Warburton, etc., in Appendix.] Philadelphia: Published by the Association of Friends for the Diffusion of religious and useful Knowledge. 1858. [H.]

Virginia. Statutes at Large; being a Collection of all the Laws of Virginia, from the first Session of the Legislature, in the Year 1619. By William Waller Hening. New York, Philadelphia and Richmond, 1819–1823. [H.]

—— Same, from October session 1792 to December session 1806, inclusive, being a continuation of Hening. 3 vols. Richmond, 1835. [H.]

Wadleigh, George. Slavery in New Hampshire — when and how abolished. *In* The Granite Monthly, VI, 377–379. Concord, N. H., 1883.

Walker, Joseph B. A History of the New Hampshire Convention for the Investigation, Discussion and Decision of the Federal Constitution. . . . [Speech of Hon. J. Atherton in Appendix, pp. 112–114.] Boston: Cupples and Hurd. 1888. [B.]

Washburn, Emory. The Extinction of Slavery in Massachusetts. A Paper read before the Massachusetts Historical Society, at their monthly meeting, April, 1857. *In* Mass. Hist Soc. Coll., 4th Series, IV, 333–346, *and* Mass. Hist. Soc. Proc., 1855–1858, pp. 188–203.

—— Historical Sketches of the Town of Leicester, Massachusetts, during the first Century from its Settlement. Boston: John Wilson and Son. 1860.

Washburn, Emory, *continued.* Slavery as it once prevailed in Massachusetts. A Lecture for the Massachusetts Historical Society at the Lowell Institute, Jan. 22, 1869. Boston: John Wilson and Son. 1869.

Washburne, E. B. Sketch of Edward Coles, second Governor of Illinois, and of the Slavery Struggle of 1823-4. Prepared for the Chicago Historical Society. Chicago: Jansen, McClurg & Company. 1882.

Washington, George. The Writings of George Washington, collected and edited by Worthington Chauncey Ford. 14 vols. New York and London, G. P. Putnam's Sons, 1891.

Watson, John F. Annals of Philadelphia, being a Collection of Memoirs, Anecdotes, & Incidents of the City and its Inhabitants from the Days of the Pilgrim Founders. . . . Philadelphia, E. L. Carey & A. Hart; New York, G. & C. & H. Carvill. 1830.   [H.]

Webster, Noah, Jr. Effects of Slavery, on Morals and Industry. Hartford, (Connecticut), Hudson and Goodwin, 1793. pp. 56.   [H.]

Webster, Samuel. A Sermon preached before the Honorable Council, and the Honorable House of Representatives, of the State of the Massachusetts Bay, in New-England. At Boston, May 28, 1777. Boston: Edes & Gill. 1777.   [B. A.]

Weeks, Stephen B. Southern Quakers and Slavery. A Study in Institutional History. Baltimore, The Johns Hopkins Press, 1896.

—— Anti-Slavery Sentiment in the South; with unpublished Letters from John Stuart Mill and Mrs. Stowe. (Southern History Association Publications. Vol. II, No. 2, April, 1898.) Washington, D. C., The Association, 1898.

Welby, Adlard. A Visit to North America and the English Settlements in Illinois, with a Winter Residence at Philadelphia; solely to ascertain the actual Prospects of the emigrating Agriculturist, Mechanic, and commercial Speculator. London: Printed for J. Drury. 1821.   [H.]

Wells, William V. The Life and public Services of Samuel Adams, being a Narrative of his Acts and Opinions, and of his Agency in producing and forwarding the American Revolution. With Extracts from his Correspondence, State Papers and political Essays. 3 vols. Boston: Little, Brown and Company. 1865.

Wesley, John. Thoughts upon Slavery. *In* The Potent Enemies of America laid open . . . London, printed: Re-printed in Philadelphia with Notes, and sold by Joseph Crukshank. 1774. pp. 83.   [H.]

Wheaton, Henry. Life of William Pinkney. (Sparks, Library of American Biography, Vol. VI.) Boston: Hilliard, Gray, and Co. London: Richard James Kennett. 1836.

Wheeler, Jacob D. A Practical Treatise on the Law of Slavery. Being a Compilation of all the Decisions made on that Subject, in the several Courts of the United States, and State Courts. . . . New York: Allan Pollock, Jr. New Orleans, Benjamin Levy. 1837.   [H.]

Whittier, John G. Samuel Hopkins. *In* Old Portraits and Modern Sketches, pp. 146-164. Boston: Ticknor, Reed, and Fields. 1850.

Williams, Peter, Jr. An Oration on the Abolition of the Slave Trade; delivered in the African Church, in the City of New-York, January 1, 1808. New-York: Samuel Wood. 1808. pp. 26. [H.]
Inscribed to the Societies for the Abolition of Slavery.

Winterbotham, W. An historical, geographical, commercial, and philosophical View of the United States of America, and of the European Settlements in America and the West-Indies. The first American Edition, with Additions and Corrections. 4 vols. New-York: Printed by Tiebout and O'Brien, for John Reid, Bookseller and Stationer. 1796.
[H.]

Winthrop, John. The History of New England from 1630 to 1649. From his original Manuscripts. With Notes by James Savage. 2 vols. Boston: Phelps and Farnham. 1825.

Woods, John. Two Years' Residence in the Settlement on the English Prairie, in the Illinois Country, United States. . . . London: Printed for Longman, Hurst, Rees, Orme, and Brown. 1822. [H.]

Woolman, John. Some Considerations on the Keeping of Negroes. Recommended to the Professors of Christianity of every Denomination. Philadelphia: James Chattin. 1754. pp. 24. [H.]

—— Considerations on Keeping Negroes; Recommended to the Professors of Christianity of every Denomination. Part Second. Philadelphia: B. Franklin, and D. Hall. 1762. pp. 52.

—— The Journal of John Woolman. With an Introduction by John G. Whittier, pp. 1–49. Boston: James R. Osgood and Company. 1873.
[H.]

—— The Works of John Woolman. In two Parts. [Part I.] A Journal of the Life, Gospel-Labours, and Christian Experiences, of that faithful Minister of Christ, John Woolman; Late of Mount-Holly, in the Province of New-Jersey. pp. 1–207. London: T. Letchworth. 1775.

—— Same. Part the Second. Containing his last Epistle and other Writings. pp. 209-320. London: T. Letchworth. 1775. [H.]

Wright, Robert. A Memoir of General James Oglethorpe, one of the earliest Reformers of Prison Discipline in England, and the Founder of Georgia, in America. London: Chapman and Hall. 1867.

INDEX

A

ABOLITION, gradual, era of, 3; by Act of Congress, resolutions in favor of, 6 *n.*

Abolition Societies, formation of, during the period of State emancipation, 4; decline of, during the wars with England, 4; revival of activity of, after 1815, 5–7; Quakers in, 40; influence of, 89, 97–111; memorials of, to Congress, reinforced by petitions of the Society of Friends, 96; appropriateness of title of, 97; policy and methods of, 97, 103; reasons for failure of, 97, 109; aims of, 97–100, 103, 105, 107; constitutions of, 98; counsellors of, 100; membership of, 100 *f.*; admission of slave-holders to, 100 *f.*; organization of, 100 *f.*; committees of, 100, 109; memorials of, to Congress against the slave-trade, 101, 106, 141; decline of, 102, 109, 110; reports of, to American Convention, 102, 107; attitude of, toward vested rights, 103; lack of aggressiveness of, 103; compilation of facts by, 103; education of public sentiment by, 103; orations and addresses of, 103, 104 *n.*; formation of, recommended, 104; distribution of literature by, 104; applications of, to Courts, 104, 106 *f.*, 109; applications of, to legislatures, 105, 105 *n.*; efforts of, against the slave-trade, 106, 108; opposition to, 109 *f.*; revival of activity in, 110; results of work of, 111; conditions necessary for success of, 112 *f.*; liberation of kidnapped negroes by, 120; protection of free blacks by, 125; efforts of, for execution and amendment of laws, 125 *f.*; liberation by, of free negroes unlawfully held, 133; victory of, over the foreign slave-trade, 142; attitude of, toward measures limiting the slave-trade, 142; enforcement of laws against the slave-trade by, 145; effects of movement against the slave-trade on, 155 *f.*; free produce movement supported by, 190.

See also American Convention.
   Alexandria Society.
   Caroline County Society.
   Chestertown Society.
   Choptank Society.
   Connecticut Society.
   Delaware Society.
   District of Columbia, Society . . . in.
   Maryland Society.
   Massachusetts and Rhode Island (*or* Providence) Society.
   New Jersey Society.
   New York (Manumission) Society.
   North Carolina (Manumission) Society.
   Pennsylvania Society.
   Tennessee (Manumission) Society.
   Virginia Society.
   Washington Society.
   Wilmington Society.

Abolitionists, immediate, 3, 7, 7 *n.*, 126; prominent, after the Revolutionary War, 89–96; in Ohio, 90; differences of method among radical abolitionists, 169, 170; greatest difficulties encountered by, 191; work of the early, 196. *See also* Dickinson, John; Dwight, Theodore; Hopkins, Samuel; Thatcher, George.

Adams, John, antipathy of, to slavery, 46.

Adams, Samuel, interest of, in cause of negro petitioners, 70.

Africa, schemes for returning negroes to, 30, 153, 153 *n.*; opposed by Benezet, 32; importation from, to be prohibited by Congress, 149. *See also* Colonization, African.